Mark Twain and Metaphor

Mark Twain and His Circle Series
Tom Quirk, Editor

Mark Twain and Metaphor

John Bird

University of Missouri Press

Columbia and London

Library of Congress Cataloging-in-Publication Data

Bird, John, 1954–
   Mark Twain and metaphor / John Bird.
        p.   cm.
   Summary: "Examines how Twain used metaphor to express his attitudes and
thoughts, revealing not only hidden facets of Twain's artistry but also new aspects
of works that we think we know well such as The Adventures of Tom Sawyer,
Adventures of Huckleberry Finn, and A Connecticut Yankee in King Arthur's
Court"—Provided by publisher.
   Includes bibliographical references and index.
   ISBN 978-0-8262-1762-2 (alk. paper)
   1. Twain, Mark, 1835–1910—Criticism and interpretation.   2. Twain, Mark, 1835–
1910—Literary style. 3. Metaphor in literature.   I. Title.
   PS1341.B57 2007
   818'.409—dc22

                                                              2007027211

♾ This paper meets the requirements of the
American National Standard for Permanence of Paper
for Printed Library Materials, Z39.48, 1984.

Designer: Jennifer Cropp
Typesetter: BookComp, Inc.
Printer and binder: Thomson-Shore, Inc.
Typefaces: Palatino, Cochin, and Pristina

To Seung Yim Lee

for her support: literal, metaphorical

Contents

Acknowledgments

I begin with one of my favorite jokes. Question: "How many PhD's does it take to screw in a lightbulb?" Answer: "One—but it takes ten years." When I tell this joke to most people, they laugh heartily, but when I tell it to fellow academics, the laughter seems a bit muted. We know the hard truth that lies at the heart of this jest. I must confess that the "lightbulb" idea to study Mark Twain's use of figurative language came to me a bit more than ten years ago. Actually, I am grateful for the time I have spent on the subject, since the luxury of time has allowed me to look deeper into both metaphor studies and Mark Twain than I would have if this idea had come to me as, say, a dissertation topic.

One reason we academics take so long to "screw in the lightbulb" is that we work, for the most part, alone. Nonetheless, we do not always work alone, and I am grateful to acknowledge the help and encouragement of many individuals and institutions.

First, I thank my students and colleagues at Winthrop University, as well as the administration for travel support and a well-timed sabbatical. The library staff at Winthrop's Dacus Library have been most helpful. I am also grateful to the staff at the Barrett Collection of the University of Virginia Library, and as all Mark Twain scholars must be, to the Mark Twain Project at the University of California, Berkeley, where Robert Hirst and his staff were invaluable as I examined Twain manuscripts.

I have shared early versions of most parts of this book at conferences, especially MLA, SAMLA, and ALA. I am grateful for the clarifying responses I have received over the years as I shared my emerging ideas. My coda, "Mark Twain Studies and the Myth of Metaphor," originally appeared in *New Directions in Mark Twain Scholarship*, ed. Michael Kiskis and Laura Skandera Trombley (Columbia: University of Missouri Press, 2001). In a slightly different form, the section on *Those Extraordinary Twins* in Chapter 4 originally appeared in *A Companion to Mark Twain*, ed. Peter Messent and Louis J. Budd (Oxford: Blackwell Publishing, 2005). I am especially thankful for friends and colleagues in the American Humor Studies Association and the Mark Twain Circle of America; at the risk of omitting a number of people who have helped me along the way, I make a short list: Joe Alvarez, Joe McCullough, Joe Csicsila, Susan Harris, Michael Kiskis, Laura Skandera Trombley, Shelley Fisher Fishkin, Ann Ryan, Kerry Driscoll, David Sloane, Lou Budd, James Leonard, Vic Doyno, Peter Messent, Jeffrey Steinbrink, Gary Scharnhorst, Judith Yaross Lee, Larry Berkove, and Alan Gribben.

Most special thanks to several readers of my manuscript at various points along the way: my colleague Kelly Richardson; Bruce Michelson, for a thorough reading at a critical juncture and for his wise suggestions and crisp ideas; an anonymous reader for the University of Missouri Press, whose suggestions for revisions certainly made my book stronger; and Tom Quirk, whose keen eye, ear, and mind helped me more than he can know. The editors and staff at the University of Missouri Press have guided this book to its completion: Beverly Jarrett, Clair Willcox, Jane Lago, Beth Chandler, Karen Renner, Blaine Duncan, and Jennifer Gravley. Very special thanks to Gloria Thomas Beckfield for her meticulous and perceptive copyediting.

Finally, I would like to thank those closest to me, my family and friends, for their support and encouragement. My late parents, Pat and Jake Bird, introduced me to Mark Twain and inculcated in me a love of words, and they would have been proud to see and read this book. My brothers, Jim and Joe, and sister, Caroline, my sisters-in-law, Hing and Karen, and brother-in-law, Larry, my cousin Anita, and my friend Craig have all given me encouragement and patiently listened to me talk about Mark Twain and metaphor. My greatest debt is to my wife, to whom this book is lovingly dedicated.

Abbreviations

AMT	*The Autobiography of Mark Twain.* Ed. Charles Neider. New York: Harper, 1959.
CTSS1	*Mark Twain: Collected Tales, Sketches, Speeches, and Essays.* Vol. 1, *1852–1890.* Ed. Louis J. Budd. New York: Library of America, 1992.
CTSS2	*Mark Twain: Collected Tales, Sketches, Speeches, and Essays.* Vol. 2, *1891–1910.* Ed. Louis J. Budd. New York: Library of America, 1992.
CY	*A Connecticut Yankee in King Arthur's Court.* Ed. Bernard L. Stein. Berkeley: University of California Press, 1979.
DRT	*The Devil's Race-Track: Mark Twain's "Great Dark" Writings.* Ed. John S. Tuckey. Berkeley: University of California Press, 1980.
ET&S1	*Early Tales and Sketches.* Vol. 1, *1851–1864,* ed. Edgar Marquess Branch and Robert H. Hirst. Berkeley: University of California Press, 1979.
ET&S2	*Early Tales and Sketches.* Vol. 2, *1864–1865,* ed. Edgar Marquess Branch and Robert H. Hirst. Berkeley: University of California Press, 1981.
FE	*Following the Equator.* Ed. Shelley Fisher Fishkin. The Oxford Mark Twain. New York: Oxford University Press, 1996.
HF	*Adventures of Huckleberry Finn.* Ed. Victor Fischer and Lin Salamo with Walter Blair. Berkeley: University of California Press, 2003.
IA	*The Innocents Abroad.* Ed. Shelley Fisher Fishkin. The Oxford Mark Twain. New York: Oxford University Press, 1996.

LFE   *Letters from the Earth.* Ed. Bernard DeVoto. New York: Harper
           and Row, 1962.
LOM   *Life on the Mississippi.* Ed. John Seelye. New York: Oxford
           University Press, 1990.
MTHL   *Mark Twain–Howells Letters.* 2 vols. Ed. Henry Nash Smith and
           William M. Gibson. Cambridge: Harvard University Press,
           Belknap Press, 1960.
MTMSM   *Mark Twain's "Mysterious Stranger" Manuscripts.* Ed. William
           M. Gibson. Berkeley: University of California Press, 1969.
PWET   *"Pudd'nhead Wilson" and "Those Extraordinary Twins."* Ed.
           Sidney E. Berger. Norton Critical Editions. New York: Norton,
           1980.
RI   *Roughing It.* Ed. Harriet Elinor Smith and Edgar Marquess
           Branch. Berkeley: University of California Press, 1993.
SSWMT   *Selected Shorter Writings of Mark Twain.* Ed. Walter Blair.
           Boston: Houghton Mifflin, 1962.
TS   *The Adventures of Tom Sawyer.* Ed. John C. Gerber and Paul
           Baender. Berkeley: University of California Press, 1982.

Mark Twain and Metaphor

Introduction

Metaphor is the privileged expression of a profound vision: a vision that goes beyond appearances and penetrates to the "essence of things."

—Gérard Genette, *Figures of Literary Discourse*

We encounter Mark Twain almost always at the level of language. We may think we know him biographically as Samuel Clemens or critically as the persona he created, but in truth, we know him primarily from words: from his words, from the words that form in our minds as we read him, and from the words of the critics who write about him. This book focuses on a particular and fundamental aspect of Mark Twain's language: metaphor. One might quickly conclude that this is another study of Mark Twain's style—and while I do analyze his style at great length, metaphor can do much more than reveal style; it can reveal patterns of thinking, the unconscious, and hidden motives. It is especially powerful in dealing with humor and with dreams, two subjects vital to an understanding of Mark Twain and his works. Overall, it can show us more clearly Twain's creativity over the course of his writing career.

Because metaphor is so essential to the way language and thought work, it can uncover concepts that might otherwise go unnoticed, and it can shed new light on what has seemingly been studied thoroughly. It opens up new ground, and it makes old ground fresh again—to speak metaphorically about the way metaphor operates, as we invariably must. Using metaphor as a way to look at Mark Twain provides an excellent means to see and re-see this American writer, to, as I suggest in my chapter titles, "figure" Mark Twain.

Metaphor theory is like Mark Twain: both seem so simple upon first introduction. Metaphor: one thing compared to another; Mark Twain: a humorist who wrote a story about a young boy tricking his friends into doing his work for him, or about a frog who can out-jump every other frog. But before we know it, as we continue to read this "mere humorist," we are in much deeper, we are encased in complexity, we are in the world of hidden desires and dreams, we are exploring the white fear of the black, the male fear of the female, the despair of "the damned human race."

This book has four chapters and a coda. In the first chapter, "Figuring 'Mark Twain,'" I examine Twain's early career, as he worked to establish the persona named in his pseudonym. Using George Lakoff and Mark Johnson's concepts from *Metaphors We Live By*, I begin by investigating "The Jumping Frog," before moving to the metaphorical conflicts that lie behind *Roughing It*. I conclude the chapter by exploring the figurative implications of the pseudonym. Working from Kenneth Burke's idea of four master tropes, I argue that "Mark Twain" is itself a figure, and that what was being established was not merely an alter ego, but a metaphorized self (an idea I return to in the final chapter). The second chapter, "Figuring the River," focuses on the Mississippi River texts: "Old Times on the Mississippi," *The Adventures of Tom Sawyer*, and *Adventures of Huckleberry Finn*. First, I argue that "Old Times on the Mississippi" is the most metaphorically rich of Twain's major writings. Then I focus on the narrator of *Tom Sawyer*, asserting that by examining his metaphorical language, we can explain what seem like inconsistencies in the novel and reveal complexities in the characterization that otherwise might go unnoticed. Two sections on *Adventures of Huckleberry Finn* examine first the characters as victims of metaphor and then metaphorical images of black and white (addressing what has become the central critical concern about the novel: race). This chapter introduces critical issues I will return to several times: Roman Jakobson's influential ideas about metaphor and metonymy and Colin Turbayne's little-known but very powerful concept that metaphor victimizes us if we do not recognize its presence.

Chapter 3, "Figuring Metaphor," looks at how Twain used metaphor and talked about it, in a variety of works and genres. I examine the deliberate confusion of metaphor in "The Private History of a Campaign That Failed," showing how metaphorical language reveals a deeper meaning at the heart of the piece. I then move to *1601*, examining psychological metaphors of bodily functions, which helps us understand both the humor and the profundity of this strange little "dirty book." Next, I look at manuscripts to see how Twain constructed metaphor in four short stories over the span of his career ("A True Story," "The Invalid's Story," "Baker's Blue-jay Yarn," and "The Man That Corrupted Hadleyburg"), as well as in the first part of *Adventures of Huckleberry Finn*. A glimpse at the way he handled figurative language during the composing process not only reveals some hidden facets of his artistry and craftsmanship, but also, especially in the case of *Huckleberry Finn*, shows us new aspects of works we think we know well. The rediscovery of the first half of the manuscript allows us to see the way Twain persistently revised to *remove* metaphor, especially in the early part of the manuscript. The chapter concludes with a look at Twain's metaphors about the writing process in his correspondence with William Dean Howells, metaphors that help us understand his attitudes toward his work.

The fourth chapter, "Figuring the End," focuses on the end of Mark Twain's writing career, beginning with a look at the metaphorical underpinnings of *A Connecticut Yankee in King Arthur's Court*, then returning to Jakobson's metaphor / metonymy concept to make an argument about identity in *Pudd'nhead Wilson*, leading to an argument for taking *Those Extraordinary Twins* more seriously. Afterward, I examine Twain's jokes, jokes that span his career, using Freud's contemporaneous joke theory as a way to see the connection between jokes and metaphor. Jokes lead me to dreams, and to the late dream narratives, especially "The Great Dark" and *No. 44, The Mysterious Stranger.* Like many recent critics and readers, I see Twain's dark late years in an essentially positive light. Yes, he ended in despair, but even in his despair he still achieved great creativity and even affirmation.

As a conclusion, as a kind of coda, I return to both Turbayne and Jakobson in "Mark Twain Studies and the Myth of Metaphor" to highlight the way metaphor has shaped—and often distorted—Twain studies, and to argue that we must be more metaphorically aware as we read and write about Mark Twain, just as Twain was himself metaphorically aware.

The Princeton Handbook of Poetic Terms provides at least a starting point for defining "metaphor": "A condensed verbal relation in which an idea, image, or symbol may, by the presence of one or more other ideas, images, or symbols, be enhanced in vividness, complexity, or breadth of implication." But after that start, the handbook admits the inadequacy of these terms: "The nature and definition of metaphorical terms and of the relations between them have both been matter for much speculation and disagreement. It is unlikely therefore that a more specific definition will at first be acceptable." The student of metaphor encounters dozens of statements about the confusion over and inadequacy of any definition of it. In *The Rule of Metaphor*, Paul Ricoeur argues that "it is impossible to talk about metaphor non-metaphorically (in the sense implied by borrowing); in short, that the definition of metaphor returns on itself." He makes the point that even the word "figure" is metaphorical, which causes him to conclude, "There is no non-metaphorical standpoint from which one could look upon metaphor, and all the other figures for that matter, as if they were a game played before one's eyes. In many respects, the continuation of this study will be a prolonged battle with this paradox."[1] While recognizing the paradox, I want to find a way to talk about this slippery term. Wayne Booth makes a cogent statement that both recognizes the paradox and provides a way to continue the discussion:

> Perhaps this broadening of meaning and explosion of interest are all to the good. If we love metaphor, we surely should not complain when we find thousands of students taking it seriously. But there is a problem for students of any subject when the word for that subject expands to cover everything. And that is precisely what has happened to this word. Metaphor has by now been defined in so many ways that there is no human expression, whether in language or any other medium, that would not be metaphoric in *someone's* definition. This could mean that the word has become useless and that we should all take up some other line of inquiry. Surely when a word can mean everything it risks meaning nothing. But the interesting thing is that in spite of differences in the scope of our definitions, we all meet everyday certain statements that everyone recognizes as metaphor and calls by that name. We seem to have a kind of common-sense agreement about a fairly narrow definition, one that survives even while our theory expands the original concept beyond recognition.[2]

I share that "common-sense agreement," and I see in Booth's argument a way to move beyond the theoretical impasse.

Any study of metaphor necessarily involves theory, but it also involves practice, the practice of the writer. The distinction between theory and practice is itself artificial and problematic, of course, but consider how this argument from Turbayne applies to Twain:

> Knowing the theory of anything is contrasted with "know-how" in all the arts such as cricket, music, baseball, walking, writing, and seeing. Babe Ruth, Sir Donald Bradman, Beethoven, Greta Garbo, Michelangelo,

Don Juan, and Shakespeare, all great exponents of "know-how," probably knew how to manipulate their instruments to achieve the desired
results long before they knew the theory of their art. Perhaps some of
them never bothered to learn the theory. On the other hand, there are
many who know the theory better than these, but lack "know-how."[3]

Twain would surely fit Turbayne's list of "know-how" exponents—we will
see the various ways he "manipulates his instrument." Although he was
no theorist, we can use theorists to help us read his work.

But how to use them and their theories? I have made a decision to focus
on a plea from Phillip Stambovsky, who notes in *The Depictive Image:
Metaphor and Literary Experience* that theorists have looked at *"what
metaphor does"* and not enough at *how* metaphor operates. Stambovsky
continues: "The consequence in metaphor scholarship has been a profu-
sion of theories on the nature of metaphoric experience with few, if any,
criteria for selecting among alternative approaches in the way of net gain
in practical understanding of how literary metaphor operates, and this is
because there have been few inquiries into how metaphoric experience in
literature is a function of *literary* experience."[4]

That is precisely what I endeavor to do in this book: to think about how
"metaphoric experience in literature" functions in the literature of Mark
Twain, with special attention to the effect of metaphor on the reader. As
Stambovsky concludes, "To apprehend a literary metaphor in its narrative
or poetic context is an enactment, indeed a celebration, of the vital imme-
diacies and refinements of sensibility and awareness that artists have
always turned to metaphor to depict."[5] I should also make clear at the out-
set that by "metaphor," I do not mean merely the rhetorical device of comparing two unlike things, but a wider concept that embraces other figures:
simile, certainly, but also related figures such as metonymy and synecdoche. The study of metaphor, as used by metaphor critics, might more
properly be called the study of figures—hence my chapter titles.

One of the first modern metaphor critics, I. A. Richards, gives us a clearer
sense of what a study of metaphor will entail and an idea of the depths to
which an attention to metaphor can take us. "Throughout the history of
Rhetoric," Richards notes, "metaphor has been treated as a sort of happy
extra trick with words, an opportunity to exploit the accidents of their ver-
satility, something in place occasionally but requiring unusual skill and
caution. In brief, a grace or ornament or *added* power of language, not its
constitutive form." But metaphor operates on a much deeper level,
Richards argues:

In philosophy, above all, we can take no step safely without an unrelax-
ing awareness of the metaphors we, and our audience, may be employ-
ing; and though we may pretend to eschew them, we can attempt to do
so only by detecting them. And this is the more true, the more severe and
abstract the philosophy is. As it grows more abstract we think increasingly by means of metaphors that we profess *not* to be relying on. The
metaphors we are avoiding steer our thought as much as those we accept.
So it must be with any utterance for which it is less easy to know what
we are saying than what we are not saying.

In fact, Richards says, metaphor permeates all language, and thus all thought:
"That metaphor is the omnipresent principle of language can be shown by
mere observation. We cannot get through three sentences of ordinary fluid
discourse without it, as you will be noticing throughout this lecture."[6] I could
say the same for this book; when I chose the word "permeates," for example, I subsequently recognized its metaphorical nature, although I was not
conscious of seeking a metaphor as I initially chose my words.

Richards's thoughts on the purpose of metaphor study certainly apply
to my book: "Our skill with metaphor, with thought, is one thing—prodigious and inexplicable; our reflective awareness of that skill is quite another
thing—very incomplete, distorted, fallacious, over-simplifying. Its business is not to replace practice, or to tell us how to do what we cannot do
already; but to protect our natural skill from the interferences of unnecessarily crude views about it; and, above all, to assist the imparting of that
skill—that command of metaphor—from mind to mind." That connection
"from mind to mind"—specifically from Twain's mind to the reader's
mind—is an ever-present concern. Connections occurred in Twain's mind
as he wrote, and those connections, communicated through metaphor, are
revealing. To quote Richards again, "The mind is a connecting organ, it
works only by connecting and it can connect any two things in an indefi-
nitely large number of different ways. Which of these it chooses is settled
by reference to some larger whole or aim, and, though we may not discover its aim, the mind is never aimless."[7] Twain's "connecting organ" connected with the readers of his day, and it continues to connect with us, with
our own "connecting organs."

Therefore, metaphor can reveal much, as Richards concludes: "A 'command of metaphor'—a command of the interpretation of metaphors—can
go deeper still into the control of the world that we make for ourselves to
live in."[8] I begin, then, with a study that attempts to do no less than that:
to go deeper into and to reveal world, self, and life, both Twain's and his
readers'.

I am not alone, of course, among Mark Twain scholars and critics in focusing on metaphor, although no one else has yet done so at length. In his fine 1976 book, *The Art of Mark Twain*, William M. Gibson comments on the centrality of figurative language in Twain's works, noting "how persistently, self-consciously, and functionally he made use of figurative speech, both simile and metaphor." Gibson continues: "It [figurative language] helps also to explain why his enduring work, whether in speeches or private letters or persuasive prose, or fiction, so often strikes readers as still fresh and new. And it may serve as a new point of departure for the criticism of Mark Twain's fiction—particularly if we consider Howells's belief that the novel has its own laws of creation (mostly uninvestigated), whereas the 'romance' may be understood in fair part through the older, better understood laws of poetry." Gibson notes that, as of 1976, "few critics have addressed themselves to the figurative strain in Mark Twain's writings." Gibson does that quite ably in his book, demonstrating that "metaphor serves as a prime force in Mark Twain's writings."[9] My book extends the examination that Gibson began, and my purpose is to open some new ground in the study of Mark Twain and his works. That ground has already been so fully plowed, but metaphor is a mighty tool, and its blade strikes deep.

1

Figuring "Mark Twain"

It is a great thing, indeed, to make a proper use of the poetical forms, as also of compounds and strange words. But the greatest thing by far is to be a master of metaphor. It is the one thing that cannot be learnt from others; and it is also a sign of genius, since a good metaphor implies an intuitive perception of the similarity in dissimilars.

—Aristotle, *Poetics*

While we might agree with Aristotle that mastery of metaphor is a mark of genius in a writer, we would not agree that it is one thing that cannot be learned. If Twain's skill with metaphor were some supernatural gift bestowed on him from birth, that skill would be much less interesting. In fact, tracing the progress of his mastery of metaphor is one of the delights of reading and studying Mark Twain, as this book will show. We can see, however, that he was already skillful in the use of metaphor early in his writing career, which his 1865 story "Jim Smiley and His Jumping Frog" certainly demonstrates.[1] Metaphor lies at the heart of this polished jewel of a short sketch, a good jumping-off point for a study of Mark Twain and metaphor.

The two narrators, the genteel narrator of the outer frame and the vernacular narrator of the inner frame, have markedly different approaches to metaphor. They live, in fact, in two different metaphorical worlds, a contrast and conflict in language that we will see Twain explore repeatedly throughout his career. The outer narrator, "Mark Twain,"[2] uses formal, stuffy diction, as was common in the frame-tale tradition of southwestern humor. The inner narrator, Simon Wheeler, is informal, rambling, and lively. This distinction has been fully explored by commentators on the sketch, but closer attention to the contrasting ways they each use metaphor is revealing.

From the start, "Mark Twain" sounds like a lawyer: "In compliance with the request of a friend of mine . . . and I hereunto append the result" (*SSWMT*, 13). His most obvious metaphor is decidedly abstract: "I have a lurking suspicion that Leonidas W. Smiley is a myth." The narrator's mythic figure is "a young minister of the gospel" (*SSWMT*, 13)—as far removed as possible from the Jim Smiley we will soon meet. The outer narrator's only other figurative expressions have the air of dead metaphor: "[H]e would *go to work* and *bore me to death* . . ." (*SSWMT*, 13; my emphasis). Twain creates a character who seems to live in a stuffy world of abstract and even dead metaphor—an effect we will encounter more fully in *Roughing It* and *The Adventures of Tom Sawyer*.

The contrast with inner narrator Simon Wheeler's figurative language is palpable. Wheeler's similes are especially striking. Describing the bull-pup "Andrew Jackson," Wheeler says, "[H]is under-jaw'd begin to stick out like the fo'castle of a steamboat, and his teeth would uncover, and shine savage like the furnaces" (*SSWMT*, 15).[3] Twain's use of his piloting knowledge, which he was to draw on often for comparisons, animates the dog. His metaphorical descriptions of the frog "Dan'l Webster" are even more compelling: "He'd give him a little punch behind, and the next minute you'd see that frog whirling in the air like a doughnut—see him turn one summer-set, or maybe a couple, if he got a good start, and come down flatfooted and all right, like a cat" (*SSWMT*, 16). The comparison to a cat is somewhat conventional, but the comparison to a doughnut is visually compelling: the reader sees the scene almost as a cartoon, with the whirling frog becoming a round blur, a hole at the center of his spinning form. The next time his jumping is described, we are told that "he'd spring straight up and snake a fly off'n the counter there, and flop down on the floor ag'in as solid as a gob of mud, and fall to scratching the side of his head with his hind foot as indifferent as if he hadn't no idea he'd done any more'n any frog might do" (*SSWMT*, 16). "Solid as a gob of mud" is a master stroke of an image, drawing simultaneously on the senses of sight, hearing, touch, and smell. Further, it is particularly suitable in a description of a frog, given its usual environment. *Frog* and *mud* are linked metonymically, but here Twain (through Wheeler) turns the metonymy into metaphor. As we shall see, Twain is particularly adept at drawing metaphor from the domain of the subject he is discussing, creating images that resonate so strongly with us because they seem to be at once so outlandish and so natural.

The description of Dan'l after the stranger has filled him with shot ranks with Twain's best uses of metaphorical language: "Dan'l give a heave, and hysted up his shoulders—so—like a Frenchman, but it warn't no use—he couldn't budge; he was planted solid as a church, and he couldn't no more stir than if he was anchored out" (*SSWMT,* 18). Two similes and a metaphor, an incongruous movement from "Frenchman" to "church" to "anchor," is such a figuratively rich concentration. The image of a frog shrugging his shoulders, underscored by Wheeler's demonstration, marks the height of the absurd comedy of this piece, and the vivid comparison to a Frenchman only makes the humor more delicious: what does Simon Wheeler know of a Frenchman? To be sure, in the variegated world of the mining camps, he might have met a Frenchman, although one wonders. Perhaps he has been to France, although that too seems highly improbable. He does not strike the reader as a theatergoer, in which case he might have encountered caricatures of this emblematic gesture. The image comes, of course, from Twain, who had not yet become an innocent abroad, but certainly knew Frenchmen from his travels and his reading. Thus closely examined, the simile draws attention to itself as a simile, a simile that makes fun not only of Frenchmen, but of similes themselves. As Richard Wilbur puts it in his poem "Lying," "Odd that a thing is most itself when likened."[4] This contradiction—that the act of comparing two unlike things paradoxically makes the thing seem more real—lies at the heart of metaphor's power.

The image packs even more punch when we recognize Twain's implied joke that the reader must supply: the unspoken slur for a Frenchman. A Frenchman is a "frog," a metaphorical slur that began as a metonymy— the French eat frogs, hence the metonymic link. The frog is a Frenchman by the shrugging of his shoulders, even if a frog has no shoulders. As we shall see, Twain so often alludes to an unspoken joke, a joke embedded in figurative language, a jewel waiting to be dug out by the perceptive reader.

The outer narrator, Mark Twain posing as "Mark Twain," sees none of this richness, none of this humor, none of this absurdity. Like the stranger in the tale, he doesn't "see no p'ints about that frog that's any better'n any other frog" (*SSWMT,* 17). The contrast between the metaphorical visions of the outer narrator and Simon Wheeler becomes for us a portal into Twain's use of language, particularly his use of figurative language, and shows us early on the way attention to metaphor can open up and freshen our reading of his work.

The way Twain fulfilled his promise with metaphor subsequently in his writing is the subject of this book. To begin, however, I look at metaphor in a different way, not as an aspect of language that Twain controlled, but as a vehicle that he used unconsciously.

I. "The Jumping Frog" and the Metaphors Mark Twain Lives By

In their 1980 book, *Metaphors We Live By*, George Lakoff and Mark Johnson suggest how metaphor can define our sense of reality. Rather than examining metaphor as poetic language or as a rhetorical device, they look at what they call "ordinary language," at metaphorical language so common we often do not even recognize it as metaphorical. Taken as a whole, they argue, this pervasive, common metaphorical language defines our conceptual systems. For example, they cite the conceptual metaphor "argument is war," then show how everyday metaphorical language not only reflects but constructs that concept: "Your claims are *indefensible*. . . . His criticisms were *right on target*. I *demolished* his argument. . . . You disagree? Okay, *shoot!*" Part of their argument is that embracing such a conceptual metaphor governs our actions: if we think metaphorically of "argument as war," we will argue accordingly; if, on the other hand, we choose another conceptual metaphor—"argument is dance," for example—we will argue much differently. And such metaphorical concepts, they claim, are culturally driven: different cultures define themselves by different metaphors. One of their main points is the way orientational or spatialization metaphors organize most of our fundamental concepts. Whole conceptual systems are formed by seemingly simple spatialization concepts: "up/down," for example, constructs a number of analogous metaphorical concepts—happy/sad, conscious/unconscious, health/sickness, high status/low status, virtue/depravity—that we see reflected constantly in our everyday language.[5]

Applying Lakoff and Johnson's ideas to a literary work—looking not as we usually do at intentional metaphor, but at these common metaphors that pervade language—we can understand more clearly the conceptual systems faced by characters, cultural contexts, and the authors that create them all. A look at the metaphorical underpinnings of Mark Twain's "Jumping Frog" reveals the conceptual systems of the characters—Jim Smiley, Simon Wheeler, "Mark Twain" (the narrator)—as well as the conceptual systems of the culture. Even further, it reveals something about Twain at this critical juncture in his decision to commit to writing as a career and provides a first step in figuring Mark Twain. We see first the way three spatialization metaphors—up/down, inside/outside, and level/crooked—combine to reveal the conceptual metaphors that govern "The Jumping Frog."

As a long line of Mark Twain critics have shown, "The Jumping Frog" in its multiple versions (and titles) is complex despite its apparent simplicity, with a framework structure that gives it several narrative levels, each yielding contrast and conflict between narrators and characters, and with a number of thematic concerns.[6] At the center of the framework is the story of the frog that gives the story its title, and unlike Simon Wheeler, I begin there and examine three spatialization metaphors in operation to see what larger conceptual metaphor they reveal.

As one might expect in a frog story, there's a lot of up and down—most of it literal, but some of it metaphorical in the sense Lakoff and Johnson note. Simon Wheeler's description of the way Jim Smiley educates the frog shows this clearly (some of the description has already been quoted, but the full passage bears attention):

> He'd give him a little punch behind, and the next minute you'd see that frog whirling in the air like a doughnut—see him turn one summer-set, or maybe a couple, if he got a good start, and come down flat-footed and all right, like a cat. He got him up so in the matter of ketching flies, and kep' him in practice so constant, that he'd nail a fly every time as fur as he could see him. Smiley said all a frog wanted was education, and he could do most anything—and I believe him. Why, I've seen him set Dan'l Webster down here on the floor—Dan'l Webster was the name of the frog—and sing out "Flies, Dan'l, flies!" and quicker'n you could wink he'd spring straight up and snake a fly off'n the counter there, and flop down on the floor ag'in as solid as a gob of mud, and fall to scratching the side of his head with his hind foot as indifferent as if he hadn't no idea he'd been doin' any more'n any frog might do. (*SSWMT*, 16)

This literal up and down motion dominates the frog story, finally amounting to a metaphoric condition, as above, when Smiley got him "up so in the matter of ketching flies," "up" here becoming a metaphor for education. Of course, Jim Smiley gets him "up" so he can use him as an object of betting. Up and down are closely allied with gambling and money: "Smiley would ante up money on him as long as he had a red"; "he used to fetch him downtown sometimes and lay for a bet"; "[the stranger] put up his forty dollars along with Smiley's and set down to wait" (*SSWMT*, 17). Smiley's other animals, the mare and the bull-pup, are also up and down, in this same metaphorical sense. The mare is down in the race early on, "but," the narrator tells us, "always at the fag end of the race she'd get excited and desperate like, and come cavorting and straddling up, and scattering her legs around limber, sometimes in the air, and sometimes out to one side among the fences, and kicking up m-o-r-e dust and raising m-o-r-e racket with her coughing and sneezing and blowing her nose—and *always* fetch up at the stand just about a neck ahead, as near as you could cipher it down" (*SSWMT*, 15). The description of the dog is similar: "And he had a little bull-pup, that to look at him you'd think he warn't worth a cent but to set around and look ornery and lay for a chance to steal something. But as soon as the money was up on him he was a different dog . . ." (*SSWMT*, 15). In the dogfight he would be down "till the money was all up," then he would grab the other dog and "hang on till he throwed up the sponge" (*SSWMT*, 15). It becomes obvious that this is Jim Smiley's gambling method: educating up an animal to look down, then, when the bets are up, put the opponent down at the end.

Two other spatialization metaphors operate in "The Jumping Frog": inside/outside and level/crooked. On the outside, the animals don't appear to be much; the mare "always had the asthma, or the distemper, or the consumption," and the dog looks "ornery," and the stranger "don't see no p'ints about that frog that's any better'n any other frog" (*SSWMT*, 15, 17). But the inside is different: the dog "would have made a name for hisself if he'd lived, for the stuff was in him and he had genius"; the frog is "indifferent" and "modest" and "straight-for'ard," "for all he was so gifted" (*SSWMT*, 16). Like up/down, inside/outside is deceptive, and again forms the basis of Jim Smiley's gambling method.

Deception is also a part of the last spatialization metaphor, level/crooked: "[W]hen it come to fair and square jumping on a dead level, he could get over more ground than any animal of his breed you ever see. Jumping on a dead level was his strong suit, you understand" (*SSWMT*, 16–17)—but it is clear that there is nothing "fair and square" or "level" about betting on a frog who has been educated up to appear down, who looks so common on the outside but is so gifted on the inside.

All three metaphors converge in the climactic scene. When Jim Smiley goes "down" to the swamp to find a frog to put "up" against Dan'l, the stranger fills Dan'l's insides with quail-shot—"filled him pretty near up to his chin" (*SSWMT*, 17), Simon Wheeler says. They set the frogs "even," and count (everything is on the level), then "him and the feller touched up the frogs from behind, and the new frog hopped off lively, but Dan'l give a heave, and hysted up his shoulders—so—like a Frenchman, but it warn't no use—he couldn't budge; he was planted solid as a church, and he couldn't no more stir than if he was anchored out" (*SSWMT*, 18). Smiley looks "down at Dan'l a long time," then "he ketched Dan'l by the nap of the neck, and hefted him, and says, 'Why blame my cats if he don't weigh five pound!' and turned him upside down and he belched out a double handful of shot" (*SSWMT*, 18). Turning the frog upside down reveals what anchored him down, what was inside, what was not level. The metaphors all come together—and they are all reversed.

Taken together, these spatialization metaphors reveal the metaphor Jim Smiley lives by: life is a game of chance. Lakoff and Johnson cite this conceptual metaphor as one example of a metaphor people use to define their worldview, and they give instances of everyday speech that reflect this metaphorical stance: "I'll *take my chances*. The *odds are against me*. I've got *an ace up my sleeve*. . . . It's a *toss-up*. . . . He's *bluffing*. . . . Let's up the *ante*." Even though such phrases would not usually be taken as metaphorical expressions in everyday speech, they demonstrate, according to Lakoff and Johnson, that "your way of talking about, conceiving, and even experiencing your situation would be metaphorically structured."[7] And we can recognize that the three spatialization metaphors—up/down, inside/outside, level/crooked—are all crucial in the figurative language favored in gambling: to be up or down in a game, down on your luck, in or out of luck, to bet on inside information, to be on the level, or to be crooked, and so on.

Of course, we don't need metaphorical language to know this about Jim Smiley; after all, Simon Wheeler tells us that Jim "was the curiousest man about always betting on anything that turned up you ever see" (*SSWMT*, 14), and his whole story concerns a series of bets. But examining what Lakoff and Johnson call the entailments of the metaphor will reveal some aspects not only of Jim Smiley, but also of the sketch, its world, and its author.

When we say "life is a game of chance," we make a number of assumptions about the vehicle of the metaphor, assumptions that define life, the metaphor's tenor.[8] To say "life is a game of chance" assumes that it has rules, that we play at life, but that outcomes are random and cannot be predicted. Further, life is a conflict between at least two players, and the game is based on difference. Life has winners and losers, and we can never be sure of being either. Since life is a game, it is not serious, but we are often serious about the odds, the stakes, and the outcomes. In other words, what begins as a game often becomes quite serious. We can see from such assumptions what Jim Smiley values, and perhaps even more importantly, what he does not value. To live by the metaphor "life is a game of chance" means *not* living by metaphors that define life in terms of work, love, or religion, for example. Why devote life to work if you can make a living by play, by gambling? Similarly, gambling argues against most forms of love, since affection might get in the way of one's ability to bet. Carried to an extreme, the metaphor even precludes the idea of a supreme being, since life is based on chance and nothing is preordained.

In Simon Wheeler's description of him, Jim Smiley runs on all of these assumptions. He works only at gambling, a kind of play at which he "works" constantly. Apparently he has no love for any man, woman, or even animal; he values other living creatures only as objects to bet on or against. Men are valuable only as potential adversaries for a bet; the only woman mentioned is Parson Walker's wife, who becomes merely an object for betting whether or not she will die; and a succession of animals are valued not for the work they can do or for their value as companions, but because they are valuable in Jim's betting schemes. Everyone, then, is reduced to an object, an object to be used or beaten. Even religion is valuable only as a wager: "If there was a camp-meeting, he would be there reg'lar to bet on Parson Walker, which he judged to be the best exhorter about here" (*SSWMT*, 14). (Not a good enough exhorter, of course, to persuade Jim of the evils of gambling.) Such is Jim Smiley's world, and by extension, the world of the mining camp, a world of chance, of constant "work" at finding enough money never to have to work again, a world that excludes women and family and commitment, a world that excludes God. No small irony that the camp is named "Angel's."[9]

Interestingly, a contradiction lies at the heart of Jim Smiley's metaphor. Simon Wheeler tells us Jim would bet on anything, "if he could get anybody to bet on the other side; and if he couldn't he'd change sides" (*SSWMT*, 14). But in the case of the mare, the bull-pup, and the frog, the side is carefully chosen and he doesn't switch; indeed, the games are all fixed. Life may be a game of chance, but for Jim Smiley, it is often a fixed game, designed so that he'll usually be up, made crooked by the insider. But because others share his metaphor, they fix him: they put up a dog with no hind legs or they fill his frog with shot. According to Simon Wheeler, Jim "was lucky, uncommon lucky; he most always come out winner" (*SSWMT*, 14), but in two of the three cases, he loses to someone who is luckier—or, in actuality, to someone who fixes the game better than he does.

If we look at the other narrative levels of the sketch, we see the same metaphors in operation, again involving conflicts and contradictions, especially in the exchange between Simon Wheeler and "Mark Twain." Simon Wheeler is first down, "dozing comfortably by the barroom stove," then he "roused up," and then he backs "Mark Twain" into a corner and blockades him with a chair (*SSWMT*, 13–14). Simon Wheeler is the insider, "Mark Twain" the outsider; Simon Wheeler is monotonously level in his delivery, while "Mark Twain" is decidedly not level in some of his reactions (especially in the early version, where he mutters at the end, "O, curse Smiley and his afflicted cow!" [*ET&S2*, 288]). At the heart of the conflict between the two is again the conceptual metaphor "life is a game of chance." Simon Wheeler seems to see life that way: random, casual, and rambling. "Mark Twain" sees life as ordered, fixed, and useful. His language, as we have seen, is the language of law and business.[10] He calls Simon Wheeler's story "useless" (*SSWMT*, 13) and values it only as "information" (*SSWMT*, 18), unable to recognize the great worth of the story's humor.

But once again, the details of the story undercut and reverse such a duality. As others have noted, Simon Wheeler's narrative is anything but random.[11] He has a thesis (that Jim Smiley would bet on anything), an overview (an ordered succession of bets, from horse to dog to cat to chickens to "two birds setting on a fence" to Parson Walker—showing very clearly a preacher's place in the great chain of being, at least in this world that elevates chance over God's order—then down slightly, to a straddle bug), and particular examples, again in an ordered succession (horse, dog, frog). And despite the description by "Mark Twain" of his "monotonous narrative"—"He never smiled, he never frowned, he never changed his voice from the gentle-flowing key to which he tuned his initial sentence, he never betrayed the slightest suspicion of enthusiasm"—despite that, Simon Wheeler's many pauses and underlined words convey the sense of a lively story. Indeed, anyone who has ever read the piece aloud knows just how hard it would be to read this as a "monotonous narrative." The stance of "Mark Twain" is similarly contradictory: if he finds the story long, tedious, monotonous, boring, and useless, why then does he commit it to memory and write it all down for someone else to read? Or could these two, as a number of critics have argued, be engaged in a "double deadpan," each putting on the other but refusing to admit it?[12] And what of the friend from the East, who set up this whole up/down, inside/outside, level/crooked story in the first place?

What is most revealing, I think, is to look at what all these conflicts and oppositions tell us about Mark Twain. As biographers and critics have shown, "The Jumping Frog" represents a crucial point in Twain's decision to be a writer. In *Mark Twain: The Fate of Humor*, James M. Cox calls a letter written to Twain's brother Orion soon after the composition of "The Jumping Frog" "one of his most important letters." In that letter, dated October 19, 1865, Twain uses both religious and gambling conceptual metaphors: "I *have* had a 'call' to literature, of a low order—i.e., humorous. It is nothing to be proud of, but it is my strongest suit."[13] I would argue that just as clearly as this letter, the conflicting metaphors of the sketch show us Twain's conflicted state of mind at the time, that "The Jumping Frog" can be read as nothing less than a dramatized version of the writer's consciousness. In a purely biographical sense, we know that by leaving behind the mining camps and becoming a writer, he had already tried and rejected Jim Smiley's world, the world of chance, of laying for a bet, although his lifelong fascination with get-rich-quick schemes and inventions shows that he never quite rejected that metaphor fully.[14]

The conflict between Simon Wheeler and "Mark Twain," then, reveals Twain's conflicted attitude about his art. If he aligned himself with "Mark Twain," he would see the story as work, as something that must be useful, as a commodity. If he aligned himself with Simon Wheeler, he would see the story as interesting and important, but as something you reel off without any apparent thought or understanding. At stake here are conflicting metaphors about life and art. Is art, like life, random, or is it ordered? Is it a joke, or is it serious? Is it play, or is it work? The story would seem to indicate the first of the pairs: random, a joke, play. And art certainly is all three. But within itself it also contains contradictions that reverse all three: it is ordered, it is serious, and as Twain's long history of revision clearly shows, it is work. Once again, metaphorical language reveals both the pairs and their reversal.

Mark Twain's "Jumping Frog" embraces the conceptual metaphor, reverses it, then transcends it, yet all the while appearing to be simple, random, and chaotic. Like the frog and Simon Wheeler (he seems to be metaphorically aligned with both, more with them than with his own namesake within the story), Twain had more in him than appeared on the surface. When his art was at its best, when he was able to embrace and transcend those conflicting metaphors he lived by, he too "most always come out winner." Moving on, we see him again negotiate among conflicting metaphors in a longer narrative, written a few years later, but set in these same crucial formative years.

II. Metaphorical Conflict in Roughing It

Mark Twain's early travel book, *Roughing It,* was important for him as he tried to define and establish the persona he was in the process of creating. Published in 1872, its setting is ten years earlier. The period of the travel book's composition marks a time when Twain was figuring out who he was as a man, as a writer, and as a character.[15] The book has usually been viewed as dealing with a conflict between opposites: the vernacular vs. the genteel, the West vs. the East, the tenderfoot vs. the old-timer.

Those oppositions, still influential nearly a half century after they were proposed, are set forth in Henry Nash Smith's chapter "Transformation of a Tenderfoot" in his 1962 book, *Mark Twain: The Development of a Writer:*

> . . . Mark Twain is not simply reporting fact or reciting elegant associations, but writing an imaginative interpretation of his experience in the Far West. When the narrator speaks in the first person, the pronoun "I" links two quite different personae: that of a tenderfoot setting out across the plains, and that of an old-timer, a veteran who has seen the elephant and now looks back upon his own callow days of inexperience. Both are present in the narrative from the start. The contrast between them, which is an implied judgment upon the tenderfoot's innocence and a corresponding claim for the superior maturity and sophistication of the old-timer, is the consequence of precisely that journey which the book will describe.

Smith cites the race in chapter 5 between a coyote and a town dog as paradigmatic of the whole text; the "sick and sorry-looking" coyote outruns and outsmarts the seemingly superior town dog. Smith argues,

> This anecdote embodies a view of the relation between vernacular and conventional values. It involves a tenderfoot (that is, a representative of the dominant culture) with a higher opinion of himself than he can make good in the Far Western environment; a veteran who looks disreputable by town-bred standards but is nevertheless in secure command of the situation; and the process by which the tenderfoot gains knowledge, at the cost of humiliation to himself. The anecdote announces a reversal of values as the traveler passes from the accustomed life of towns to the strange life of the Far West.[16]

Without explicitly using the word "metaphor," Smith has outlined a metaphorical conflict that governs and informs the entire text, and as I have said, the metaphors Smith sets up have in large part governed criticism of the text. While I agree with Smith about the paradigmatic nature of this metaphorical conflict, I disagree about which side Twain is on. In fact, *Roughing It,* perhaps more than any other of his longer works, enacts Twain's attempt to figure out early on exactly who he is and where he stands in this pivotal conflict between East and West, between the genteel and the vernacular. A close examination of the metaphorical language in the text is the best way to see this conflict, specifically the often-reprinted story of Buck Fanshaw's funeral, which occurs a little more than halfway through the text, in chapter 47. This story serves as a paradigm of the metaphorical conflict in *Roughing It,* a key to an understanding not only of the text but also of Twain's emerging persona and his attitudes—an important continuation of the kind of self-defining begun in "The Jumping Frog" and other early tales and sketches.[17]

The pretext for the story is to give an example of the style of funerals in Virginia City, ostensibly to make a contrast between the way "the distinguished public benefactor" and "the distinguished rough" are buried, but the narrator tells only of one: the funeral of Buck Fanshaw, a saloon keeper, fireman, and "representative citizen" who had "killed his man" (*RI,* 308).[18] Actually, the story is more about a conversation between Scotty Briggs, a fireman and "stalwart rough," and the minister, "a fragile, gentle, spirituel [*sic*] new fledgling from an eastern theological seminary, and as yet unacquainted with the ways of the mines" (*RI,* 309). The description of Scotty that follows is more than "something of a contrast," as the narrator puts it with understatement: "Scotty was a stalwart rough, whose customary suit, when on weighty official business, like committee work, was a fire helmet, flaming red flannel shirt, patent leather belt with spanner and revolver attached, coat hung over arm, and pants stuffed into boot-tops. He formed something of a contrast to the pale theological student" (*RI,* 310). Their attempts to make funeral arrangements provide great linguistic comedy:

He [Scotty] was on a sorrowful mission, now, and his face was the picture of woe. Being admitted to the presence he sat down before the clergyman, placed his firehat on an unfinished manuscript sermon under the minister's nose, took from it a red silk handkerchief, wiped his brow and heaved a sigh of dismal impressiveness, explanatory of his business. He choked, and even shed tears; but with an effort he mastered his voice and said in lugubrious tones:

"Are you the duck that runs the gospel-mill next door?"

"Am I the—pardon me, I believe I do not understand?"

With another sigh and a half-sob, Scotty rejoined:

"Why you see we are in a bit of trouble, and the boys thought maybe you would give us a lift, if we'd tackle you—that is, if I've got the rights of it and you are the head clerk of the doxology-works next door."

"I am the shepherd in charge of the flock whose fold is next door."

"The which?"

"The spiritual adviser of the little company of believers whose sanctuary adjoins these premises."

Scotty scratched his head, reflected a moment, and then said:
"You ruther hold over me, pard. I reckon I can't call that hand. Ante and pass the buck." (*RI*, 310–11)

Critics are divided over Twain's sympathies in this scene. Richard Bridgman says that "Mark Twain's linguistic preference is never in doubt. He placed the highest value on the slang of Nevada"; Kenneth Lynn sees in "[t]he conflict between two radically different styles . . . the enduring drama of American humor, representing as it does a conflict between two utterly different concepts of what American life should be. . . . The anecdote makes it quite clear that . . . the narrator prefers Scotty Briggs's." But Henry Nash Smith says that, while "[t]he sketch exploits the familiar contrast between colloquial and pedantic speech, . . . the narrator no longer has the point of view of one of the boys," that he "is now fully identified with the point of view of an upper class that considers itself to be custodian of the official values."[19] Like three recent critics of the passage, Pascal Covici, David Sewell, and Don Florence, I would argue that neither position is correct, that Twain's position is both more ambivalent and more problematic than a simple alignment with one side or the other. Covici and Sewell reach that position by focusing on the linguistic nature of the conversation, specifically the slang Scotty uses in conflict with the minister's lofty diction. But rather than the slang, I focus, as does Florence, on the metaphorical conflict underlying this exchange.[20]

After the exchange between Scotty and the minister quoted above, the minister continues: "My friend, I seem to grow more and more bewildered. Your observations are wholly incomprehensible to me. Cannot you simplify them in some way? At first I thought perhaps I understood you, but I grope now. Would it not expedite matters if you restricted yourself to categorical statements of fact unencumbered with obstructing accumulations of metaphor and allegory?" (*RI*, 311). Rather than Scotty's slang, which the narrator has highlighted in his introduction, the minister focuses on the metaphorical nature of Scotty's language, the metaphors of poker, betting, fighting, and commerce that underlie the slang. What I find interesting is the way *both* speakers are using "obstructing accumulations of metaphor." Scotty's metaphors are obvious: "You ruther hold over me, pard. I reckon I can't call that hand. Ante and pass the buck" (*RI*, 311). The minister's are less obvious, making the reader and the minister himself think he is, in his words, restricting himself "to categorical statements of fact." The minister is "ignoring what his own language does," Florence points out, and thus "[h]is conversation with Scotty is not so much a clash of correct versus slang as it is an engagement between different symbolic systems."[21] So, rather than the two speaking on two different levels, metaphorical and literal, and thus not understanding each other, both are speaking on metaphorical levels, and despite Florence's point about "different symbolic systems," they are sometimes even in the same domain of metaphor—but they are still not able to communicate. A look back at the opening of their exchange will show what I mean. Scotty asks the minister if he is "the duck that runs the gospel-mill next door," metaphorically comparing the church to a business (and a low tradesman's business, at that.) In his next attempt, he employs the same domain of metaphor, asking if the minister is the "head clerk of the doxology-works next door." The minister answers this metaphorical question with a metaphorical answer: "I am the shepherd in charge of the flock . . . next door." Rather than "categorical statements of fact unencumbered with obstructing accumulations of metaphor," the minister uses his own metaphorical language as easily as Scotty uses metaphors of poker and commerce. To the minister, as well as to an audience steeped in biblical metaphor, such language has lost its metaphorical nature and seems literal. Scotty, having no such grounding, is still perplexed, so the minister moves to Scotty's metaphorical domain, echoing his business metaphor: "The spiritual adviser of the little *company* of believers whose sanctuary adjoins these *premises*" (my emphasis). The two still do not understand one another; the conflicting metaphors, even the metaphors within the same domain, do not meet and make meaning.

In terms of J. R. Searle's speech-act theory, what has happened here is a fundamental breakdown of the way metaphor operates; as Searle says, "The basic principle on which all metaphor works is that the utterance of an expression with its literal meaning and corresponding truth conditions can, in various ways that are specific to metaphor, call to mind another meaning and corresponding set of truth conditions." The reason this speech act breaks down is that neither speaker can move to that level of "another meaning and corresponding set of truth conditions." Lakoff and Johnson, in *Metaphors We Live By*, would explain the breakdown as a failure on the level of conceptual metaphor, the place where the metaphorical language we use all the time shows the way we view the world, either culturally or individually.[22] With his constant use of gambling metaphors, Scotty Briggs shows his metaphorical worldview, and shows himself to be a brother to Jim Smiley: for Scotty, as it is for Jim, life is a game of chance. The minister, of course, would have a quite different worldview. Thus, a failure of language through conflicting metaphors really shows a conflicting conception of the nature of existence. Their next exchange underscores this point:

> "Now we're all right, pard. Let's start fresh. Don't you mind my snuffling a little—becuz we're in a power of trouble. You see, one of the boys has gone up the flume—"
>
> "Gone where?"
>
> "Up the flume—throwed up the sponge, you understand."
>
> "Thrown up the sponge?"
>
> "Yes—kicked the bucket—"
>
> "Ah—has departed to that mysterious country from whose bourne no traveler returns."
>
> "Return! I reckon not. Why, pard, he's *dead!*"
>
> "Yes, I understand." (*RI*, 311–12)

Again, both are speaking metaphorically, within the same domain—death as a journey, death as an action—but failing to communicate because each has such a different philosophical view of death, as they do of life. Despite the minister's "I understand," the two do *not* understand each other, as their continuing dialogue shows. As Philip Beidler has argued in an important essay on *Roughing It*, the exchange between Scotty and the minister shows "the existence not simply of two conventions of discourse but of two complete and separate ways of knowing the world in its totality." He concludes that the conversation ends "in an outright impasse."[23] The impasse, I am arguing, is an impasse over metaphor.

The question of Twain's sympathy with these two is a tricky one. Smith's contention that, by this time in the text, the narrator is fully identified with an upper class doesn't seem to me to be borne out by the evidence, considering that the minister's stilted diction constantly makes him a target of ridicule. Smith bases his assertion on what he sees as condescension in the narrator's tone as he describes Scotty Briggs, which is partly true, but I think Smith overlooks a key explanation from the narrator as he initially introduces the story: "Slang was the language of Nevada. It was hard to preach a sermon without it, and be understood" (*RI*, 309). Obviously, this statement makes a very pointed criticism against the "fledgling from an eastern theological seminary" (*RI*, 309), as the narrator describes the minister. Even though the focus of the story seems to be on Scotty Briggs's colorful language and the humor of the incongruous exchange, a clear subtext concerns the need to be able to speak the local language and, even more importantly, to use the local conceptual metaphors in order to do one's job and be understood. Clearly, a mastery of the vernacular has important ramifications for

Twain, too, embarking as he was on a career of using language to communicate, and trying to find the language that would let him do that.

Does Twain's sympathy lie, then, with Scotty Briggs and his more colorful metaphorical language? At first, that seems to be the case. As David Sewell argues in *Mark Twain's Languages*, "We are more sympathetic toward Scotty because he is by far the more fully realized character of the two; moreover, Twain's major object in this chapter was to create a tour de force of Western slang, the success of which is certified by his contemporaries' appreciative response." But according to Sewell, the real target "is language itself, which creates as much opportunity for misunderstanding as for communication." The target is indeed language, but more specifically metaphorical language: Twain is attacking not only the minister's inability to use the local metaphorical slang, but also Scotty's inability to speak in any other figurative language. Scotty's slang, as colorful as it appears to be at first, soon becomes highly clichéd; his "throwed up the sponge" and "kicked the bucket" are as much clichés as the minister's "departed to that mysterious country from whose bourne no traveler returns." To a writer embarking on a career in which his first devotion is to finding fresh, precise language to recount his perception of experience, both forms of cliché are targets. Even worse, Scotty's expressions increasingly become meaningless and absurd; he repeats the phrase "no Irish need apply" in nearly any circumstance, including as a benediction after the prayer at Buck Fanshaw's funeral, apparently, the narrator says, as a heartfelt tribute to Buck, but the phrase is at best meaningless and at worst, as Sewell argues, "exclusive and even xenophobic." Indeed, the reader has trouble sympathizing with Scotty as he eulogizes his dead friend while making offhand derogatory remarks about Micks, Catholics, Greasers, and niggers. Surely Twain's allegiance is not completely with *either* character; he is, as Covici argues, quite ambivalent.[24]

The case becomes even more complicated, and the complications concern both characters. As a kind of coda to the story, the narrator tells of Scotty's later career:

> Scotty Briggs, in after days, achieved the distinction of becoming the only convert to religion that was ever gathered from the Virginia roughs; and it transpired that the man who had it in him to espouse the quarrel of the weak out of inborn nobility of spirit was no mean timber whereof to construct a Christian. The making him one did not warp his generosity or diminish his courage; on the contrary it gave intelligent direction to the one and a broader field to the other. If his Sunday-school class progressed faster than the other classes, was it matter for wonder? I think not. He

talked to his pioneer small-fry in a language they understood! It was my large privilege, a month before he died, to hear him tell the beautiful story of Joseph and his brethren to his class "without looking at the book." I leave it to the reader to fancy what it was like, as it fell, riddled with slang, from the lips of that grave, earnest teacher, and was listened to by his little learners with a consuming interest that showed that they were as unconscious as he was that any violence was being done to the sacred proprieties! (*RI*, 316–17)

Smith cites this comment as another example of the narrator's condescension toward Scotty and a mark of his stance: "The narrator is now fully identified with the point of view of an upper class that considers itself to be custodian of the official values."[25] But our focus on metaphor shows that he is certainly not "fully identified"; and while there are without a doubt traces of condescension, if one recalls his remark about the impossibility of preaching a sermon without slang, it becomes clear that even this stance also contains admiration; whatever the improprieties, Scotty, unlike the minister, can communicate his message.

The case with the minister is also somewhat complicated. Before he begins the story, the narrator says of Scotty's visit that "in after days it was worth something to hear the minister tell about it" (*RI*, 309–10). Therefore, not only was this pale eastern minister able to remain in the rough western mining town, but he also was able to appreciate the humor of the situation, as well as, one supposes, at last to understand Scotty's slang and be able to repeat it. The minister, then, at least in after days, is aligned more with the narrator, who is after all a master of both levels of metaphor—similar to the stance Twain finally holds in "The Jumping Frog." The minister is like the coyote in that early passage: he looks like less, but in the end, he "wins." For one thing, he converts Scotty. But even more importantly, because the minister is telling the story with relish and understanding, he has mastered both languages—like Twain, the minister seems to have become a master of metaphor. Metaphor often combines the high and the low in one compact, fresh expression. That is what the mining camp does, what the West does, what *Roughing It* does. As Florence argues, "Love, compassion, and reverence for the dead may be expressed as aptly through the metaphors of poker as through those of the Bible and Shakespeare: all metaphors have their common ground in the imagination."[26]

Twain was learning how to use metaphor to its full artistic value, and what the Scotty Briggs episode metaphorically shows us is that process. Here, as in all of *Roughing It*, he is trying to find his voice, trying to negotiate a register of language somewhere between the vernacular of what the narrator calls the "vast bottom-stratum of society" (*RI*, 308) that Scotty Briggs represents and the heightened diction of the pale eastern minister and, by extension, the accepted literary diction of the day. Covici sums up the point well in his entry on the episode in *The Mark Twain Encyclopedia:* "Celebrating wild western slang as it becomes an eastern tool of domestication, Twain here fashions a wonderfully successful linguistic tour de force and a comprehensive, albeit brief, survey of attitudes and values that will concern him for the rest of his writing life."[27] More inclusively and precisely, I am arguing, he creates this linguistic tour de force through a conflict of metaphors, a conflict that on the surface seems relatively straightforward and uncomplicated, apparently on the side of the West and the vernacular at the expense of the East and the genteel, but a conflict that on closer examination reveals ambivalence and complexity—and in its conflict, enacts before the reader Mark Twain's evolving skill with metaphor.[28]

We can see this metaphoric conflict throughout *Roughing It,* as an examination of some key passages will show. It begins even before the narrative starts, in Twain's "Prefatory," where he insists, "This book is merely a personal narrative, and not a pretentious history or a philosophical dissertation" (*RI*, xxiv). He continues for a full paragraph, promising "information concerning an interesting episode in the history of the Far West, about which no books have been written by persons who were on the ground in person, and saw the happenings of the time with their own eyes" (*RI*, xxiv). His tone is serious and proper, and his language is formal, even Latinate. The next paragraph marks a radical shift in attitude and language, with an extended metaphor that borders on the absurd: "Yes, take it all around, there is quite a good deal of information in the book. I regret this very much; but really it could not be helped; information appears to stew out of me naturally, like the precious ottar of roses out of the otter. Sometimes it has seemed to me that I would give worlds if I could retain my facts; but it cannot be. The more I caulk up the sources, and the tighter I get, the more I leak wisdom. Therefore, I can only claim indulgence at the hands of the reader, not justification" (*RI*, xxiv). This comment serves as an excellent introduction to the book, which contains not only much information, but also much absurdity, on the order of "precious ottar of roses out of the otter."[29] The metaphorical conflict is thus waged from the very beginning.

Twain packs for his upcoming journey with literal linguistic baggage. From the start, we see language—eastern language—unnecessarily carried to the West. The narrator tells us that among the baggage is "six pounds of Unabridged Dictionary; for we did not know—poor innocents—that such things could be bought in San Francisco on one day and received in

Carson City the next" (*RI*, 45). This unnecessary baggage soon begins to assault the passengers: "Every time we avalanched from one end of the stage to the other, the Unabridged Dictionary would come too; and every time it came it damaged somebody. One trip it 'barked' the Secretary's elbow; the next trip it hurt me in the stomach, and the third it tilted Bemis's nose up till he could look down his nostrils—he said" (*RI*, 58). The literal baggage is converted to metaphorical baggage, baggage that assaults, a metaphor that prefigures the conflicts of language that are to mark the text.

As the narrative gets under way, and as the travelers are passing many milestones on their journey west, an important linguistic (and metaphoric) milestone is passed at breakfast. The narrator describes the gruff men's table manners:

> We could not eat, and there was no conversation among the hostlers and herdsmen—we all sat at the same board. At least there was no conversation further than a single hurried request, now and then, from one employé to another. It was always in the same form, and always gruffly friendly. Its Western freshness and novelty startled me, at first, and interested me; but it presently grew monotonous, and lost its charm. It was:
> "Pass the bread, you son of a skunk!" No, I forget—skunk was not the word; it seems to me it was still stronger than that; I know it was, in fact, but it is gone from my memory, apparently. However, it is no matter—probably it was too strong for print, anyway. (*RI*, 25–26)

His concluding sentence underscores the importance of the strong language, a link to the conflict of metaphor between Scotty Briggs and the pale young minister: "It is the landmark in my memory which tells me where I first encountered the vigorous new vernacular of the occidental plains and mountains" (*RI*, 26). That landmark is not only "the vigorous new vernacular," but also the vigorous metaphor that propels the vernacular.

The coyote and town-dog episode that Henry Nash Smith justly cites as paradigmatic of the whole book immediately follows this linguistic landmark, and it is, as Smith argues, a landmark that shows the conflict between eastern and western values.[30] Like any of the animals in "The Jumping Frog," the coyote does not at first appear to be very much; in the race with a town dog who "has a good opinion of himself," he does the same as Andrew Jackson the bull-pup or Dan'l Webster the frog: he doesn't look like he is fast at all, but then toys with the dog, leading him on, even letting up on purpose. Finally, in an unstated but clear comparison to thunder and lightning, he disappears into the distance: "[F]orthwith there is a rushing sound, and the sudden splitting of a long crack through the atmosphere, and behold that dog is solitary and alone in the midst of a vast solitude!" (*RI*, 32). Smith sees the metaphorical relationship between the coyote and dog and the veteran and tenderfoot, and further between vernacular and conventional values (without ever explicitly calling the relationship metaphorical), but errs, I think, in seeing the relationship as clear-cut. The situation outlined in *Roughing It* is more complex than an initiation story, a "transformation of a tenderfoot," as Smith calls it in his chapter title; and the Mark Twain we are presented with is more complex than a comparison of a naive young traveler and a grizzled veteran. As participant, Twain is indeed the tenderfoot, and by the end he is the veteran, but as narrator, he is in yet another position. He is more like the minister in after years, who is able to tell the story of Scotty Briggs with relish, a master finally of both domains of metaphor, and able to see his former self as a somewhat ridiculous figure. The figurative language constantly highlights this complexity and conflict.[31]

We can see evidence of this narrative stance throughout, as when a stagecoach driver says "the Apaches used to annoy him all the time down there, and that he came as near as anything to starving to death in the midst of abundance, because they kept him so leaky with bullet holes that 'he couldn't hold his vittles'" (*RI*, 55–56). The incongruous hyperbolic figurative language and the implied metaphor are presented in a mixture of formal and vernacular language, seemingly separated by the quotation marks, but with the vernacular actually imbedded in the indirect discourse—"came as near as anything to starving to death"—and the formal immediately following—"in the midst of abundance." The similarity to the narrator's leaky metaphor in the preface is highlighted even further by his concluding sentence, dripping with understatement: "This person's statements were not generally believed" (*RI*, 56). The passive-voice construction hides from us the attitude being presented here: not generally believed by whom? The tenderfoot? The old-timer? Perhaps both—but certainly by the narrator, who can manipulate the language of all stances, skillfully blending it, in control.

The narrator stands in contrast to Joseph Smith, a contrast we see in a passage of literary criticism that tells us much about the narrator's control and his response to a lack of mastery. The comments on the Mormon Bible are incisive, humorous, and loaded with metaphor: "The book is a curiosity to me, it is such a pretentious affair, and yet so 'slow,' so sleepy; such an insipid mess of inspiration. It is chloroform in print" (*RI*, 107). The chloroform metaphor is followed, characteristically, with a joke that extends the metaphor: "If Joseph Smith composed this book, the act was a miracle—

keeping awake while he did it, at any rate" (*RI*, 107). His further comments contain yet more metaphor: "The author labored to give his words and phrases the quaint, old-fashioned sound and structure of our King James's translation of the Scriptures; and the result is a mongrel—half modern glibness, and half ancient simplicity and gravity. The latter is awkward and constrained; the former natural, but grotesque by the contrast" (*RI*, 107). Such a textual "mongrel" is precisely what Twain could have written in *Roughing It* had he not been so skillful with language, with all domains of metaphor. Instead, we have a book where the levels of language are in conflict, but because they are so tightly controlled, the formal is not "awkward and constrained," and the vernacular is not "grotesque by the contrast." The mixture is, instead, rich and delightful, as the Scotty Briggs episode proves.

In one more example, Twain combines the vernacular and the formal view in a way that seems effortless, but is actually quite skillful in negotiating conflicting levels of language. In this episode, spanning chapters 31–33 (often reprinted with the title "Lost in a Snowstorm"), Twain moves to a new place with language by transcending the positions of *both* Scotty Briggs and the pale young minister.

The three characters are Ollendorff, the Prussian Ballou (whose speech is riddled with malapropisms), and "Mark Twain." Despite the rich possibilities for conflicting vernaculars with these three, the narrative generally avoids direct quotation, peppering the dialogue occasionally with Ballou's eccentric use of language, and giving Ollendorff's one long speech in very correct, even formal English, rather than the doggerel German dialect one might expect. The result is a long passage of narration from Mark Twain's stance, with most of the dialogue concealed in indirect discourse. Ballou's malapropisms add to the humor, as when the travelers discover that they have not been following a troop of soldiers that is increasing in numbers, but instead walking in circles: "Boys, these are our own tracks, and we've actually been circussing round and round in a circle for more than two hours, out here in this blind desert. By George this is perfectly hydraulic!" (*RI*, 208). In the next paragraph, the narrator says, "Then the old man waxed wroth and abusive. He called Ollendorff all manner of hard names—said he never saw such a lurid fool as he was, and ended with the peculiarly venomous opinion that 'he did not know as much as a logarythm!'" (*RI*, 208). Ballou's anger stems from the fact that Ollendorff had claimed an infallible sense of direction, and the narrator uses an especially good simile, and an unexpected one if coming verbatim from Ollendorff: "He said that if he were to straggle a single point

out of the true line his instinct would assail him like an outraged conscience" (*RI*, 207). The narrator's language dominates the rest of the
episode, and therein lies much of its power. The paragraph describing their
attempts to start a fire by firing a pistol at the firewood, something they
had learned in books, is a good example:

> We huddled together on our knees in the deep snow, and the horses put
> their noses together and bowed their patient heads over us; and while
> the feathery flakes eddied down and turned us into a group of white stat-
> uary, we proceeded with the momentous experiment. We broke twigs
> from a sage-brush and piled them on a little cleared place in the shelter
> of our bodies. In the course of ten or fifteen minutes all was ready, and
> then, while conversation ceased and our pulses beat low with anxious
> suspense, Ollendorff applied his revolver, pulled the trigger and blew the
> pile clear out of the county! It was the flattest failure that ever was. (*RI*,
> 211)

This passage serves as a linguistic paradigm for the whole episode: formal
language driven by formal metaphor ("feathery flakes eddied down and
turned us into a group of white statuary") is halted by the literal explosion
of the gun, then punctuated by the figurative vernacular ("blew the pile
clear out of the county"). Throughout the episode, Twain sets up the
reader's expectations with heightened formal metaphoric diction, border-
ing on the edge of melodrama and even sentimentality, then blows up the
tone with his vernacular metaphoric vision, as when he describes the young
Swede who landed his canoe among them "and took his pedestrian way
Carsonwards, singing his same tiresome song about his 'sister and his
brother' and 'the child in its grave with the mother,' and in a short minute
faded and disappeared in the white oblivion" (*RI*, 209). After ridiculing
the sentimental songs, the narrator himself wades deep into the conventional language of death and loss, then punctures the metaphorical vision
with a joke: "He was never heard of again. He no doubt got bewildered
and lost, and Fatigue delivered him over to Sleep and Sleep betrayed him
to Death. Possibly he followed our treacherous tracks till he became
exhausted and dropped" (*RI*, 209). What Twain manages here is language
that is sentimental and at the same time a lampoon of sentimentality. The
mixture, rather than being a "textual mongrel," is a skillful blend that con-
tinually sets up, then frustrates, the reader's expectations, with delightfully
humorous results.

   After the failed attempt at lighting the fire with a pistol, they try rub-
bing two sticks together, to no avail: "At the end of half an hour we were

thoroughly chilled, and so were the sticks" (*RI*, 213). The remainder of
this paragraph exemplifies Twain's blending of metaphorical levels:

> At this critical moment Mr. Ballou fished out four matches from the rub-
> bish of an overlooked pocket. To have found four gold bars would have
> seemed poor and cheap good luck compared to this. One cannot think
> how good a match looks under such circumstances—or how lovable and
> precious, and sacredly beautiful to the eye. This time we gathered sticks
> with high hopes; and when Mr. Ballou prepared to light the first match,
> there was an amount of interest centred upon him that pages of writing
> could not describe. The match burned hopefully a moment, and then
> went out. It could not have carried more regret with it if it had been a
> human life. The next match simply flashed and died. The wind puffed
> the third one out just as it was on the imminent verge of success. We gath-
> ered together closer than ever, and developed a solicitude that was rapt
> and painful, as Mr. Ballou scratched our last hope on his leg. It lit, burned
> blue and sickly, and then budded into a robust flame. Shading it with his
> hands, the old gentleman bent gradually down and every heart went with
> him—everybody, too, for that matter—and blood and breath stood still.
> The flame touched the sticks at last, took gradual hold upon them—hes-
> itated—took a stronger hold—hesitated again—held its breath five heart-
> breaking seconds, then gave a sort of human gasp and went out. (*RI*,
> 213–14)

The personification of the matches and the fire is handled skillfully, with
the proper formal solemnity, through understated metaphor rather than
attention-grabbing similes, and overall amounts to an apt metaphorical
view of their situation. The scene that follows, in which each man gives up
his pet vice, is set up by this solemnity, with the reader somewhat unsure
how to react. The scene is serious, but as the metaphorical language continues to build, we begin to suspect we are being had. Ollendorff's reform
from drinking is presented in indirect discourse and contains the metaphorical language of temperance reform that it parodies:

> Then he got out his bottle of whisky and said that whether he lived or
> died he would never touch another drop. He said he had given up all
> hope of life, and although ill-prepared, was ready to submit humbly to
> his fate; that he wished he could be spared a little longer, not for any self-
> ish reason, but to make a thorough reform in his character, and by devot-
> ing himself to helping the poor, nursing the sick, and pleading with
> people to guard themselves against the evils of intemperance, make his
> life a beneficent example to the young, and lay it down at last with the

precious reflection that his reform should begin at this moment, even here in the presence of death, since no longer time was to be vouchsafed wherein to prosecute it to men's help and benefit—and with that he threw away the bottle of whisky. (*RI,* 214–15)

The chapter ends with the three holding on to one another, as they "awaited the warning drowsiness that precedes death by freezing" (*RI,* 216), and then the final, metaphor-rich ending: "It came stealing over us presently, and then we bade each other a last farewell. A delicious dreaminess wrought its web about my yielding senses, while the snow-flakes wove a winding sheet about my conquered body. Oblivion came. The battle of life was done" (*RI,* 216). This satiric burlesque of romantic death scenes is well controlled, adopting the metaphorical stance of sentimental fiction, yet at the same time co-opting it, in control of it, with the conflict between the vernacular and formal vision deeply embedded in its heart. The vernacular reemerges as the men wake up, with the inevitable puncturing of the whole scene: "Will some gentleman be so good as to kick me behind?" (*RI,* 217). They have, of course, carried out their drama of reform and death within a few feet of the stage station. With one further twist, so true to human psychology, and so deliciously funny, Twain wants to smoke after breakfast, already going back on his vow of reform. He searches for his pipe in a snowdrift, and the conflict between the formal and vernacular visions reaches its climax:

> I discovered it after a considerable search, and crept away to hide myself and enjoy it. I remained behind the barn a good while, asking myself how I would feel if my braver, stronger, truer comrades should catch me in my degradation. As last I lit the pipe, and no human being can feel meaner and baser than I did then. I was ashamed of being in my own pitiful company. Still dreading discovery, I felt that perhaps the further side of the barn would be somewhat safer, and so I turned the corner. As I turned the one corner, smoking, Ollendorff turned the other with his bottle to his lips, and between us sat unconscious Ballou deep in a game of "solitaire" with the old greasy cards! (*RI,* 219)

Never again, after this, can one read either a tale of freezing to death or one of character reform the same way; as the narrator concludes, "Absurdity could go no farther. We shook hands and agreed to say no more about 'reform' and 'examples to the rising generation'" (*RI,* 219). In one final grim point, he tells us that two men actually *had* died in the snowstorm—yet another turn of the screw.

I would suggest that this episode represents the heart of Mark Twain's comic genius, offered early in his writing career. At the center of his achievement is his control of language, specifically control of the conflict over metaphorical visions and control of metaphor itself. We see this control at the level of language, at the level of metaphor, but the ramifications extend outward to include much more: the creation of a prose style, but also the creation of a persona, the negotiation between young, bachelor life in the West and adult, married life in the East. James Cox says *Roughing It* embodies "the myth of Mark Twain," defining "myth" this way:

> Myth, after all, is the narrative from which we cannot escape. It is what remains after our skepticism trims experience to the core. Yet if myth is consciously adopted, it becomes not the inescapable narrative of our lives but an experience we are trying to recover. It is the forgotten language, the buried life, the undiscovered mode of awareness which, having existed all the time, must be brought up from the depths of the memory or out from behind the appearance of the world. Whether such a myth lies outside or inside the self, its values are discovered through struggle, sacrifice, initiation, and recognition.

The power of metaphor is its ability to give us precisely those powers of recovery and discovery, of struggle and recognition. Perhaps metaphor is the key to remembering "the forgotten language," to finding "the undiscovered mode of awareness." Although metaphor is a matter of style, it goes much deeper and reveals more than we would at first imagine. Gérard Genette makes this important point in an analysis of Proust: "Thus metaphor is not an ornament, but the necessary instrument for a recovery, through style, of the vision of essences, because it is the stylistic equivalent of the psychological experience of involuntary memory, which alone, by bringing together two sensations separated in time, is able to release their *common essence* through the *miracle of an analogy*—though metaphor has an added advantage over reminiscence, in that the latter is a fleeting contemplation of eternity, while the former enjoys the permanence of the work of art."[32]

Genette's words lie at the heart of what I am arguing about Mark Twain and metaphor; his words are so important that I will return to them again at several junctures in this book. The way Twain learned to negotiate the conflicts of metaphor in *Roughing It* shows us more than a writer trying to establish his style; it shows him in the act of creating, as Cox argues, his persona and his myth. Perhaps one way to better understand the persona and myth of Mark Twain is to take a closer look at "Mark Twain"—at the metaphorical underpinnings of the famous pseudonym.

III. "Mark Twain" and the Four Master Tropes

Who is Mark Twain? That has always been the question.

Susan Gillman makes the point in the introduction to her book *Dark Twins* (1989): "Ever since William Dean Howells insisted in his memoir *My Mark Twain* on defying his own title and calling his friend 'Clemens . . . instead of Mark Twain, which seemed always to mask him,' the peculiarly double personality Samuel Clemens/Mark Twain has continued to elude and to fascinate. A critical language of twinning, doubling, and impersonation has subsequently developed around this writer, in part fostered by what James Cox calls 'the primal act of inventing Mark Twain.'"[33] This is not only "a critical language of twinning," but a *metaphorical* language of twinning—a rich and complex metaphor that underlies and shapes the critical language, often without the critics' knowledge—an idea I explore at the end of this book. For now, I will pose a slightly different question: "*What is* 'Mark Twain'?"—a double shift, from "who?" to "what?" and from Mark Twain to "Mark Twain"—to analyze not Mark Twain the man, whoever he is or was, but "Mark Twain" the pseudonym. It turns out that the pen name is almost as puzzling and ambiguous as the man.

Even the history of the name is interesting and puzzling. Samuel Clemens first used the pseudonym "Mark Twain" in "Letter from Carson City," a short piece for the *Territorial Enterprise,* published February 3, 1863 (*ET&S1*, 192). As Edgar Marquess Branch and Robert H. Hirst, the editors of *Early Tales and Sketches,* suggest, "his remark 'I feel very much as if I had just awakened out of a long sleep' seems deeply appropriate" (*ET&S1,* 192). Though his own explanations about the name's origins are a bit murky, we commonly accept the association with the cry of the leadsman on a steamboat as he sounded the water for safe passage: "mark one" means six feet, or one fathom; "mark twain" means twelve feet, or two fathoms, and safe water for passage. The other story comes from his Washoe mining days, when the call "mark twain" was an indicator to the bartender to give two drinks on credit, then make two marks for future payment—making the pseudonym what John Gerber calls "an in-joke among Sam Clemens's drinking companions."[34] I will return to these stories of the name, including some interesting inconsistencies, but first we should consider the figurative implications of the words in the name.

Rich enough in itself are the name's metaphorical implications, but in reading Kenneth Burke, I found an even richer and more comprehensive approach, what Burke calls "the four master tropes": metaphor, metonymy, synecdoche, and irony. In an appendix to *A Grammar of Motives,* seemingly as a literal afterthought to his monumental book, Burke lays out his proposal concerning the four figures: "[M]y primary concern with them here will be not with their purely literal usage, but with their rôle in the discovery and description of 'the truth.' It is an evanescent moment that we shall deal with—for not only does the dividing line between the figurative and literal usages shift, but also the four tropes shade into one another. Give a man but one of them, tell him to exploit its possibilities, and if he is thorough in doing so, he will come upon the other three."[35] Though I do not share Burke's assurance that such an examination will result in "the discovery and description of 'the truth,'" subjecting the name to these four perspectives can help shed light not only on the name, but on the writer who took the name as his pseudonym, as his mask, as his alter ego. By circling the name from several perspectives, we will gain a fuller understanding of its complexities.

First, then, "Mark Twain" as metaphor. Its metaphoric implications are obvious, and explain why the name resonated with audiences from the very beginning and enduringly, in a way that other pseudonyms from the time—Petroleum V. Nasby, Orpheus C. Kerr, Josh Billings—have not. In fact, the name has from the beginning shaped the way we read and interpret the writer. The metaphoric implications of doubles and twins and splits that derive from "twain" show, as Gillman and others have argued, the author's fascination with dualities of all kinds, and the history of Twain criticism is a history of doubling and splits.

While we have always paid attention to "twain," we have paid less attention to "mark," since we have always taken the word as a first name and are less likely to read it figuratively. But "mark" by itself is rich in meaning. *Webster's Third New International Dictionary* (1993) lists two main meanings for "twain": "two, a couple, a pair," and, as a verb, "divide, part, sunder." By contrast, "mark" takes up nearly two columns, with more than sixty possible meanings. When we unite the two words, the complexity becomes staggering. If the "mark" is an "impression or trace made on something," it becomes either two impressions or one impression split into two, since "twain" always carries that double meaning of a pair, or of a unity that has been split. That ambiguity—a single entity split in two, or two separate entities that strangely mirror each other—is like Twain's fascination with Siamese twins. Are they two individuals, or one divided organism? And is the divided nature of the name really a trope for the conflicted and divided writer himself, as so many have argued for so long?

Moving to some other meanings for "mark," we could see this paradoxically unified split as a doubled "written or printed symbol," a doubled "grade, as in school," or, enticingly, I think, a doubled "target," or "an object of attack, ridicule, or abuse," or even "the victim of a confidence game." No less than four of the dictionary meanings concern quality: "character, device, label, brand, or seal . . . to show the maker or owner, to certify quality, or for identification" or "a standard or acceptable level of performance." "Mark," rather than "twain," comes to the fore when we think in this way. When we add "end in view; goal, object" or "set up as a guide or to indicate position," "mark" takes on qualities associated with piloting, the domain from which the name supposedly springs (in fact, one definition is "bits of leather or colored bunting on a sounding line"). From the verb form, the most suggestive meaning is "to notice or observe critically"; the name, then, becomes a *command* to pay close attention to duality—"mark my doubleness," it seems to be telling us. Even the etymology is interesting: "from Old English, *maerc*, boundary, landmark, sign." "Mark Twain" is a doubled boundary—and surely a doubled (at least) sign.

Such a quick look at just some of the entailments of the metaphor suggests, I hope, the richness of the name. What is "Mark Twain" as a metaphor? It is two of something, or, paradoxically, it is one thing split. We can choose what that something is from all the many meanings of "mark," and whether we settle on one meaning or hold them all in our minds simultaneously, they are still either paired units or units split. That paradox lies at the center of the way we think about Mark Twain, not just because of the way he wrote or the persona he projected, but because of the figures that the words themselves contain. By its double nature, "twain" is always a paradox; joined with the nearly endless meanings of "mark," it becomes all the more complex.

It may have already occurred to the reader that I am using "mark" here more as a metonymy than as a metaphor. I think that is so, and unavoidable, but in proximity to the overwhelmingly metaphorical "twain," "mark" inevitably gets drawn into the metaphor. That is why Burke's division into master tropes is helpful for purposes of analysis and proves his point that the tropes "shade into one another."[36] The overwhelmingly metaphorical nature of "twain" makes it natural to think of "Mark Twain" as a metaphor, but the overwhelmingly metonymic nature of "mark" pulls us the other way.

Considering "Mark Twain" as metonymy, "mark" is again the overlooked term because, as I suggested earlier, we think of it literally, as a name. In all its entailments mentioned above, "mark" is a thing closely associated with something else, standing beside it, taking its place. When you write your name, it becomes your mark, and it is able to stand for you, to represent you. For this particular writer, all his words are his mark, and they are all doubled or split. In fact, the concept of "pen name" is itself a metonymy: the utensil an author uses to write with is so closely associated with the author that a new name, a new identity, becomes attached to the author, somewhat displacing or even replacing the original name. Take the example of George Orwell, a pen name that has effectively erased the identity of Eric Blair. With other pen names, the new name is accepted alongside the real name, but we do not perceive the added name as indication of any kind of psychological or psychic split—no one attributes any kind of psychic angst to Theodore Geisel for calling himself "Dr. Seuss" to write children's books. In Mark Twain's case, however, the new identity is *added* to Samuel Clemens, and we think of his identity as either doubled or split— and in a way that informs interpretations of his work and overshadows the reading of his life. He seems almost alone among pseudonymous writers: why is it that Samuel Clemens becomes both himself and his own metonymy, a metonymy that shifts to become strongly metaphoric?

What is "Mark Twain"? Neither the cry of the leadsman nor of the bartender, it is the cry of the writer, or perhaps the critic. We are dealing no longer with an individual, or even with a writer, but with a creation closely associated through a metonymic relation with the very act of writing. The shift in identity has long fascinated us: is he Samuel Clemens or Mark Twain?[37] Does that split reveal a basic insecurity in his personality? Does it mask a kind of schizophrenia? Or is it just a game, an innocent play with words by a man who lived a life of wordplay? The name itself leads us in both directions, always with that inherent contradiction and conflict.

Or, rather than metaphor or metonymy, is "Mark Twain" a synecdoche?[38] If we consider "Mark Twain" as a part for the whole, we see the name in a new light. I would suggest that we normally do think of him in this way, more than we think of "Mark Twain" as metonymy. The whole is Samuel Clemens, and the part that we take for the whole, the synecdoche, is "Mark Twain." The ramifications of this linguistic relationship are very important for the way we view the writer and his work. Mark Twain is an entity we can refer to and discuss and analyze, but since we are thinking of him as a part for the whole, we are ultimately thinking of him as only a part *of* the whole. Mark Twain always carries for us, then, a residue of incompleteness, of fragmentation, in a way that, for example, Henry James or William Dean Howells never do. James or Howells (or any other writer) could have just as fragmented or split a self as Samuel Clemens/Mark Twain, but the two names highlight, always, his supposed duality and incompleteness. Every writer is also a person, and those two roles sometimes coincide, sometimes conflict. The synecdochic relationship between Mark Twain and Samuel Clemens exploits and exemplifies these two complex roles, making them seem more separate than they really are, more split, more visible. Further, I think the two roles sometimes serve to denigrate Mark Twain as a writer—although he was certainly adept at self-denigration, as in his metaphorical label for himself, "jack-leg novelist."[39] We valorize Samuel Clemens because we see him as the whole, and thus somehow more authentic; and we see Mark Twain as a fragment, as somehow suspect and an evasion, perhaps even as a fraud. Biographers for a century have established that Samuel Clemens was a complex person, a man of splits, conflicts, and contradictions; but the name itself colors the way we see him and the way we interpret him.

Finally, to the fourth of Burke's master tropes: "Mark Twain" as irony. As others have noted, the name is highly ironic: on the river, "mark twain" means two fathoms, safe passage for a steamboat, but only if the leadsman's cry is signaling a move toward deeper water. If the boat's movement is toward shallower water, "mark twain" signals impending danger.[40] The scene in "Old Times on the Mississippi" where Horace Bixby tricks the cub into thinking that a supposedly bottomless crossing is not so deep dramatizes this irony very clearly:

> Then came the leadsman's sepulchral cry—
> "D-e-e-p four!"
> Deep four in a bottomless crossing! The terror of it took my breath away.
> "M-a-r-k three! . . . M-a-r-k three . . . quarter less three! . . . Half twain!"
> This was frightful! I seized the bell-ropes and stopped the engines.
> "Quarter twain! Quarter twain! *Mark* twain!"
> I was helpless. I did not know what in the world to do. I was quaking from head to foot, and I could have hung my hat on my eyes, they stuck out so far. (*SSWMT,* 95)

In this context, rather than signaling safety, "mark twain" is the cry that freezes the blood. It marks the boundary between safety and danger, a line that requires constant vigilance, a dangerous edge to walk. "Mark Twain," a name that is supposed to invoke humor (the name is itself a joke), becomes an ironic marker—metaphorically, the double boundary that the name's etymology inscribes.

Even the story of how Clemens chose the name is ironic. As he recounts it in *Life on the Mississippi,* he "confiscated" the name from Captain Isaiah Sellers, who used to sign the pen name "Mark Twain" to his "brief paragraphs of plain practical information about the river" (*LOM*, 324). Ironically, the name "Mark Twain" was an object of ridicule; according to *Life on the Mississippi*, "the . . . other old pilots . . . used to chaff the 'Mark Twain' paragraphs with unsparing mockery" (*LOM*, 324). Supposedly, Clemens wrote a parody of Sellers's reports, and other pilots had it printed in the *New Orleans True Delta*. In a partly serious, partly mocking tone, Twain tells of Sellers's angry reaction, his own remorse, and Sellers's subsequent hatred of him. He ends with the account of taking the name: "He never printed another paragraph while he lived, and he never again signed 'Mark Twain' to anything. At the time that the telegraph brought the news of his death, I was on the Pacific coast. I was a fresh new journalist, and needed a *nom de guerre*; so I confiscated the ancient mariner's discarded one, and have done my best to make it remain what it was in his hands—a sign and symbol and warrant that whatever is found in its company may be gambled on as being the petrified truth; how I have succeeded, it would not be modest in me to say" (*LOM*, 325). Clearly, that last claim is a joke, but it is also ironic: the name "Mark Twain" is associated with anything *but* the "petrified truth"—in fact, the reference to "petrified" would have evoked for his audience a memory of one of his first famous western hoaxes, the petrified man. Generations of readers have come to expect from this Mark Twain much play with the "petrified truth": sometimes a petrified lie, often a stretcher, very often a hoax—and sometimes, as with the petrified man, not only a hoax, but a literal and figurative thumbing of the nose. To further the irony, the very story seems to be anything but the truth: Clemens took the name before Sellers's death, and there is not even any evidence that Sellers ever signed his name as "Mark Twain."[41] So why the elaborate story? Partly, of course, this is Mark Twain's myth-making, but it is also a part of the ironic bundle that is "Mark Twain." If we closely examine the story, the name, and the stance, we find a series of ironic reversals—much as we saw in both "The Jumping Frog" and *Roughing It*.

All four figures are revealing, but metaphor has a way of predominating over the others. In "Metaphor and the Twinned Vision," Walter Ong proposes metaphor as a fundamental mode of perception, especially when we are trying to figure out something that puzzles us, which by this point the name "Mark Twain" certainly is: "Faced with an object, the human intellect is simply not equipped to assimilate it *en bloc*—not the object nor even the tiniest aspect of it. Man knows *componendo et dividendo*—by putting together and setting apart. Even after it has built up a reserve of symbols or concepts, if the mind is to get at the truth of a thing, it must always make two passes at it. One never suffices. The mind needs two items to set against each other." Ong offers subjects and predicates as his example of the two items set against each other: "By manipulating two items so that one thus for a brief instant controls the other we 'know' in the full sense, we possess—for a brief moment—truth."[42] What if we look at Samuel Clemens and Mark Twain as the two items set against each other? That is nearly the history of criticism on the author, and using Ong's idea, explains why we *must* do so to "know" the writer. And in this writer's case, he himself has made the split and provided us with the two items.

But Ong goes on to explain why we are not satisfied with duality: "Intellection is polarized to simplicity. It yearns to reduce everything to one principle, one starting point, not two. This polarization is so strong that the intellect wants to cut back of the enunciation itself, a poor, two-membered thing. Over the ages we can actually observe the human intellect as, by a chronic compulsion, it beats about apprehension, a single concept, an idea out of which it can draw everything. It wants a plenary or elemental experience of truth which is absolutely simple, a one."[43] This, too, is the impetus of much Mark Twain criticism: the quest to find "the real Mark Twain" or "the real Samuel Clemens." Critics and biographers have flitted back and forth between the two terms, trying to find in one or the other that elusive unity. Since "Mark Twain" is among other things a metaphor, it becomes especially tantalizing.

Further tracing the pull of metaphor, Ong continues: "This [a metaphor] creates the impression of extraordinary unity or condensation, and it accounts for the brilliance, the glow of resplendent intelligibility which we sense in metaphor and which Quintilian long ago referred to as 'light.' Since the metaphor must be based on some similarity, however elusive, the impression of unity rests on more than a pure illusion." Thus, "Mark Twain" creates an "impression of extraordinary unity," and that unity, because it is based on some similarity, "rests on more than a pure illusion." The unity of "Mark Twain" is both true *and* an illusion. Ong describes the duality: "The metaphor is thus an intellectual monad and dyad all at once. In it the mind senses the twinning suggestive of the enunciation, by which it is best equipped to lay hold of truth intellectually, but it senses this twinning in one single term, so as to suggest that the mind is, for once, functioning with single, not with double vision." In this way, "Mark Twain" gives us a sense of both unity and doubleness. This paradox explains why one critic looks at him and sees unity, another duality. Both are present in the name at the same time, as they are present in the writer, as they are in his works, and ultimately, as they are in us, his readers.[44]

Ong demonstrates his point with a reading of the Shakespeare poem "The Phoenix and the Turtle." He makes an interesting and insightful interpretation. Coincidentally, each half of the pen name "Mark Twain" appears here:

> Metaphor, in its strange double focus, brings us quickly to the quest for unity with which the phoenix and the turtle are preoccupied and which conditions their appearance in this poem—the quest for unity set in motion by the mysterious structure of a composite being, man, nostalgic for a simplicity which he cannot find within his own consciousness, resentful of everything short of this simplicity, ultimately discontent with his grasp of truth in statements, which are poor divided things like man himself, bearing the *mark* [my emphasis] of their own destruction within themselves. Even when they contain no margin of error, when everything they assert is absolutely true, our statements have a way of leaving us unsatisfied by not meaning so much as we had thought ourselves on the point of uttering. . . .
>
> The difficulty goes deep, for it lodges in the structure of human cognition itself. Hence it is not surprising that among the elemental, archetypal symbols he is operating with, Shakespeare encounters human reason itself, nonplussed by the divided unities and the united divisions with which it must deal:
>
> > "Reason in itself confounded,
> > Saw division grow together,
> > To themselves yet either neither,
> > Simple were so well confounded,
> >
> > That it cried, How true a *twain*
> > Seemeth this concordant one!" [my emphasis]

Those last two lines surprised me when I first read them, and Ong's conclusion could speak for me: "Although more explicitly focused on something else, this last phrase hits off the metaphorical situation to perfection, because it touches the depths of the human situation out of which the need for metaphor grows."[45]

We need this metaphor that is "Mark Twain," this twinned vision, this dyadic monad, this unified duality, not only to tell us something about this particular writer, but to tell us something about our own condition. Samuel Clemens named his own self, and we have been grappling not only with that unified duality ever since, but also with our own twinned vision. I can only repeat in a sort of wonder: "How true a twain / Seemeth this concordant one!" And I wonder, too, yet again, at the power of metaphor to uncover for us what has seemed buried, hidden, lost.

2

Figuring the River

> On any level, Mark Twain makes you see the River, as it is and was and always
> will be, more clearly than the author of any other description of a river known
> to me. But you do not merely see the River, you do not merely become
> acquainted with it through the senses; you experience the River. . . . But Mark
> Twain is a native, and the River God is his God. It is as a native that he accepts
> the River God, and it is the subjection of Man that gives to Man his dignity.
> For without some kind of God, Man is not even very interesting.
>
> —T. S. Eliot, Introduction to *Adventures of Huckleberry Finn*

For Mark Twain, the river is central: to his biography, to his writing, to
his career, to the way he is conceived in the popular imagination. The river
in many ways is at the heart of the persona and the myth of Mark Twain.
The river is literal, yet it is metaphorical at the same time, so much so that
it transcends metaphor to become symbol.

The river is central, but in Twain's early career, it seems in some ways to
have been what was hidden, buried, lost—at least to his imagination. His
rediscovery of the river came when he decided to write a series of articles on
steamboating for the *Atlantic*. After he had sent *Atlantic* editor William Dean
Howells "A True Story" in 1874, Howells asked for more contributions, but
Twain wrote back that he did not have anything at the time. The very same
day, in a walk with his friend the Reverend Joseph Twichell, he began talking about his piloting days on the Mississippi. Twain wrote Howells back,
quoting Twichell as exclaiming, "Now there's virgin stuff to hurl into a

magazine!" (*MTHL*, 1:34). He could not have forgotten the river, of course, and he had plans as far back as the 1860s to write a book on the subject, but writing about his own experiences seems not to have occurred to him until then. The idea of memory is central to "Old Times on the Mississippi," and the spark for the narrative began with memory rekindled.

Something profound happened to Mark Twain as an artist when he began to write "Old Times," and metaphor lies at the heart of the discovery he made. As Gérard Genette observes, metaphor is not just a matter of style or an ornament, "but the necessary instrument for a recovery, through style, of the vision of essences." "Old Times" resonates so deeply in Twain's career because it shows us, at least in part, his "psychological experience of involuntary memory."[1] That psychological experience was to shape his works that focus on the river, on his experience there, and on the river's centrality to American life and to the American consciousness, and especially to the conflict and complexity of race and slavery.

Metaphor is itself like a river, and indeed like Mark Twain's river, a comparison made clear in this definition by Philip Wheelwright in *Metaphor and Reality*: "What really matters in a metaphor is the psychic depth at which the things of the world, whether actual or fancied, are transmuted by the cool heat of the imagination. The transmutative process that is involved may be described as *semantic motion*; the idea of which is implicit in the very word 'metaphor,' since the motion (*phora*) that the word connotes is a semantic motion—the double imaginative act of outreaching and combining that essentially marks the metaphoric process."[2] The depth and motion of metaphor are like the depth and motion of the river—and perhaps not surprisingly, "Old Times" is the most richly metaphorical of Twain's works. The decade from the mid-1870s to mid-1880s shows Twain at the height of his powers, and it also shows him at the height of his power with metaphor.

I. Navigating Metaphor in "Old Times on the Mississippi"

The opening passage of "Old Times on the Mississippi" has often been read as emblematic of Mark Twain's realistic style and descriptive power. Reading it with attention to its metaphor is illuminating. The narrator begins by talking about the "one permanent ambition" of all the boys on the river: to be a steamboatman. In speaking of the "transient ambitions," he uses interesting metaphors to describe their appeal: "When a circus came and went, it left us all *burning* to become clowns; the first negro minstrel show that ever came to our section left us all *suffering* to try that kind of life; now and then we had a hope that, if we lived and were good, God would permit us to be pirates" (*SSWMT*, 64; my emphasis). ("Suffering" to be a negro minstrel is especially apt and ironic, I think.) But it is in the long description of a steamboat arriving that he really hits his stride and shows the depths of recovered memory that are working on his imagination, showing us at once the town, the boy, and the writer, in breathless thrall—and moving the reader to that same state.

A number of critics have read this passage closely, but a helpful way to read it is to focus on the relationship between metaphor and metonymy.[3] Although the opposition of metaphor and metonymy has a long critical history, dating back to Russian formalism, most credit the formulation to Roman Jakobson's article "Two Aspects of Language and Two Types of Aphasic Disturbances" (1956), which David Lodge calls "[t]he most systematic and comprehensive (though highly condensed) exposition of the idea . . . and the source most often cited in modern structural criticism." In a study of the linguistic nature of speech dysfunction, Jakobson proposes that "[a]ny linguistic sign involves two modes of arrangement": combination and selection. According to Jakobson, in any given message, "[t]he addressee perceives that the given utterance (message) is a COMBINATION of constituent parts (sentences, words, phonemes, etc.) SELECTED from the repository of all possible constituent parts (the code). The constituents of a context are in a state of CONTIGUITY, while in a substitution set signs are linked by various degrees of SIMILARITY which fluctuate between the equivalence of synonyms and the common core of antonyms." He aligns similarity with metaphor and contiguity with metonymy:

> The development of a discourse may take place along two different semantic lines: one topic may lead to another either through their similarity or through their contiguity. The METAPHORIC way would be the most appropriate term for the first case and the METONYMIC way for the second, since they find their most condensed expression in metaphor and metonymy respectively. In aphasia one or the other of these two processes is restricted or totally blocked—an effect which makes the study of aphasia particularly illuminating for the linguist. In normal behavior both processes are continually operative, but careful observation will reveal that under the influence of a cultural pattern, personality, and verbal style, preference is given to one of the two processes over the other.[4]

Jakobson found that aphasics, those who had suffered speech loss through brain damage, made meaning either by connecting words or by substituting them, but that they were incapable of doing both, as a normal speaker does. From this observation, he postulated that, because of their particular form of brain damage, aphasics were operating linguistically according to a principle of either metaphor or metonymy. Further, he postulated that these two poles are in opposition to one another in people with normal speech, and that we are all constantly shifting between the two.[5]

Though the thrust of Jakobson's article is mainly an attempt to diagnose speech dysfunction linguistically, what has proved important for literary study are his brief but suggestive comments in his final pages, in which he looks at the way metaphor and metonymy divide and underlie all forms of discourse. Jakobson proposes that all discourse is principally structured either metaphorically, by similarity, or metonymically, by contiguity. He applies the distinction to literature, painting, film, psychoanalysis, and anthropology, showing how the language of each is structured either by similarity or by contiguity, by metaphor or by metonymy. For example, poetry, romanticism, and dream symbolism are structured metaphorically, while prose, realism, and dream condensation are structured metonymically. As Jakobson's editors summed it up, "With one stroke he defined a fundamental polarity of language, culture and human thought in general."[6] That polarity has been explored by scholars in a variety of disciplines, and has been extremely important in structuralist and post-structuralist thought, from Levi-Strauss to Derrida, and is key to the theories of Lacan.

In his 1977 book-length study of the figures, *The Modes of Modern Writing: Metaphor, Metonymy, and the Typology of Modern Literature*, David Lodge addresses this question: "[I]t may be asked whether anything that offers to explain so much can possibly be useful, even if true. I believe it can, for the reason that it is a binary system capable of being applied to data at different levels of generality, and because it is a theory of dominance of one quality over another, not of mutually exclusive qualities. Thus the same distinction can serve to explain both the difference between category A and category B and the difference between item X and item Y in category A."[7] Visualizing the concept as an X-Y graph helps us to understand its power. On the graph, metaphor / similarity / paradigmatic would be plotted along the vertical axis, while metonymy / contiguity / syntagmatic would be plotted along the horizontal axis. Rather than seeing X and Y as static axes, we should imagine that the vertical axis can slide along the horizontal axis, as well as move up and down. This model can illustrate any number of operations. For example, focusing on the paradigmatic and syntagmatic labels, we can see the way the construction of a sentence occurs: the paradigmatic axis slides along the syntagmatic axis, stopping at points labeled "article," "modifier," "subject," "predicate," "object," each time moving up and down and supplying a word that fits each function of speech. We can use the model to explain the choices that make up any sign system—the semiotics of clothing, for example. The various articles of clothing—hat, shirt, belt, pants, shoes—are syntagmatic, on the horizontal axis; and the particular items that can be chosen from these categories—a derby, a tunic, an alligator belt, jeans, cowboy boots—are paradigmatic, on the vertical axis. Or we can use the axes to explain narrative structure, moving along a syntagmatic series of plot conventions, each time choosing different paradigmatic items to plug into the conventions.

The interaction between metonymy (syntagmatic) and metaphor (paradigmatic) operates in a similar way. Language operates in an interplay between these two figurative poles, both always present, but one or the other usually in domination, as Jakobson argues. The opening of "Old Times on the Mississippi" becomes a new passage when read this way.

The beginning has a metonymic focus on the boat itself, but then moves to metaphor as a way to frame the entire piece: "Once a day a cheap, gaudy packet arrived upward from St. Louis, and another downward from Keokuk. Before these events, the day was glorious with expectancy; after them, the day was a dead and empty thing" (*SSWMT*, 64). The tensions Twain sets up here are multiple: from the start, we know that we are seeing a "cheap, gaudy packet," but despite that, the expectation of the sight and the event make the day "glorious." This tension runs throughout the passage, as he builds up long strings of metonymic images, punctuated with metaphors that animate the images in concentrated bursts of linguistic power. The scene has a cinematic feel to it, with each image related to the next by contiguity; indeed, Jakobson argued in his hints about his theory's application that film and realistic fiction are predominantly governed by the pole of metonymy. While reading the passage, it is helpful, as Lodge demonstrates in *The Modes of Modern Writing*, to read as if we are watching a film, which lets us see the metonymic relation of the images, as well as appreciate the moments when metaphor interrupts the metonymy, which are often scenes of great interest and power.[8] If we read the famous passage again, but this time focus on the succession of images, we can see the way they relate to each other and we can see their movement between metonymy and metaphor:

> After all these years I can picture that old time to myself now, just as it was then: the white town drowsing in the sunshine of a summer's morning; the streets empty, or pretty nearly so; one or two clerks sitting in

front of the Water Street stores, with their splint-bottomed chairs tilted
back against the wall, chins on breasts, hats slouched over their faces,
asleep—with shingle-shavings enough around to show what broke them
down; a sow and a litter of pigs loafing along the sidewalk, doing a great
business in watermelon rinds and seeds; two or three lonely little freight
piles scattered about the "levee;" a pile of "skids" on the slope of the
stone-paved wharf, and the fragrant town drunkard asleep in the shadow
of them; two or three wood flats at the head of the wharf, but nobody to
listen to the peaceful lapping of the wavelets against them; the great
Mississippi, the majestic, the magnificent Mississippi, rolling its mile-
wide tide along, shining in the sun; the dense forest away on the other
side; the "point" above the town, and the "point" below, bounding the
river-glimpse and turning it into a sort of sea, and withal a very still and
brilliant and lonely one. (*SSWMT*, 64–65)

"The white town drowsing in the sunshine" is clearly a metonymy for the
sleepy inhabitants of the town, but I think we are more inclined to see this
image as a metaphor, a metaphor that is descriptively filled out by the string
of metonymic details that follows, especially the sleeping clerks. The town
drunkard is asleep too, but the metaphoric adjective "fragrant" packs a
punch, coming as it does in the midst of such metonymic detail. The focus
shifts almost wholly to metaphor when he describes the river, contrasting
it with the metonymic town—the power comes in metaphor, especially
metaphor among so much metonymy—and by the end, the "majestic" river
is actually a metaphorical "sea."

In the second half of the passage, metaphor and metonymy interpene-
trate in interesting ways: "Presently a film of dark smoke appears above
one of those remote 'points;' instantly a negro drayman, famous for his
quick eye and prodigious voice, lifts up the cry, 'S-t-e-a-m-boat a-comin'!'
and the scene changes!" (*SSWMT*, 65). The metonymic "dark smoke" cuts
to the image of the dark man, a striking metaphoric dissolve; then we see
the drayman only as a synecdoche, as eye and voice. The action that follows begins with metonymy, then resolves into the central metaphor of the
passage—and indeed of the whole narrative: "The town drunkard stirs, the
clerks wake up, a furious clatter of drays follows, every house and store
pours out a human contribution, and all in a twinkling the dead town is
alive and moving" (*SSWMT*, 65). The following scene is the exact counterpart to the drowsing town scene, with metonymic details of description
and action, the "cheap, gaudy packet" transformed and now seen by the
town (and the narrator) as "rather a handsome sight" (*SSWMT*, 65). Once
again, the occasional move to metaphor rather than metonymy stands out

for the reader, creating bursts of heightened energy and emphasis. In this passage of mostly metonymic details, the reader feels the effect of metaphorical phrases such as "gilded rays" and "black with passengers":

> She is long and sharp and trim and pretty; she has two tall, fancy-topped chimneys, with a gilded device of some kind swung between them; a fanciful pilot-house, all glass and "gingerbread," perched on top of the "texas" deck behind them; the paddle-boxes are gorgeous with a picture or with gilded rays above the boat's name; the boiler deck, the hurricane deck, and the texas deck are fenced and ornamented with clean white railings; there is a flag gallantly flying from the jack-staff; the furnace doors are open and the fires glaring bravely; the upper decks are black with passengers; the captain stands by the big bell, calm, imposing, the envy of all; great volumes of the blackest smoke are rolling and tumbling out of the chimneys—a husbanded grandeur created with a bit of pitch pine just before arriving at a town; the crew are grouped on the forecastle; the broad stage is run far out over the port bow, and an envied deckhand stands picturesquely on the end of it with a coil of rope in his hand; the pent steam is screaming through the gauge-cocks; the captain lifts his hand, a bell rings, the wheels stop; then they turn back, churning the water to foam, and the steamer is at rest. (*SSWMT*, 65)

The climax here comes in a metaphor, as "the pent steam is screaming through the gauge-cocks." That personified, metaphorical image at the end of the long accumulation of metonymy stands out in stark contrast, so that the reader can almost hear the sounds screech off the printed page.

The passage concludes with a return to the "dead" metaphor, completing the frame, but also giving the last finish to the extended metaphor that resonates throughout the whole narrative: "Then such a scramble as there is to get aboard, and to get ashore, and to take in freight, all at one and the same time; and such a yelling and cursing as the mates facilitate it all with! Ten minutes later the steamer is under way again, with no flag on the jack-staff and no black smoke issuing from the chimneys. After ten more minutes the town is dead again, and the town drunkard asleep by the skids once more" (*SSWMT*, 65). Similarly, the art and science of piloting, seemingly dead in memory and imagination, come to life for the narrator and the reader in the ensuing pages of the narrative, then die again as the golden age of piloting passes. The metaphoric thrust of the opening frames this cycle, the metaphor emerging from Mark Twain's vision and memory, whether or not he was conscious of the process, the "necessary instrument for a recovery, through style, of the vision of essences," as Genette describes it.[9]

We encounter several categories of metaphor in "Old Times on the Mississippi"—cursing, animals, piloting, and most importantly, the central metaphor of the text, the river as a book. In fact, this metaphor becomes something more, and accounts for much of the enduring power of the short piece, giving it a value for the reader and for its writer that transcends the river. Finally, metaphor, or its lack, can help explain the anticlimactic nature of the ending, as well as help us to understand the relationship between this 1874 text and 1883's *Life on the Mississippi*. I begin, then, with cursing.

In the early description of the "fragrant" night watchman, the narrator asks, "What was it to me that he was soiled and seedy and fragrant with gin? What was it to me that his grammar was bad, his construction worse, and his profanity so void of art that it was an element of weakness rather than strength in his conversation?" (*SSWMT*, 70). What is this "art of profanity" that he alludes to? We can learn by comparing the night watchman with the mate, who the narrator tells us, "in the matter of profanity . . . was sublime" (*SSWMT*, 69). The narrator describes the mate with a combination of simile and metaphor: "When he gave even the simplest order, he discharged it like a blast of lightning, and sent a long, reverberating peal of profanity thundering after it" (*SSWMT*, 69). The order as lightning is vivid enough, but the art of the construction is the metaphorical thunder, the noun phrase "long, reverberating peal of profanity" and the gerund "thundering" linking the metaphor's tenor with its vehicle so economically that we almost cannot extract one from the other, and we hear the metaphor rumbling after the simile. As in the ending of the paragraph, cursing becomes metaphor when the mate calls someone a "dash-dash-*dashed* split between a tired mud-turtle and a crippled hearse-horse!" (*SSWMT*, 70). Indeed, almost all cursing *is* figurative. You call someone a thing he or she is not, metaphorically comparing them to an animal or other object, or metaphorically wishing on them a particular action, or metonymically associating them with a particular body part. (I leave it to the reader to fill in the dash-dash-dashes.)

We see this metaphorical power of cursing most clearly with Horace Bixby, the cub's captain and teacher. In the scene where he asks the cub the names of all the points he has taught him, and the cub replies that he doesn't know, the narrator describes Bixby's anger: "Oh, but his wrath was up! He was a nervous man, and he shuffled from one side of his wheel as if the floor was hot. He would boil awhile to himself, and then overflow and scald me again" (*SSWMT*, 75). In this extended metaphor, as he does often in "Old Times," Twain forms the vehicle of the metaphor by choosing terms from the current domain, that of steamboating and piloting (as he did in

"Jumping Frog," comparing the frog with a gob of mud). The effect of this linkage is to highlight and underscore steamboating and piloting, to use the figurative as literal and the literal as figurative, a form of metaphor that seems almost organic. In this case, Bixby's boiling, overflowing, and scalding comes out as speech and eventually as cursing. When the cub replies that he thought Bixby had told him the names of the points "to be entertaining," the pilot explodes:

> This was a red rag to the bull. He raged and stormed so (he was crossing the river at the time) that I judged it made him blind, because he ran over the steering-oar of a trading-scow. Of course the traders sent up a volley of red-hot profanity. Never was a man so grateful as Mr. Bixby was: because he was brim ful, and here were subjects who would *talk back*. He threw open a window, thrust his head out, and such an irruption followed as I had never heard before. The fainter and farther away the scowmen's curses drifted, the higher Mr. Bixby lifted his voice and the weightier his adjectives grew. When he closed the window he was empty. You could have drawn a seine through his system and not caught curses enough to disturb your mother with. (*SSWMT,* 75)

Mr. Bixby's being "brim ful" begins the metaphor that Twain extends until Bixby "empties" himself, the process of emptying seeming to follow the laws of physics and gravity. A lesser writer might have stopped there, but Twain pushes the metaphor (and the joke) further with the concluding seine comment. Again, the use of the fishing domain, so closely associated with the river, enriches the metaphorical complexity of the description, the same technique he early on employed with the jumping frog.

These Bixby cursing passages reach their culmination when the pilot asks the cub, "What is the shape of Walnut Bend?" The narrator's initial thought is one of the great lines in Twain's humor, with a metaphor implied, and the choice of comparison perfect for the joke: "He might as well have asked me my grandmother's opinion of protoplasm" (*SSWMT,* 83). The narrator continues, and we get another remarkable extended metaphor: "I reflected respectfully, and then said I did n't know it had any particular shape. My gunpowdery chief went off with a bang, of course, and then went on loading and firing until he was out of adjectives" (*SSWMT,* 83). This time, instead of a simile-metaphor combination, he uses a string of metaphors, five in that last sentence. With one figurative bullet left, the narrator continues, pushing his metaphor as far as he can: "I had learned long ago that he only carried just so many rounds of ammunition, and was sure to subside into a very placable and even remorseful old smooth-bore as soon as they were all gone" (*SSWMT*, 83). The pun on "bore" finishes the passage brilliantly.

Aside from the general proprieties of the age that Twain always had to deal with as a writer, the special constraints of writing for the *Atlantic* had an effect on the way he dealt with profanity. But paradoxically, the constraint he had to show in dealing with profanity actually makes his presentation stronger. Rather than present the cursing directly, he had to present it figuratively, and artistically he gained by that move. Direct profanity would be, as I have argued, figurative in itself, but a figure that might not register with us because it is overpowered by the impact of the profanity. By presenting figurative profanity in a substitute figure, Twain recovered a metaphorical presence that would likely have been obscured by the more overt cursing.

But the rich metaphorical nature of "Old Times on the Mississippi" extends beyond profanity. The text contains some of Twain's most memorable metaphorical language. "Pilots bore a mortal hatred to" rafts, the narrator tells us, "and it was returned with usury" (*SSWMT*, 97). Shifting from what would be the expected and mundane "interest" to "usury" makes the phrase come alive and transforms it from a dead metaphor to a very live one, a skill we will soon see again with *The Adventures of Tom Sawyer*. Twain does something similar in his description of the effects of the June rise on the poor river people: "And yet these were kindly dispensations, for they at least enabled the poor things to rise from the dead now and then, and look upon life when a steamboat went by" (*SSWMT*, 100). The grim humor of that joke echoes the opening metaphor of the dead and live town, and the mixture of the literal "rise" with its metaphorical sense is yet another example of the crossing between literal and figurative. The pilot Mr. Brown describes someone with this vivid simile: "Sallow-faced, red-headed fellow, with a little scar on the side of his throat, like a splinter under the flesh" (*SSWMT*, 111). In the narrator's description of learning the shape of the river and the landscape, he uses this especially memorable simile: "No prominent hill would stick to its shape long enough for me to make up my mind what its form really was, but it was as dissolving and changeful as if it had been a mountain of butter in the hottest corner of the tropics" (*SSWMT*, 86–87).

As he often does in his works, and as we have already seen with "The Jumping Frog," Twain makes great use of animal metaphors. The sounding-boat was "long, trim, graceful and as fleet as a greyhound" (*SSWMT*, 106). One particular night is "as dark as the inside of a cow" (*SSWMT*, 98). The cub says he is "brimful of self-conceit and carrying my nose as high as a giraffe's" (*SSWMT*, 114)—and the reader knows how quickly Mr. Bixby will bring that nose and self-conceit down. On two occasions, a pilot spins around the wheel "like a squirrel" (SSWMT, 102, 115). Twain's favorite animal—the cat—becomes especially associated with Horace Bixby, who "stood by his wheel, silent, intent as a cat, and all the pilots stood shoulder to shoulder at his back" (SSWMT, 81). In another cat metaphor, he refers to "the solid firmament of black cats that stood for an atmosphere" (SSWMT, 85). A lover of animals, Twain used them constantly, often for humor, but later in his career, for a larger and more serious comparison to man, "the lowest animal."

The central concern of the text, the science of piloting, also provides one of its most important metaphors. The term "cub" is itself metaphorical, and "pilot," although quite literal, grows in meaning as the narrative unfolds, becoming a metaphor for one who masters any craft, then finally reaching the status of symbol.[10] As we have seen, Twain makes good use of piloting as the domain from which to construct many of his metaphorical terms. In one category are the metaphorical terms the pilots themselves used, whether or not they recognized them as metaphorical: "Here, take her," Bixby tells the cub, "shave those steamships as close as you'd peel an apple" (SSWMT, 72). But Twain can take these and extend their metaphorical sense; the pilots "hug" the bank on an upstream run, but the narrator describes Bixby as "hugging the shore with affection" (SSWMT, 72). The metaphorical sense is largely dead to the pilots when they speak of hugging the shore, but its sense is recovered when Twain adds what might seem to be a redundancy. Clearly, there is nothing affectionate about "hugging the shore," but Twain's addition of the term changes the way we see Bixby's piloting. This pilot really does love to hug the shore.

In another category are the piloting and steamboating terms the narrator uses to describe other processes, especially the mental process of learning the river. He does this repeatedly: "I dreadfully wanted to ask a question, but I was carrying about as many short answers as my cargo-room would admit of, so I held my peace"; "My late voyage's notebooking was but a confusion of meaningless names. It had tangled me all up in a knot every time I had looked at it in the daytime"; "Oh, don't say any more, please! Have I got to learn the shape of the river according to all these five hundred thousand different ways? If I tried to carry all that cargo in my head it would make me stoop-shouldered"; "I haven't got brains enough to be a pilot; and if I had I wouldn't have strength enough to carry them around, unless I went on crutches" (SSWMT, 74, 79, 84, 88). These metaphors of learning the river reach their culmination in the most fully developed and probably the most memorable metaphor in the narrative.

Of course, I am referring to the river as a metaphor for a book. Leo Marx in *The Machine in the Garden* points out the way this passage pertains not only to "Old Times on the Mississippi," but also to *Huckleberry Finn,* and to a great extent, to Mark Twain's realist vision.[11] I quote part of the passage to remind us of the way Twain extends the metaphor:

> The face of the water, in time, became a wonderful book—a book that was a dead language to the uneducated passenger, but which told its mind to me without reserve, delivering its most cherished secrets as clearly as if it uttered them with a voice. And it was not a book to be read once and thrown aside, for it had a new story to tell every day. Throughout the long twelve hundred miles there was never a page that was void of interest, never one that you would leave unread without loss, never one that you would want to skip, thinking you could find higher enjoyment in some other thing. There never was so wonderful a book written by man; never one whose interest was so absorbing, so unflagging, so sparklingly renewed with every re-perusal. The passenger who could not read it was charmed with a peculiar sort of faint dimple on its surface (on the rare occasions when he did not overlook it altogether); but to the pilot that was an *italicized* passage; indeed, it was more than that, it was a legend of the largest capitals, with a string of shouting exclamation points at the end of it. . . . (*SSWMT,* 91–92)

Here, Twain brings together the two crafts he had learned—piloting and typesetting—using the terms of one to highlight the other. His famous lament about "whether he has gained most or lost most by learning his trade" (*SSWMT,* 93) is mitigated somewhat, I would argue, by the fact that he has united both crafts in his more recent but more valuable trade: being a writer. In this passage, all the parallel metaphors of "Old Times on the Mississippi" merge, just as all the points about teaching and learning converge. The power of the passage lies not only in the considerable amount it reveals about Mark Twain and his work, and that really is considerable, as Marx and others have shown, but also in the power this passage holds for each individual reader. The metaphor allows us to read the passage very personally. I have found that "Old Times" is one of the best works to teach Mark Twain. I tell my students to substitute for piloting and learning the river any complex craft or skill they have mastered or are trying to master, and they find this comparison illuminating and applicable, whether the skill is ballet dancing, biology, playing baseball, or, as in my case, playing the mandolin, or my more recent impossible and endless pursuit, fly fishing. We can all put ourselves in the place of the cub as he tries to master this apparently impossible skill. The power of the narrative for the reader comes, I think, from each reader's substitution of himself as the cub and recognition of the apparent impossibility of mastering any craft. The river as a book transcends metaphor to become a symbol, a variable symbol that expands to incorporate the interests of each reader. Metaphorically, we each become the cub in our own ways, and, one hopes, we begin to make the move from cub to pilot.

If we take the metaphor literally, emphasizing not the river, but the book, we can read the text as a text about books themselves, about reading and writing. This focus is powerful for Twain as a writer and for each one of us as readers—and as writers ourselves. Like the river, the book is hard, the book is complex. Mastering the book is seemingly impossible, especially as we start out. Writing is hard; reading is hard. As soon as we master one skill, up pops another that we have to learn, then another, endlessly. Then up pop the rules and the exceptions to the rules and the contradictions and the paradoxes. Mastering the book is a lifelong process for those brave enough, or foolish enough, to begin at all. Seen this way, "Old Times on the Mississippi" is the figurative embodiment of a life of the mind, if not of life itself. This is why I see the story as so central to Mark Twain's work and so important to readers intellectually and emotionally. And metaphor provides that power.

Yet a serious problem remains with this text. Along with many other readers, I have always found the ending of "Old Times on the Mississippi" curiously flat.[12] The last two chapters, "Rank and Dignity of Piloting" and "The Pilot's Monopoly," always made the narrative seem anticlimactic, and even somewhat truncated, and certainly did not provide a suitable ending. Reading again with a focus on metaphorical language, I expected a relative lack of figures from what had come before, but I was a little surprised to find *no metaphor at all* in these two chapters. Coming at the end of a narrative so rich in metaphor makes the contrast all the more striking and certainly contributes to the flatness and anticlimax I have always felt as I read. A formalist might suggest that the flatness and anticlimax mirrors the message: the death of steamboating, brought on partly by the pilot's monopoly, but more by the coming of the war and the railroad. The abrupt ending is itself like the sudden end of steamboating that Twain describes. In any case, ending with the death of steamboating mirrors the death/life/death metaphor of the opening: through metaphor, "the dead town is alive and moving"; then, with the passing of steamboating, it is "dead again." Did Twain purposely eliminate figurative language in these chapters to give that effect? Impossible to say, but my study of his metaphorical practice suggests that his figurative language springs from his subject matter or from the stance and character of his narrator. The prosaic, matter-of-fact subject matter of the ending yields language devoid of metaphor—or perhaps it is the other way around. In any case, the absence of metaphor proves revealing. Perhaps the best explanation is that Twain here is responding to an unconscious process, the mysterious process Genette describes as "the stylistic equivalent of the psychological experience of involuntary memory."[13] Piloting was dead to him, and the lack of metaphor here shows that clearly.

Of course, in one sense, that ending is not really an ending, since Twain returned to the river and to the book, inserting "Old Times on the Mississippi" into what was to become *Life on the Mississippi*. John Seelye, in his introduction to the Oxford paperback edition, points out the prevalence of business metaphor in his argument that Twain was more interested in commerce than art when he returned to the river for his fourth travel book. Seelye's textual evidence gives us a sense of what Twain was up to:

> The river we hear "remained out of the market" for a hundred and fifty years after De Soto discovered it; and though by the time La Salle explored it the Mississippi was "ready for business" another seventy years had to pass before the "business" actually began. Further, we read that the shifting channel of the river has caused entire islands to "retire from business" and towns and plantations to "retire to the country"; a boasting crew member is said to take confidence from his association with a large steamboat, and thereby "was not putting on all those airs on a stinted capital"; Mark Twain himself, drawing humorous and exaggerated conclusions from scientific data, "gets wholesale returns of conjecture out of . . . trifling investments of fact."

In Seelye's analysis, "[t]he consistent parade of commercial figures of speech reveals the author's essential attitude toward his materials, that 'trifling investment of fact' from which he hopes to receive a 'wholesale return' by means of his 'conjectures.'"[14] Whether or not one agrees with Seelye's assessment of *Life on the Mississippi*, it is instructive to compare the metaphorical concerns of the two texts to gauge Twain's attitude toward his subject. It is like the change in the view of the river, from "all manner of beautiful pictures" for the passenger to "the grimmest and most dead-earnest of reading-matter" for the pilot. But rather than see such a drastic change from the earlier text to the later, I think we can see that the change is already evident in "Old Times," coming in the last two chapters' difference from the rest of the text.

If Mark Twain was the master of metaphor that I am claiming him to be, how can we explain a narrator who often depends on dead metaphor and cliché? That is precisely the kind of narrator we encounter in his next great river book.

II. *Figuring* Tom Sawyer:
The Narrator's Metaphorical Vision, Dead and Alive

"I perhaps made a mistake in not writing in the first person," Mark Twain wrote to Howells on July 5, 1875, as he finished the first draft of *The Adventures of Tom Sawyer* (*MTHL*, 1:91). This admission, as well as the success of his subsequent, first-person sequel, has colored our perception of the novel's narrator ever since. John Gerber, probably the best commentator on the way Mark Twain uses point of view, offers this assessment in his entry on *The Adventures of Tom Sawyer* in *The Mark Twain Encyclopedia*:

> As in almost all of Mark Twain's works, the style in [*Tom Sawyer*] results from the point of view. It is a shifting style because the point of view slides from that of the middle-aged writer to that of the approximately twelve-year-old boy. As the middle-aged author, Twain writes in the conventional, stilted, "literary" manner that characterizes other novels of the period. But when he adopts Tom's point of view, his language immediately freshens. The boy forces him to do what he does best: report concrete happenings in simple pictorial language. In style, therefore, [*Tom Sawyer*] represents a transition between the mannered discourse in *The Gilded Age* and the vernacular in *Huckleberry Finn*.

Others have agreed about the narrator's weakness; William M. Gibson maintains, "[W]henever the narrator spoke to the adult reader about his young characters he tended to weaken these parts of the book; whereas in the strong episodes he presented the boys' actions—both overt and psychological—dramatically, without editorial comment." In a recent study, Peter Messent blames the lack of unity on the "omniscient and retrospective narration," asserting that "Twain's use of satire, burlesque and sentimentality often run in uneasy relationship to one another."[15]

Indeed, the narrator *is* conventional and stilted, and perhaps even worse, at times stuffy, clichéd, and trite. And as Messent points out, the shifts between satire and sentimentality are often abrupt and hard to reconcile. We can blame these problems on various things: Twain's relative inexperience with extended fiction—this was, as Gibson notes, only his second novel; or his psychological state after his marriage, as Walter Blair suggests; or "the instability of his attitudes toward his material," as Henry Nash Smith argues. The question of whether he was writing for adults or children is one that Twain discussed with Howells both at the time of composition and over a number of years, and one that had an effect on the kinds of revisions he made. Also, as Alan Gribben and Marcia Jacobson have shown, the model of Thomas Bailey Aldrich's *Story of a Bad Boy* had an effect on the construction of the narrator.[16] Though all these explanations seem sound, the problems with the narrator of *Tom Sawyer* raise a number of questions. How could Mark Twain, at the height of his powers, create such a narrator, one so full of cliché and conventionality? More to the point, *why* would he, when in other works of the same period he was able to create narrators with fresh, vital vision? If the narrator is so problematic, how did the novel rise above its continuously weak narrative presence to achieve its status as, to quote Gerber again, "a book one never forgets" (*TS*, xiv)?

I propose that the answer to these questions may lie in our close identification of the narrator with the author, an identification fueled by the text, but one that I believe is at least partly erroneous. In this stilted and conventional narrator, Mark Twain created a character distinct from himself, distinct from his usual persona, and a character that, I will argue, we are *supposed* to find stilted and trite. Further, I propose that there is not just one narrator of *Tom Sawyer*, but two: this stilted, conventional narrator and the fresher, more lively narrator that Gerber and others see in the scenes that shift closer to Tom's point of view. I suggest that we can best see this distance and distinctness by examining both narrators' language, specifically their metaphorical language. Because metaphor is so fundamental to both a writer's linguistic characteristics and his personal vision, it can function as a kind of linguistic fingerprint. If we look at each narrator's metaphorical language, comparing it to that in other writings from the period that plainly do have Mark Twain as narrator, we will see a definite distinction. We can most clearly see the way the narrator becomes more lively when his point of view nears Tom's in the way his metaphors shift from clichéd and dead to fresh and alive. In other words, this shift is not merely one from literary language to vernacular language, as Gerber sees it; rather, it is a shift in metaphorical vision. Because these shifts are so carefully controlled, the narrative point of view works consistently on a double level. Thus, this seemingly flawed narrator is actually two separate narrators, and rather than constituting a flaw, this narrative split actually contributes to the depth and success of the novel. Further, the narrative split not only explains the confusion often felt by an earlier generation of largely formalist critics, but also answers the serious charges of more recent cultural critics concerning the novel's putative moral blindness.[17]

We can get a clear sense of what I am calling the "conventional narrator" by quoting any of the idyllic set pieces that open many chapters. The first paragraph of chapter 2, the introduction to the whitewashing scene, shows this narrator very well: "Saturday morning was come, and all the summer world was bright and fresh, and brimming with life. There was a song in every heart; and if the heart was young the music issued at the lips. There was cheer in every face and a spring in every step. The locust trees were in bloom and the fragrance of the blossoms filled the air. Cardiff Hill, beyond the village and above it, was green with vegetation, and it lay just far enough away to see a Delectable Land, dreamy, reposeful, and inviting" (TS, 10). Part of the effect of this paragraph comes, I think, from the preponderance of dead metaphor, so dead it is worse than cliché: "the summer world was bright and fresh, and brimming with life"; "a song in every heart"; "cheer in every face and a spring in every step." The one original metaphor, comparing Cardiff Hill to "a Delectable Land," complete with capital letters, is so stilted and literary that it loses any intended metaphorical flavor. Another chapter opening, describing Tom in school, strings together cliché after cliché:

> The harder Tom tried to fasten his mind on his book, the more his ideas wandered. So at last, with a sigh and a yawn, he gave it up. It seemed to him that the noon recess would never come. The air was utterly dead. There was not a breath stirring. It was the sleepiest of drowsy days. The drowsing murmur of the five and twenty scholars soothed the soul like the spell that is the murmur of bees. Away off in the flaming sunshine, Cardiff Hill lifted its soft green sides through a shimmering veil of heat, tinted with the purple of distance; a few birds floated on lazy wing high in the air; no other living thing was visible but some cows, and they were asleep. (TS, 57)

This narrator can string together dead metaphor at will: "These despised themselves, as being the dupes of a wily fraud, a guileful snake in the grass" (TS, 34); "Tom was introduced to the judge; but his tongue was tied, his breath would hardly come, his heart quaked" (TS, 35); "how her tears would fall like rain" (TS, 22); "would she heave one little sigh to see a bright young life so rudely blighted, so untimely cut down?" (TS, 25).

Yet the novel also contains metaphorical language that is lively and inventive, revealing a vernacular vision and attitude rather than the conventional literary vision typified by the clichés just quoted. For example, here is the description of Tom after his Sunday morning bath: "But when he emerged from the towel, he was not yet satisfactory; for the clean territory stopped short at his chin and jaws, like a mask; below and beyond this line there was a dark expanse of unirrigated soil that spread downward in front and backward around his neck" (*TS*, 28). Or the description of the Sunday school superintendent, a description that uses vivid metaphors and similes to make a brief but indelible portrait of a village type:

> This superintendent was a slim creature of thirty-five, with a sandy goatee and short sandy hair; he wore a stiff standing-collar whose upper edge almost reached his ears and whose sharp points curved forward abreast the corners of his mouth—a fence that compelled a straight look-out ahead, and a turning of the whole body when a side view was required; his chin was propped on a spreading cravat which was as broad and as long as a bank note, and had fringed ends; his boot toes were turned sharply up, in the fashion of the day, like sleigh-runners—an effect patiently and laboriously produced by the young men sitting with their toes pressed against a wall for hours together. (*TS*, 31–32)

Just as ably as one narrator can string together dead metaphors, the other can reel off memorable metaphors and similes: the poodle who sat down on the pinch-bug in church "was but a wooly comet moving in its orbit with the gleam and the speed of light" (*TS*, 43); Aunt Polly "scrubbed [Tom] down with a towel like a file" (*TS*, 93); Aunt Polly "calculated his capacity as she would a jug's, and filled him up every day with quack cure-alls" (*TS*, 94). The description of Tom's and Joe's attempt to smoke a pipe ably employs extended metaphor:

> So the talk ran on. But presently it began to flag a trifle, and grow dis-jointed. The silences widened; the expectoration marvelously increased. Every pore inside the boys' cheeks became a spouting fountain; they could scarcely bail out the cellars under their tongues fast enough to pre-vent an inundation; little overflowings down their throats occurred in spite of all they could do, and sudden retchings followed every time. Both boys were looking very pale and miserable, now. Joe's pipe dropped from his nerveless fingers. Tom's followed. Both fountains were going furi-ously and both pumps bailing with might and main. Joe said feebly:
> "I've lost my knife. I reckon I better go and find it." (*TS*, 124)

How can one novel contain such conflicting metaphorical visions? Is this a sign of Twain's inexperience as a fiction writer, or an indication of his conflicted mental state, or his inability to write in a sustained vernacular style? I don't think it's any of these things, and we have already seen ample proof of his skill in his works up to this time, particularly in "Old Times on the Mississippi," which he wrote at about the same time as *Tom Sawyer*.

In both river narratives, an older narrator looks back nostalgically at his boyhood hometown, describing a sleepy scene. "After all these years I can picture that old time to myself now, just as it was then," the narrator of "Old Times" begins, and we, coming fresh from such scenes in *Tom Sawyer*, brace ourselves for a stream of clichés. Instead, we get the vivid picture that I quoted above of the sleeping town brought to life by the arrival of a steamboat, with concrete detail piled on detail, figurative language spare but powerful: "the fragrant town drunkard"; "the upper decks . . . black with passengers"; "the pent steam screaming through the gauge-cocks" (*SSWMT*, 64–65). This narrator sounds nothing like the conventional narrator of *Tom Sawyer*, and what is more, as we have seen, Mark Twain could sustain this vision throughout most of "Old Times on the Mississippi." Why could he not do so in *Tom Sawyer*? I propose that he could, but chose not to, that the conventional narrator of parts of *Tom Sawyer* is not the familiar persona Mark Twain, but another persona, one that we are supposed to recognize and reject. There are *two* narrators here, the novel is richer for it, and we can see that only by examining metaphorical language.

At the end of the whitewashing incident, the narrator interrupts the scene to tell us that Tom "had discovered a great law of human action, without knowing it" (*TS*, 16). Henry Nash Smith notes, "The incident is reduced to an exemplum illustrating a generalization that has nothing to do with the story." Smith sees this as a result of the "burlesque interpos[ing] a considerable psychological distance between himself and his characters," but I would argue instead that Twain is giving us a clear signal about the identity of the narrator and, more importantly, how we are supposed to respond to his dead vision. The key language is this: "If he [Tom] had been a great and wise philosopher, like the writer of this book, he would have comprehended . . ." (*TS*, 16). Smith comments, "Something tells the writer he is on the wrong tack and he confuses things further by mocking at himself," but I propose that Twain is satirizing here the very notion of "The Author." We are to take the phrase "great and wise philosopher" not as Twain's mocking himself, but as Twain's mocking writers who see themselves as "great and wise philosophers," who see themselves as "Author," which is the name I give to this narrator with the dead metaphorical vision.[18]

An extended sequence in the Examination Evening scene offers further and more substantial proof of the existence of two narrators. After all the recitations, "the prime feature of the evening" is "original 'compositions' by the young ladies" (*TS*, 156). The narrative voice is the lively narrator, the satiric Mark Twain we are used to from works such as *Life on the Mississippi*, especially the parts that follow what was originally "Old Times." The narrator tells us:

A prevalent feature in these compositions was a nursed and petted melancholy; another was a wasteful and opulent gush of "fine language;" another was a tendency to lug in by the ears particularly prized words and phrases until they were worn entirely out; and a peculiarity that conspicuously marked and marred them was the inveterate and intolerable sermon that wagged its crippled tail at the end of each and every one of them. No matter what the subject might be, a brainracking effort was made to squirm it into some aspect or other that the moral and religious mind could contemplate with edification. (*TS*, 156)

Then we get several examples of these "prize authors":

The first composition that was read was one entitled "Is this, then, Life?" Perhaps the reader can endure an extract from it:

"In the common walks of life, with what delightful emotions does the youthful mind look forward to some anticipated scene of festivity! Imagination is busy sketching rose-tinted pictures of joy. In fancy, the voluptuous votary of fashion sees herself amid the festive throng, 'the observed of all observers.' Her graceful form, arrayed in snowy robes, is whirling through the mazes of the joyous dance; her eye is brightest, her step is lightest in the gay assembly." (*TS*, 156–57)

This narrator may as well be describing and lampooning the narrator I am calling "Author." The last composition, "A Vision," concludes with this immortal simile: "A strange sadness rested upon her features, like icy tears upon the robe of December, as she pointed to the contending elements without, and bade me contemplate the two beings presented" (*TS*, 159). As the narrator comments, "This nightmare occupied some ten pages of manuscript and wound up with a sermon so destructive of all hope to non-Presbyterians that it took the first prize" (*TS*, 159).

Rather than being an anomaly in the text, this lampooning of overwrought literary language has actually been going on throughout, as the two narrative visions have been conflicting with one another. In a typical chapter in the first half of the novel, "Author" begins; then the narrator with the fresher metaphorical vision takes over; then the scene shifts totally to dialogue and action. At the end of a typical chapter, "Author" is apt to return and make a comment. In the scenes where the language becomes most overwrought, as in the scenes where Tom mopes around wishing for death because Becky Thatcher has rejected him, the lively narrator emerges and dashes dirty washwater on the prostrate Tom, metaphorically splashing "Author" back to reality. John Gerber has noted this split, but he saw the livelier narration occurring when the scene shifted closer to Tom's point of view.[19] As true as that sometimes is, it is often not the case. In the scenes just mentioned, which are very close to Tom's vision, the language is the most overwrought, the metaphor most dead. Significantly, after the lively narrator exposes "Author" so fully in the examination scene, "Author" largely disappears from the narrative for a long period.

"Author" reemerges much later in the novel, when Injun Joe's corpse is found. The description of how "the poor unfortunate had starved to death" is deliciously purple:

> The captive had broken off the stalagmite, and upon the stump had placed a stone wherein he had scooped a shallow hollow to catch the precious drop that fell once in every three minutes with the dreary regularity of a clock-tick—a dessert spoonful once in four and twenty hours. That drop was falling when the Pyramids were new; when Troy fell; when the foundations of Rome were laid; when Christ was crucified; when the Conqueror created the British empire; when Columbus sailed; when the massacre at Lexington was "news." It is falling now; it will still be falling when all these things shall have sunk down the afternoon of history, and the twilight of tradition, and been swallowed up in the thick night of oblivion. (TS, 239–40)

"Author" goes on to draw a message from this sermon, making his "composition" worthy of a first prize on Examination Evening. Henry Nash Smith misreads the passage, I think; he argues that "such a burst of eloquence is quite out of keeping with the tone of the book. It serves no purpose except to demonstrate that the narrator can produce the kind of associations held in esteem by the dominant culture."[20] I see the language as perfectly in keeping with the tone of the book, at least the part of the tone that is set by "Author," and as serving the purpose not of pleasing the dominant culture, but of showing the dominant culture the hollowness and deadness of its prized language.

The lively narrator makes this point clearly in the passage following "Author's" peroration:

> This funeral stopped the further growth of one thing—the petition to the Governor for Injun Joe's pardon. The petition had been largely signed; many tearful and eloquent meetings had been held, and a committee of sappy women been appointed to go in deep mourning and wail around the Governor and implore him to be a merciful ass and trample his duty under foot. Injun Joe was believed to have killed five citizens of the village, but what of that? If he had been Satan himself there would have been plenty of weaklings ready to scribble their names to a pardon-petition and drip a tear on it from their permanently impaired and leaky water-works. (*TS*, 240–41)

The metaphorical linkage of drips shows us very clearly the attitude we are being induced to have toward the "drippy" "Author."

By the end of the narrative, as many critics have noted, Huck Finn's presence and vision have taken over, leading Mark Twain to his greater triumph with point of view and, I would add, with metaphor. But I am not so sure that he was right when he remarked that he had "perhaps made a mistake in not writing in the first person" in *Tom Sawyer;* in any case, the point of view he chose is certainly more complex than it might seem on first reading, and that complexity adds a great deal to the novel he did write. Henry Wonham, in seeing the narrative as split between a single narrator and Tom Sawyer, says the "unstable discrepancy . . . complicates the reader's interpretive task." How much more, then, does the presence of yet another narrator complicate the task? I certainly agree with Wonham that "this discrepancy may also be read as a measure of Twain's increasing dexterity as a writer." Rather than being a flaw, these multiple narrators make *Tom Sawyer* a richer, more complex novel, and they help to explain what seem like inconsistencies in attitude.[21] The questions that Smith raises in *Mark Twain: The Development of a Writer*, for example, can be answered by recognizing the presence of more than one narrator. According to Smith,

> The structural problems of the novel, like those of Mark Twain's earlier books, reflect the instability of his attitudes toward his material. He was not clean in his own mind whether he was writing a story for boys or a story about boys for adults. The burlesque love story presupposes a grown-up audience; it depends for its effect on the reader's perception of the comic parallels between Tom's behavior and that of an adult. Tom's fantasies about pirates and robbers and Robin Hood, again, are relatively

meaningless unless the reader can enjoy the ironic contrast between the glamorous fantasy world of romance and the everyday reality of life in St. Petersburg. Both these modes of burlesque interpose a considerable psychological distance between the novelist and his characters, and make it difficult for him to do justice to whatever values may be latent in the Matter of Hannibal.

As I noted earlier, Smith sees the early reference to "a great and wise philosopher" as an example of Twain's "mocking at himself," but if we see this passage instead as one of the first places where the lively narrator undercuts "Author," we read it much differently. The same holds true for other passages Smith questions. For example, in the Sunday school examination scene, Smith notes the "patronizing air" of the narrator as the superintendent is described, and in "the resumption of fights and other recreations among certain of the bad boys, and by fidgetings and whisperings that extended far and wide, washing even to the bases of isolated and incorruptible rocks like Sid and Mary," Smith recognizes the metaphor, but not its source: "In themselves, the witty understatement of 'recreations' and the equally witty comparison of Sid and Mary to rocks with waves breaking against them are amusing, but they represent a kind of exhibitionism on the part of the writer."[22] Such a comparison would be uncharacteristic for "Author," but not for the lively narrator.

Recognizing multiple narrators also answers the serious charge brought against the novel and against Mark Twain by Forrest G. Robinson in *In Bad Faith*. Robinson defines bad faith "as the reciprocal deception of self and other in the denial of departures from public ideals of the true and the just." The society of St. Petersburg is guilty of this self-deception, Robinson argues, summing up what he calls "the leading paradoxes of St. Petersburg social life": "the shameless, virtually unconscious, resort to devious means; the enlistment of an ostensibly scrupulous God in the endorsement of a bald deception; and, at the root of it all, there is bad faith, the deep, if deeply uneasy, acquiescence in a culture of lies." More seriously, according to Robinson, Twain is implicated in bad faith by failing to recognize and expose that society's hypocrisy; indeed, he is so deeply inculcated in his culture that he cannot fully see the hypocrisy. Robinson's use of Carolyn Porter's comment on one of Twain's contemporaries sums up his position: "I believe that it is accurate to say of Mark Twain in *Tom Sawyer* what Porter says of Henry Adams in *The Education*—that his 'narrative strategy . . . is designed primarily to deny what the act of writing it demonstrates,' that the novelist 'was a participant in the social process he presumed merely to observe.'" Robinson maintains that "Mark Twain was too deep inside his world to see it from without."[23]

We as readers are guilty of the same bad faith, Robinson contends, because we are so taken in by the story and by the narrator that we refuse to see the harsh reality of the culture: "[O]ur inclination to smile knowingly at the novel, and then to dismiss it as 'a light book suitable for children and for adults satisfied with a funny story,' is the leading symptom of our immersion in the culture of bad faith that the story portrays."[24] These charges are indeed serious, especially since what lies at the heart of this bad faith, Robinson argues throughout his book, is what he calls "race-slavery."

Robinson's point hinges on his close identification of Mark Twain with a single narrator of the novel, and on the reader's close identification with both. That close identification is where his argument breaks down and shows us how important it is to recognize the presence of more than one narrator. Robinson does not recognize this, and in fact seems to make no distinction between the narrator(s) and Mark Twain. We are all caught up in bad faith, he contends, and "Mark Twain is our guide." "For in following him through *Tom Sawyer*," Robinson continues, "we have been consistently acquiescent in his refusal to acknowledge fully the manifestations of bad faith, even when they are baldly present to sight." The conclusion of his point raises a direct challenge:

> The most compelling evidence of this shortsightedness is the nearly total failure of scholars and critics to focus their analysis on those frequent, if brief, intervals in the novel when the narrator pauses over, and then recoils from, the perception of fractures beneath the placid surface of St. Petersburg society. When such insights occur, Mark Twain is suddenly angry and satirical; for a moment he loses his detachment. Yet in every case his impulse is to regain composure as quickly as possible, at the price of suppressing the truth that he has glimpsed. Rather than confront his unsettling thoughts, he turns immediately away; and, once again, his readers have been willing to follow.

Because Robinson sees only one narrator (and because he sees that narrator as identical with Mark Twain), he sees these numerous inconsistencies as evidence of *the author's* bad faith, evidence that affects the whole book, all turning on the character of the narrator: "Had his own hands been less evidently dirtied in the culture of bad faith, *Tom Sawyer* would have been a much different—which is to say, a much more overtly angry—book. As it is, and at times against nearly irresistible promptings, Mark Twain settled into the safe, rather nervously studied, and thoroughly untoward persona of an urbane, slightly condescending outsider."[25]

When we recognize not one, but two narrators, one dead to metaphor, the other alive to it and using language that satirizes and undercuts his wooden counterpart, we see the flaws in Robinson's argument. That is certainly not to say that St. Petersburg (and nineteenth-century America, or twentieth- and twenty-first-century America, for that matter) is not implicated in bad faith, but it does exonerate Mark Twain of much of the guilt Robinson and other cultural critics charge him with. The contesting of metaphorical visions in the narrative stances of *The Adventures of Tom Sawyer* shows that clearly. "Author" is certainly guilty of bad faith, but Twain, through his more lively narrator, exposes that bad faith to all.

Did Mark Twain do all this consciously? Again, as with the absence of metaphor in the final two chapters of "Old Times on the Mississippi," there is no way of knowing. He was certainly capable of writing with one consistent voice if he wanted to, as other texts show. I realize that he wrote heuristically, and that sometimes he was not in perfect control of his material. But I do not think that is true of *Tom Sawyer*. Walter Blair notes that Twain's "shifting memories and moods" had an effect on the way he wrote the novel, and quotes two letters to Will Bowen. The first, written soon after Twain's marriage, is nostalgic, even overwrought: "Heavens what eternities have swung their hoary cycles about since." The second was written in the summer of 1876, the year *Tom Sawyer* was published: "As to the past, there is but one good thing about it, . . . that it *is* the past. . . . I can see by your manner of speech, that for more than twenty years you have stood dead still in the midst of the dreaminess, the melancholy, the romance, the heroics, of sweet but sappy sixteen. Man, do you know that this is simply mental and moral masturbation? It belongs eminently to the period usually devoted to *physical* masturbation, and should be left there and outgrown. . . . You need a dose of salts. . . ." Blair concludes, "The mood of *Tom Sawyer* is that of the earlier letter."[26] I disagree. *Both* moods are in the novel, and it seems clear to me which one Twain preferred. His vivid metaphor in the second letter underscores that for me. As is often the case, metaphor serves as the telling light that reveals.

I began this section by quoting Twain's letter to Howells about perhaps making a mistake in not choosing a first-person narrator for his boy book. We know what astonishing results came when he did choose to do so, and what a world of trouble he raised by finding that remarkable voice and style. What we have not fully seen yet is how crucial metaphor is to voice and style, and even more deeply, to vision and theme. Metaphor carries us to the heart of the novel that is the heart of Mark Twain's career.

III. Huckleberry Finn *and the Victims of Metaphor*

Among the many triumphs that Mark Twain achieved in *Adventures of Huckleberry Finn* is its relative lack of metaphor in Huck's narrative, especially when compared to some of his other works with first-person, vernacular narrators. This achievement owes much to his creation of Huck as a character, and even more to his fidelity to Huck's voice. It would have been artistically easy, and even characteristic and natural for Twain, to create a narrator whose speech was full of colorful backwoods metaphor. Twain was unquestionably a master of that kind of speech when he wanted to use it, and rarely fell into the kind of false metaphor that has become such a commonplace in novels, movies, and television that attempt a vernacular flavor. The relative lack of metaphor in Huck's narration reveals something important about Huck's vision and even his psychology; as David Sloane points out, "Huck is more than uneducated, he is overpoweringly literal."[27] We can see this literal stance best in the exchange that occurs when Buck Grangerford asks Huck where Moses was when the candle went out:

> I said I didn't know; I hadn't heard about it before, no way.
> "Well, guess," he says.
> "How'm I going to guess," says I, "when I never heard tell about it before?"
> "But you can guess, can't you? It's just as easy."
> "*Which* candle?" I says.
> "Why, any candle," he says.
> "I don't know where he was," says I; "where was he?"
> "Why, he was in the *dark!* That's where he was!"
> "Well, if you knowed where he was, what did you ask me for?" (*HF*, 135)

Huck is "in the dark" about both riddles and metaphor.

As an artist, having imagined such a determinedly literal-minded character, Twain seems to have purposefully squelched his own use of metaphor. In this way, he is like a great musician in an improvisational genre, Miles Davis in jazz or Bill Monroe in bluegrass, who can play all the notes but deliberately chooses to underplay in the service of a particular song or mood. "The notes you don't play are just as important as the notes you do," goes the old jazz adage. Or it could be a testament to how deeply Twain was able to enter into the psychology of Huck, his fictional creation, becoming Huck so fully that he thought and spoke like Huck, and no longer thought or spoke like himself.

This is not to say that Twain's greatest novel is devoid of metaphor. That would be impossible in English or any other language. But clearly, the novel is not as rich in metaphor as most of his other works, and certainly not as rich as we might expect it to be, given how brightly its language glows in the reader's mind, during the reading and long afterward. As it turns out, the recovery of the first half of the manuscript allows us to see the way Twain arrived at this vision, and that interesting process will be examined in the next chapter. Here, I focus on metaphor from a slightly different angle: looking at how the characters of the novel are themselves victims of metaphor, and what that means for Huck, for the novel, and for the reader. This first examination will lead to an even closer look at the racial metaphor of the novel, giving us fresh perspectives on some of the problems that dominate discussions of *Huckleberry Finn*.

The concept of "victims of metaphor" comes from Colin Turbayne's *Myth of Metaphor,* first published in 1962. In the vast, interdisciplinary field of metaphor studies, I have rarely seen this book cited, and I have never seen it cited in a study of literary metaphor. Even so, Turbayne's book is among the most illuminating and insightful of the many books on metaphor. But because Turbayne focuses on the science of optics and the ways metaphors of sight have changed and distorted the history of that science, his ideas on metaphor may have been generally overlooked by many in the humanities.

Turbayne traces three stages of metaphor, passing from rejection of a word because it is "simply inappropriate . . . because it gives the thing a name that belongs to something else"; to a second stage, in which "we accept the metaphor by acquiescing in its make-believe"; to the third stage, in which "the metaphor becomes so commonplace that we don't see it as a metaphor; the two items, formerly different, become accepted as the same." Thus, according to Turbayne, "What had been models are now taken for the things modeled." Turbayne calls this process a "transition from using metaphor with awareness to being used or victimized by it, from make-believe to belief." "The victim of metaphor," he argues, "accepts one way of sorting or bundling or allocating the facts as the only way to sort, bundle, or allocate them. The victim not only has a special view of the world but regards it as the only view, or rather, he confuses a special view of the world with the world. He is thus, unknowingly, a metaphysician. He has mistaken the mask for the face."[28]

One way to read *Huckleberry Finn* is to read the characters in terms of their own "special view of the world," according to their instinctive or intuitive metaphorical visions. Huck, as I have said, the most literal-minded of characters, is having to understand and choose from among the perspectives of a number of characters who all are victims of metaphor, who all have one way of sorting the world, who all have "mistaken the mask for the face." To read the novel as a series of encounters between Huck and these victims of metaphor, and to watch Huck struggle with these competing visions, changes the way we read and helps to give us a better understanding of Huck and of the novel. Though one could argue that every character Huck encounters is just such a victim of metaphor, I focus on the views of the primary victims of metaphor in the opening quarter of the novel, before he sets out on his journey: Tom Sawyer, Pap, the Widow Douglas, Miss Watson, and Jim.[29] In this part of the novel, the competing metaphorical visions are laid out very clearly, and by examining the way Huck meets each vision, tests it, and deals with it, we can see the way each of these characters exerts a powerful and lingering influence on Huck for the rest of the novel, and how these conflicting but flawed metaphorical visions are key to an understanding of Huck's later choices. Huck struggles to see and understand these distorted visions, and he struggles to free himself from also being a victim of metaphor. Finally, the ultimate victim of metaphor may be the reader, who may also have only one way of sorting the facts, and thus a special, but distorted, view of the novel. So by being more aware of what is going on metaphorically, we can gain a clearer understanding of the novel, of its enduring controversies and puzzles, and perhaps even of our world and of ourselves.

In the opening, when Huck goes back to the widow's house, we see his first encounter with a metaphorical vision. Her name for Huck, "a poor lost lamb," shows us her way of sorting the world. The familiar passage tells us something about the way Huck reacts to metaphor and highlights his literal-mindedness, a vital part of his character and his vision: "The widow she cried over me, and called me a poor lost lamb, and she called me a lot of other names, too, but she never meant no harm by it" (*HF*, 2). Huck is rarely able to recognize metaphor, and in nearly every instance, he reacts this literally. In the face of each of these characters who are victims of metaphor, Huck has a different view. So when the widow prays over her food, Huck sees only that "you had to wait for the widow to tuck down her head and grumble a little over the victuals, though there warn't really anything the matter with them" (*HF*, 2). Huck is unable to recognize the metaphorical relation between himself and Moses, and when he finds out "that Moses had been dead a considerable long time" (*HF*, 2), he makes his famous—and for him, rare—metaphorical pronouncement: "I don't take no stock in dead people" (*HF*, 2). Indeed, he might say that he "don't take no stock in metaphor"—which we can see more clearly when he encounters Miss Watson's skewed vision.

To Miss Watson, Huck is not a "poor lost lamb." In her eyes, Huck is a poor lost sinner, or worse; her metaphorical view is diametrically opposite to her sister's. These two are the first of many opposite characters who will be paired in various formulations, and all have a big effect on Huck's development. All of these pairs hover residually over Huck for the remainder of the novel.

The widow's and Miss Watson's competing visions come to a head for Huck in the next chapter, when he finally explains the discrepancy in their visions by deciding that there are "two Providences" (*HF*, 14). To reach that conclusion, though, he must do what he often does when confronted with metaphorical visions: test them. After Miss Watson takes him into the closet to pray (and this time *she* is the literal one; she seems literally to take him into a closet), Huck says, "but nothing come of it. She told me to pray every day, and whatever I asked for I would get" (*HF*, 13). As he always must, Huck tries, but only as a test of her figurative promise that he would get whatever he asked for: "Once I got a fish-line, but no hooks. It warn't any good to me without hooks. I tried for the hooks three or four times, but somehow I couldn't make it work" (*HF*, 13). For Huck, prayer is a kind of magic trick that he, for some reason, cannot do. Still, he will not give up: "By-and-by, one day, I asked Miss Watson to try for me, but she said I was a fool" (*HF*, 13). That is her metaphorical name for Huck—and then he still has to look, characteristically, for proof: "She never told me why, and I couldn't make it out no way" (*HF*, 13).

But that is *still* not enough for Huck. As always, he must test the vision. He goes deep into the woods and thinks about it. His list of questions is characteristically literal, but also incisive about other characters, showing their preoccupation with acquisition and possessions: "I says to myself, if a body can get anything they pray for, why don't Deacon Winn get back the money he lost on pork? Why can't the widow get back her silver snuff-box that was stole? Why can't Miss Watson fat up?" (*HF*, 13). Again, he must ask—but this time, he knows enough to go to the widow, who tells him that prayer is for "spiritual gifts." As always, Huck is helpless in the face of metaphor, but others are always ready to explain: "This was too many for me, but she told me what she meant—I must help other people, and do everything I could for other people, and look out for them all the time, and never think about myself. This was including Miss Watson, as I took it" (*HF*, 13). That last conclusion is a brilliant testimony to Huck's literal vision—and sends him into the woods *again* to test the new information: "I went out in the woods and turned it over in my mind a long time, but I couldn't see no advantage about it—except for the other people—so at last I reckoned I wouldn't worry about it any more, but just let it go" (*HF*, 13–14). However, the two women are still at him about Providence, confusing him with their competing visions: "Sometimes the widow would take me one side and talk about Providence in a way to make a body's mouth water; but maybe next day Miss Watson would take hold and knock it all down again" (*HF*, 14). With so much conflicting information about the same entity, Huck's obstinately literal mind must come to a rational explanation: "I judged I could see that there was two Providences, and a poor chap would stand considerable show with the widow's Providence, but if Miss Watson's got him there warn't no help for him any more" (*HF*, 14). When he makes a decision for the widow's Providence, he still sees all this literally: "I would belong to the widow's, if he would have me, though I couldn't make out how he was agoing to be any better off then than what he was before, seeing I was so ignorant and so kind of low-down and ornery" (*HF*, 14). These competing metaphorical visions are with Huck for the rest of his journey, and a seed has been planted that will prove decisive at the very climax of the novel.

A very different metaphorical vision comes from Tom Sawyer, and Huck's observations on his interaction with Tom Sawyer's Gang are typical: "We played robber now and then about a month, and then I resigned" (*HF*, 14). Before that resignation, though, comes a long series of encounters with elaborate visions and tests of them, only some of which we see in Huck's mostly indirect discourse. In Tom's metaphorical world, hogs are "ingots," and "turnips and stuff" are "julery" (*HF*, 14). We get to see the literal and metaphorical side by side in Huck's narration, with Huck as usual testing everything. The whole affair must have been an amazing spectacle for the town, and Tom's vision is so strong that he captures the boys' imagination and makes them see the world in his own particular way:

> One time Tom sent a boy to run about town with a blazing stick, which he called a slogan (which was the sign for the Gang to get together), and then he said he had got secret news by his spies that next day a whole parcel of Spanish merchants and rich A-rabs was going to camp in Cave Hollow with two hundred elephants, and six hundred camels, and over a thousand "sumter" mules, all loaded down with di'monds, and they

didn't have only a guard of four hundred soldiers, and so we would lay in ambuscade, as he called it, and kill the lot and scoop the things. (*HF*, 14–15)

Huck's familiar response is to doubt, but test: "I didn't believe we could lick such a crowd of Spaniards and A-rabs, but I wanted to see the camels and elephants" (*HF*, 15). He is disappointed in the literal: "But there warn't no Spaniards and A-rabs, and there warn't no camels nor no elephants. It warn't anything but a Sunday-school picnic, and only a primer-class at that" (*HF*, 15). (That last comment is curious—as if a higher-up class would have made the vision any less absurd.) Still, Huck must chase the vision down and report every detail of its dissolution, from the metaphorical to the literal, reporting their "haul"—"we never got anything but some doughnuts and jam, though Ben Rogers got a rag doll, and Jo Harper got a hymn-book and a tract" (*HF*, 15)—all of which they must drop when the very real teacher intervenes.

When Huck confronts Tom, Tom builds his vision again:

I didn't see no di'monds, and I told Tom Sawyer so. He said there was loads of them there, anyway, and he said there was A-rabs there, too, and elephants and things. I said, why couldn't we see them, then? He said if I warn't so ignorant, but had read a book called "Don Quixote," I would know without asking. He said it was all done by enchantment. He said there was hundreds of soldiers there, and elephants and treasure, and so on, but we had enemies which he called magicians, and they had turned the whole thing into an infant Sunday school, just out of spite. (*HF*, 15–16)

Persistently, literal Huck is ready to act: "I said, all right, then the thing for us to do was to go for the magicians" (*HF*, 16). In their discussion of magic lamps, Huck always sees the practical side of the question. Still, he cannot let this go, just as with his testing of prayer. Again, he goes deep into the woods to test the vision, this time with "an old tin lamp and an iron ring," which he "rubbed and rubbed till I sweat like an Injun, calculating to build a palace and sell it" (*HF*, 17). Huck is always literal, always practical, always looking for the monetary value in these visions, as he did with Miss Watson and prayer. But as with prayer, Huck can't make the magic work: "[B]ut it warn't no use, none of the genies come. So then I judged that all that stuff was only just one of Tom Sawyer's lies. I reckoned he believed in the A-rabs and the elephants, but as for me I think different. It had all the marks of a Sunday school" (*HF*, 17). "Just one of Tom Sawyer's lies"—he may as well have said "just one of Tom Sawyer's metaphors." Tom's metaphorical vision is the magic of words, the magic of the romantic, and even though it looks as if Huck has rejected this vision as soundly as he has rejected Providence, the vision will linger over him. Like the widow and Miss Watson, Tom is a metaphysician, mistaking the mask for the face; like them, he is a victim of metaphor.

The most powerful character pair in the novel is Jim and Pap, starkly juxtaposed in chapters 4 and 5. Jim's metaphorical vision is magic, done with the hair-ball, and his prophecy for Huck involves metaphorical use of white and black: the white and black angels that hover around Pap, and the light and dark girl flying about Huck in his life. Then we see Pap, with his black eyes and fish-belly white skin: "not like another man's white, but a white to make a body sick, a white to make a body's flesh crawl—a tree-toad white, a fish-belly white" (*HF,* 23). Since white and black are so central a metaphorical matrix for the novel, and have, in the issue of race, become the novel's central critical concern, I discuss these images in more depth in a later section.

Pap's vision is the vision of the primitive, animalistic nihilist; he repeatedly compares himself metaphorically to a hog, for example. His vicious diatribe against "govment" comes when he has lain all night in the gutter and "was just all mud," as Huck says (*HF,* 33). Again, the imagery is persistently black and white, especially concerning the free professor from Ohio—in Pap's words, "a mulatter, most as white as a white man. He had the whitest shirt on you ever see, too, and the shiniest hat; and there ain't a man in that town that's got as fine clothes as what he had . . ." (*HF,* 33). In the case of Pap, Huck never has to take time to test the vision; much to his credit, he rejects Pap's vision without deep thought—or undoubtedly, this rejection has happened before the narrative ever began. Even so, some of Pap's ethos—about stealing, for example—lingers as an influence for Huck.

The final metaphorical vision set up in the opening chapters is Jim's. His may be the hardest to see as a metaphorical vision, for a number of reasons: because Jim is with Huck for most of the rest of the novel, because Huck is so sympathetic to Jim's vision, and because we as readers want Jim's vision so deeply. As I said, Jim's first vision is a magic vision, not only about the hair-ball, but about all the signs and folklore he knows. In a way, then, this is the third magic vision Huck encounters, after the religious magic of the widow and Miss Watson, and the romantic magic of Tom Sawyer. Unlike theirs, Jim's magic vision is intimately tied to the natural world, from birds flying to snakeskins to his poetic vision of the moon laying all the stars. "Jim knowed all kinds of signs," Huck says. "He said he knowed most everything" (*HF*, 55). But Jim's more important vision emerges only gradually, and this deeper vision is so compelling that Huck, as well as the reader, is captivated by it, until we cannot see his vision as anything but the truth. But as Turbayne reminds us, Jim too is a victim of metaphor, and ultimately that makes potential victims of us all.

Before Huck can accept Jim's metaphorical vision, he must undo the visions of Jim that he has tacitly accepted from Pap, Tom, Miss Watson, and even the Widow Douglas. His tricks on Jim—the snakeskin, notably—are a carryover from Pap and from Tom, and his notion of Jim as a slave and a "nigger" come from Miss Watson, Jim's owner, and the rest of his society. The undoing comes throughout the journey, as Huck has much to unlearn, but one pivotal moment, full of rich figurative meaning, comes after they are lost in the fog, when Huck tricks Jim into thinking their separation was all a dream. Jim's response, examined more fully in the next section, humbles Huck, and he has to undo the vision he has held all his life—"It was fifteen minutes before I could work myself up to go and humble myself to a nigger" (*HF*, 105)—but he also has to begin constructing a new vision: "I didn't do him no more mean tricks, and I wouldn't done that one if I'd knowed it would make him feel that way" (*HF*, 105). Why *didn't* he know that? Why is he surprised that Jim loves his family, the same as a white person does? It is because the metaphorical vision of Jim, and all blacks, as lower than human, as animals, as objects, was so strongly held that a whole nation could allow it, despite its own self-proclaimed vision of equality for humanity.

What, then, is Jim's metaphorical vision, the one that Huck now begins to learn, the one most readers accept as the truest? Much to Huck's surprise, and often to his horror, Jim sees himself as a human being, as a man, as a father, and as a free individual. These ideas come to an early climax in chapter 16, when Jim thinks they are about to reach Cairo and he is near freedom, and he talks out loud about his plans and expectations, gaining freedom for himself, then buying his wife, then buying, or perhaps even stealing, his two children. Huck's metaphorical response—"It most froze me to hear such talk" (*HF*, 124)—underscores the conflict between visions that happens at this point, between Jim's emerging sense of himself as a free person and, mainly, Miss Watson's vision of Jim as her property. Huck does not give Jim up to the slave traders here; the inevitable crisis is only delayed.

The problem—for Huck, for Jim, for the novel, and for the reader—is that Jim's vision of himself as a free individual, as beautiful and noble and proper and right as it is, makes Jim the ultimate victim of metaphor in the narrative. More so than the widow or Miss Watson or Pap or even Tom Sawyer, Jim is fooling himself about the world he lives in. Huck learns to share Jim's vision, at least partially, and the reader shares it even more so. Most readers buy into Jim's impossible vision—and that is what has caused so much of the trouble for this novel.[30]

With the metaphorical visions set up and the trip well under way, one way we can read the middle portions of the novel is to take episodes and see how variations and combinations of these victims of metaphor influence Huck's viewpoint. For example, in the Grangerford-Shepherdson feud, Huck undoubtedly sees the family, as he tells us, in terms of the widow's sense of aristocracy, a sense that is at its heart metaphorical: "Col. Grangerford was a gentleman, you see. He was a gentleman all over; and so was his family. He was well born, as the saying is, and that's worth as much in a man as it is in a horse, so the Widow Douglas said, and nobody ever denied that she was of the first aristocracy in our town" (*HF,* 142). But as Huck goes on, we can see that the vision is mixed with another: " . . . and pap he always said it too, though he warn't no more quality than a mud-cat, himself" (*HF,* 142). Like Miss Watson, the Grangerfords are slave owners; in, fact, each of them has a personal slave. The Grangerfords also seem to be an extension of Tom Sawyer's vision, living as they do according to the books, and living out a life of danger and excitement—for a reason none of them can remember. They become quite literally victims, and not just of metaphor; the scene where Huck cries over the dead body of his new friend Buck is one of the most poignant in the novel, so poignant that Huck can barely talk about it.[31] Surely this episode gives the lie to the metaphorical visions of aristocracy that the Grangerfords represent. Every episode in the novel shares these combinations, and Huck is constantly testing the competing visions, reacting according to the visions he has been exposed to: the king and the duke, Boggs and Colonel Sherburn, the Wilks family. Each is just another combination of the same metaphorical visions Huck already knows.

The climax comes in chapter 31, when Huck has his celebrated crisis of conscience.[32] One way to read this pivotal scene is to see it as a clash of metaphorical visions, predominantly Miss Watson's against Jim's, but with the others' visions also clearly coming into play. The letter Huck intends to write is not to Miss Watson, but to Tom, and the very act of writing such a letter seems in some ways to be Tom's kind of ploy; the idea that "everybody naturally despises an ungrateful nigger" surely comes from Pap; the conscience that "grinds" Huck comes from the widow (*HF,* 268). In the first climax of the crisis, Providence, the entity that Huck had earlier decided not to worry about, reenters—and it is not the Providence he had earlier declared tentative allegiance to: "And at last, when it hit me all of a sudden that here was the plain hand of Providence slapping me in the face and letting me know that my wickedness was being watched all the time from up there in heaven, whilst I was stealing a poor old woman's nigger that hadn't ever done me no harm, and now was showing me there's One that's always on the lookout, and ain't agoing to allow no such miserable doings to go only just so fur and no further, I most dropped in my tracks I was so scared" (*HF*, 268–69). Huck's next comment coalesces several of the metaphoric visions: "Well, I tried the best I could to kinder soften it up somehow for myself, by saying I was brung up wicked, and so I warn't so much to blame; but something inside of me kept saying, 'There was the Sunday school, you could a gone to it; and if you'd a done it they'd a learnt you, there, that people that acts as I'd been acting about that nigger goes to everlasting fire'" (*HF*, 269). The vision of his upbringing is Pap's, and the kind of rationalization Pap would make for his own low-down actions. The vision of the Sunday school is Miss Watson's, but it is also the widow's and Tom's, and even Pap's, as antagonistic to religion as we know him to be.

At this crucial moment, a moment that makes him "shiver," Huck returns to a vision he had tried but failed at earlier: "And I about made up my mind to pray," he says (*HF*, 269). His failure this time comes from the vision the widow has instilled in him, that he "can't pray a lie." The solution is to try Tom's vision of the written word as a way out: "At last I had an idea; and I says, I'll go and write the letter—and *then* see if I can pray" (*HF*, 269). The competition between the magic of religion and the magic of the word has become so tangled that Huck doesn't really know why he is doing any of this anymore. Is his purpose to do the right thing and write a letter? Or is it to pray and exonerate himself? And why is he resorting to prayer in the first place? His troubles are gone before he actually does either, expressing his relief in a simile that, while conventional, is all too rare for the literal Huck: "Why, it was astonishing, the way I felt as light as a feather, right straight off, and my troubles all gone" (*HF*, 269). After he uses the magic power of the word and writes his letter, he uses a religious metaphor that seems to have come more from the Widow Douglas: "I felt good and all washed clean of sin for the first time I had ever felt so in my life, and I knowed I could pray now" (*HF*, 269). Miss Watson's vision is still dominant; Huck's only reason for praying is to ease himself of her tormenting vision of Providence, and his thought before he prays (which he of course never does) is "how near I come to being lost and going to hell" (*HF*, 269).

The hell he envisions is Miss Watson's hell and he is condemned there by her Providence; it is the hell he wished to go to in the first chapter, drawn by the power of his friend Tom's vision.

The train of images that follows as Huck unconsciously gives himself over to Jim's vision begins as a kind of collage, the juxtapositions governed by the pole of metonymy, and then pauses with a metaphorical comment: "And got to thinking over our trip down the river; and I see Jim before me, all the time, in the day, and in the night-time, sometimes moonlight, sometimes storms, and we a floating along, talking, and singing, and laughing. But somehow I couldn't strike no places to harden me against him, but only the other kind" (*HF*, 269–70). The rest of the familiar and powerful passage is a succession of metonymic images, one dissolving into the other by contiguity, and ending with a dramatic focus on the piece of paper that has now become a metaphor for the competing visions that Huck has been struggling with throughout the whole novel:

> I'd see him standing my watch on top of his'n, stead of calling me, so I could go on sleeping; and see him how glad he was when I come back out of the fog; and when I come to him again in the swamp, up there where the feud was; and such-like times; and would always call me honey, and pet me, and do everything he could think of for me, and how good he always was; and at last I struck the time I saved him by telling the men we had small-pox aboard, and he was so grateful, and said I was the best friend old Jim ever had in the world, and the *only* one he's got now; and then I happened to look around, and see that paper. (*HF*, 270)

Huck's next words take on extra weight when we think of them as metaphor, and when we think about the competing visions that lie behind them: "It was a close place. I took it up, and held it in my hand. I was a trembling, because I'd got to decide, forever, betwixt two things, and I knowed it." When Huck says, "All right, then, I'll *go* to hell" (*HF*, 271), he is, as he says, deciding "forever, betwixt two things," but really he is making a complicated decision among several visions: rejecting Miss Watson's, but also rejecting the widow's, Pap's, and Tom's—and embracing Jim's. In the Evasion that follows, Huck embraces, again, Tom's vision, but all in the supposed service of Jim. The clash of those strong competing visions has disturbed readers for a long time, and no doubt will continue to.[33]

Ultimately, it is really the reader who is the victim of metaphor, and largely because Jim's vision is so noble, so superior to the others, so right, but at its heart, for Jim in his time and situation, so totally impossible. Jim is a victim of metaphor because he has accepted one way to bundle the facts of his existence: the American way, the vision of the Declaration of Independence and the Constitution, the metaphorical vision of the entire country. All the indignities he has to suffer at the hands of Tom (and, by his complicity, Huck) and by the mob at the Phelps farm are metaphors for what the country did in "set[ting] a nigger free that was already free before" (*HF*, 360), as Huck puts it. The country promises it, and Jim wants it so, and we as readers want it so—but it isn't going to be that way, and it wasn't that way. As readers, we indulge ourselves in a romantic vision, even though we do not want to think of Jim as a victim of metaphor.

What I am saying about the delusion of Jim's vision may seem shocking. But consider a parallel to the shocking events of September 11, 2001. Most people could see clearly that the terrorist hijackers were horribly deluded in their beliefs, that, if we applied Turbayne's terms, they were undoubtedly "victims of metaphor." They had undergone what Turbayne calls the "transition from using metaphor with awareness to being used or victimized by it, from make-believe to belief"; as victims of metaphor, to quote Turbayne again, they had accepted "one way of sorting or bundling or allocating the facts as the only way to sort, bundle, or allocate them. The victim not only has a special view of the world but regards it as the only view, or rather, he confuses a special view of the world with the world."[34] Their delusion is immediately clear to most of us, but here is my point: *our delusion eludes us so successfully that we are unable to see it as delusion.*

In our own way, we Americans (and I will speak of most Americans here) do not realize that we too are victims of metaphor. Our metaphor of freedom, independence, and what we bundle together as "the American way" is a metaphor that most of us do not see as a metaphor anymore, but as our right, as an intrinsic part of our existence, as "the way things are." We too have accepted "one way of sorting or bundling or allocating the facts as the only way to sort, bundle, or allocate them"; we too have "a special view of the world," and we see it as the "only view"—or, as Turbayne concludes, we confuse "a special view of the world with the world." This is not to excuse the terrorists in any way; their actions rightly horrify most of humanity. But it is to point out that they acted because they were victims of metaphor, and most of us reacted as we did because we are, too. Jim is a victim of a metaphor very similar to the one that we instinctively felt on September 11—which explains why most readers do not see Jim's belief in his own freedom and independence as anything other than his intrinsic right, as the nature of his existence. A vision of human freedom is a noble idea, but it is a metaphorical vision, not the only way to bundle the facts, and not the way we have bundled the facts for most of human history.

At the very end, in one of the final illustrations, "Out of Bondage" (*HF*, 360), Jim has his arms around both boys, Tom smugly holds the bullet that hangs around his neck, and Huck holds Jim's chains, with a kind of ironic, puzzled look on his face. Jim is not free, as he will soon find out, no matter where he goes in the country. Tom is not "most well now" (*HF*, 360)—the Tom Sawyers of the world never get well. And there is no territory for Huck to light out for ahead of the rest. He has "been there before," he says of being "sivilized" (*HF*, 362)—but he might as well say the same about the territory. Pap and Miss Watson are both dead, but their visions are not—no dead metaphors allowed in this grim book. The widow has been replaced by Aunt Sally. Jim's vision is the most enduring, for it is a vision that ought to come true, and perhaps someday will.

Turbayne reminds us that we can never replace metaphors with the literal truth, that we cannot get to "the facts." All we can hope to do is to be aware that we are ordering our world through comparisons, always. "We are always victims of adding some interpretation," he says. "We cannot help but allocate, sort, or bundle the facts in some way or another." He concludes, "Metaphors furnish a clear illustration of the 'imposture' or the 'delusion' or the 'cheat' of words. It is part of the nature of metaphor to appear wearing a disguise. . . . The audience has to see through this disguise. For metaphors do not come with their shared names on them. Every case of taking a metaphor literally is a case of being duped by words."[35] As readers, as citizens of the world, we are constantly being "duped by words." The most we can hope for is to remember that we are being duped, and not to mistake the mask for the face. We see in this great novel how serious the outcome can be if we are not aware. "Human beings can be awful cruel sometimes," Huck wisely says. Can it be that our cruelty always comes from being victims of metaphor?

Race, even if it is a metaphorical vision, has become so important for the novel that it demands a still closer look. A deeper dive into metaphor may help us understand this central issue a bit more clearly.

IV. "Trash is what people is dat puts dirt on de head er dey fren's":
The Metaphor and Metonymy of Race in Huckleberry Finn

In chapter 12 of *Adventures of Huckleberry Finn*, as Huck and Jim are about to depart on their escape and what will turn out to be a long journey, Huck says, "It warn't good judgment to put *everything* on the raft" (*HF*, 77). In recent years, it seems as if critics of the novel are in danger of doing just that. While earlier generations of critics did not comment on the racial issues of the novel as fully or with as much complexity as they might have, its racial elements became a dominant, if not *the* dominant, critical concern about the novel in the 1990s and after.[36] I touched on the issue of race in the previous section, but now I zoom in closer.

As others have done, I focus on the racial language of the novel, but examine it in light of its metaphorical underpinnings, looking for nuances of language and attitude that might otherwise go unnoticed. Because metaphor is such a vital and omnipresent part of language, it contains much and can reveal much. As Paul Ricoeur has said, "[M]etaphor is the rhetorical process by which discourse unleashes the power that certain fictions have to redescribe reality."[37] The way this fiction redescribes the reality of racism in America, then and now, has certainly been powerful, and is still a matter for argument. Metaphor will shed some more light on what has become the most controversial side of Mark Twain's great novel.

As we well know, and as becomes very clear whenever one teaches the novel, racial language, particularly one offensive word, pervades the text, so that we do not have to look far for it. Rather than begin with racial language in general or the offensive term in particular, I wanted to think more broadly about metaphorical images. In an attempt to get past obvious occurrences and find concentrations of racial language, I looked for clusters of words and images that might relate to race in either a literal or a metaphorical sense. I began my examination of metaphors of race at one such cluster. A word search of the novel reveals three large concentrations of the words "white" and "black": Jim's hair-ball prophecy, Pap's speech on "govment," and the descriptions of Emmeline Grangerford's pictures. After a closer examination of the metaphorical imagery in these scenes, I move on to the offensive word and to some of the other issues figurative language can help us understand more clearly.

When Jim reads the hair-ball, he sees two angels hovering around Pap: "One uv 'em is white en shiny, en t'other one is black" (*HF*, 22). Jim reads these two angels with their conventional metaphorical meanings: "De white one gits him to go right, a little while, den de black one sail in en bust it all up" (*HF*, 22). The rest of the passage underscores Jim's interpretation, as well as his privileging of white over black: "Dey's two gals flyin' 'bout you in yo' life. One uv 'em's light en t'other one is dark. One is rich 'en t'other is po'" (*HF*, 22). If we align these terms, we have positive associations for "white/light/rich" and negative associations for "black/dark/poor." Why would Jim, a black person, make such an interpretation? He could have such ideas so ingrained in him that he sees the world this way, and some of his later comments about whites and blacks seem to show that: "I wouldn' think nuff'n; I'd take en bust him over de head. Dat is, ef he warn't white. I wouldn't 'low no nigger to call me that" (*HF,* 97). Or is that comment, and the conventional white and black interpretation, just a survival strategy? Perhaps Jim is putting Huck on, interpreting in the terms he would expect a white boy to believe in also. Or, moving to the level of the author, is this Mark Twain, consciously or unconsciously, inscribing the scene with his own racial attitudes? Perhaps even Twain is putting us on, as Jim may be with Huck, telling the reader what the reader expects.[38] Thus, in its first important occurrence, white/black, seemingly such a clear-cut opposition, is somewhat confused. And these images recur, twin angels themselves hovering around the entire text.

Adding to the impact of the imagery is the dramatic situation, in which a white boy is seeking advice from a black man. Significantly, in the next chapter, on the next page, so close that it could be considered a continuation of the hair-ball scene, Huck meets Pap. The juxtapositions are striking: Huck has just sought magic counsel from a black man concerning his white father, and now the father almost magically appears. Seen in these terms, the combinations of white and black imagery in the description of Pap become all the more intriguing:

> He was most fifty, and he looked it. His hair was long and greasy, and hung down, and you could see his eyes shining through like he was behind vines. It was all black, no gray; so was his long, mixed-up whiskers. There warn't no color in his face, where his face showed; it was white; not like another man's white, but a white to make a body sick, a white to make a body's flesh crawl—a tree-toad white, a fish-belly white. (*HF,* 23)

These are rare moments of metaphor-making for the literal-minded Huck. This is literal description, to be sure, but Huck uses exceptionally powerful and vivid figurative language. It is almost as if the horror of Pap is so strong that the usually literal Huck is driven to figurative language to express his disgust and fear. The images of black and white burn in the reader's memory: the eyes behind the black, greasy hair, "shining through like he was behind vines," contrasted with his sickening, "tree-toad white" face. As artistically striking as the metaphors are, they are in perfect keeping with Huck's character and his knowledge, and the association, unlike Jim's conventional one, is most unconventional, reminiscent of Melville's "Whiteness of the Whale" or prefiguring Frost's "Design." For Huck, as for Frost's speaker, whiteness appalls; it "make[s] a body's flesh crawl." The meaning of the metaphors, already somewhat unclear, becomes even more complicated. I refer again to Genette's observation that metaphor is not merely an "ornament," but "the stylistic equivalent of the psychological experience of involuntary memory."[39] The metaphorical description, then, is not just a powerful picture of Pap, but a revealing picture of Huck's psychological state, both at the moment of seeing Pap within the narrative and when remembering his living and dead father at the moment of narration. The confusion over white and black in Jim's prophecy continues, as does the juxtaposition of black Jim and white Pap, setting up not only a contrast but also a pattern for the story.

The next interpretation comes from Pap, when he speaks about whiteness in his speech about "govment": "Oh, yes, this is a wonderful govment, wonderful. Why, looky here. There was a free nigger there, from Ohio; a mulatter, most as white as a white man. He had the whitest shirt on you ever see, too, and the shiniest hat; and there ain't a man in that town that's got as fine clothes as what he had; and he had a gold watch and chain, and a silver-headed cane—the awfulest old gray-headed nabob in the State" (*HF*, 33). Pap's emphasis on the man's clothes is in direct contrast to his own, just as the emphasis on their whiteness is a direct contrast to his; according to Huck, Pap is "all mud," and Pap himself says his clothes "ain't fitten for a hog" (*HF*, 33). The whiteness of the clothes also reminds the reader of Pap's extreme whiteness, but now the interpretation has shifted again. For Pap, whiteness is negative, but for a very different reason than Huck's. Although Pap recognizes the association of white with cleanliness and quality, its association with someone even half black makes him see it negatively. David L. Smith has noted that "Pap's final description of this Ohio gentleman as 'a prowling, thieving, infernal, white-shirted free nigger' almost totally contradicts his previous description of the man as a proud, elegant, dignified figure." Pap is able to take a positive association, see it negatively, then transform it even further into a distortion of what he himself has just given us, suggesting perhaps that he is describing not the free black man, but himself, Pap Finn, who is certainly a prowling, thieving, infernal, dirty-shirted free *white* man.[40]

In the last important cluster of black and white, Huck describes Emmeline Grangerford's artwork. His description includes incongruous similes, "cabbage" and "chisel" used to help us picture the woman's clothing:

There was some that they called crayons, which one of the daughters which was dead made her own self when she was only fifteen years old.

They was different from any pictures I ever see before; blacker, mostly, than is common. One was a woman in a slim black dress, belted small under the arm-pits, with bulges like a cabbage in the middle of the sleeves, and a large black scoop-shovel bonnet with a black veil, and white slim ankles crossed about with black tape, and very wee black slippers, like a chisel, and she was leaning pensive on a tombstone on her right elbow, under a weeping willow, and her other hand hanging down her side holding a white handkerchief and a reticule, and underneath the picture it said "Shall I Never See Thee More Alas." (*HF*, 137)

Emmeline's other pictures are similarly blackened, and Huck's comment—"These was all nice pictures, I reckon, but I didn't somehow seem to take to them, because if ever I was down a little, they always give me the fantods" (*HF*, 138)—only begins to show his reaction to them. He tells us a few pages later that "many's the time I made myself go up to the little room that used to be hers and get out her poor old scrap-book [containing her poetry] and read in it when her pictures had been aggravating me and I had soured on her a little" (*HF*, 140–41). In this case, none of the black-and-white images have any clear racial connotation; instead, the conventional association of black with death is highlighted, and Huck, as we know, "don't take no stock in dead people" (*HF*, 2). But Huck's extreme reaction against the color is still instructive, and could have some application to race, especially if we pair it with his horror at Pap's whiteness. In Huck's world, black would always have at least a trace of racial meaning, even if it is on a level he does not fully recognize, and it certainly holds more than a trace for us, especially in the way we now read the novel.

We might conclude from these scenes that Huck rejects both the black and the white angels hovering around him, although the evidence of the text suggests otherwise. Huck repeatedly shows a positive reaction to black images and metaphors: he says the storm on Jackson's Island is "all blue-black outside, and lovely" (*HF*, 59), and that "the king's duds was all black, and he did look real swell and starchy" (*HF*, 204). At the Grangerfords', he speaks approvingly of the colonel's "blackest kind of eyes, sunk so deep back that they seemed like they was looking out of caverns at you" (*HF*, 142), as well as his black hair, in contrast to his "full suit from head to foot made out of linen so white it hurt your eyes to look at it" (*HF*, 142). The contrast to Pap's shining eyes, his black hair, and his own hurting whiteness is palpable.

All of these pairings of white and black carry a residue for Huck and for the reader. They make even more poignant the moment in chapter 16 when the slave traders ask Huck, "Is your man white, or black?" (*HF*, 125). The choice, seemingly so clear, is metaphorically confused and confusing. Huck hesitates, and in language that is both richly metaphorical and a foreshadowing of the crisis in chapter 31, he tells us:

> I didn't answer up prompt. I tried to, but the words wouldn't come. I tried, for a second or two, to brace up, and out with it, but I warn't man enough—hadn't the spunk of a rabbit. I see I was weakening; so I just give up trying, and up and says—
>
>   "He's white." (*HF,* 125)

Significantly, there are very few such pairings of "white" and "black" explicitly talking about race. The reason, of course, is that another word is used for one of the racial terms.

That word is spread throughout the text, as we know from all the controversy and from the difficulty and discomfort we have in reading aloud almost any passage in the novel. As we did with "Old Times on the Mississippi," we can examine the word in terms of metaphor and metonymy, then make some connection to the clusters of black-and-white imagery. If we look at the racial terms themselves according to Jakobson's principle, we see that both "white" and "black" would be metonymic, at least in referring to a person's race, identity being named by skin color, but what of "nigger"? In the strictest sense, it too would be a metonymy, since it derives from "Negro," and hence from the color black, and it is most often used that way: "Miss Watson's big nigger, named Jim" (*HF,* 6), for example. On just a few occasions, the term is overtly metaphorical, standing for a quality, as in the description of cheap chewing tobacco as "nigger-head" (*HF,* 183), or, more disturbingly, when Huck expresses his disgust over the King and Duke by saying, "Well, if ever I struck anything like it, I'm a nigger" (*HF,* 210). (Ironically, Huck's disturbing comment is immediately followed by his oft-quoted statement "It was enough to make a body ashamed of the human race" [*HF,* 210].) If we see "nigger" purely as a metonymy, pointing only to a person's color, it might not be that offensive, no more offensive than "Negro" or even "black"; clearly, though, we always see it as a metaphor, with all its strong entailments, regardless of how it is used. Part of the argument over the term is really about its status as a metaphor or a metonymy—defenders of Mark Twain's use of it for verisimilitude are taking it as metonymy, but attackers always take it metaphorically, no matter its intention. In the case of "nigger," metaphor overpowers metonymy, as it usually does. "Nigger" is never simply an identifying label; it always carries loads of metaphorical baggage.

"Nigger" and "white," then, operate as a metaphorical and metonymical axis, in opposition to each other, and with their meanings constantly penetrating into each other. Adding to the confusion, the terms shift from metonymy to metaphor, making a chiasmus, or crossover, as metaphor and metonymy are apt to do. Looking back, then, at the earlier uses of "white" and "black" and considering them in the light of metaphor and metonymy, we can see a number of these crossovers. In Jim's hair-ball prophecy, the metonymic black and white become fully metaphorical, and conventionally so, while Huck in describing Pap uses the metonymic white in an unconventional metaphorical association. Pap uses the Ohio professor's white clothes—a metonymy—as a metaphor for the man's pretensions and as proof of the problems with "govment." And in describing Emmeline's pictures, Huck uses their metonymic blackness as a metaphoric comment on the death that pervades the house and the family. This constant crossover helps explain the confusion surrounding the two racial terms.

We might expect the term "white trash" to be used in opposition to "nigger." Interestingly, "white trash" never occurs in the novel. The only use of the word "trash" is in the passage where Huck and Jim get separated in the fog. After Huck plays the trick on Jim of making him think he has dreamed the whole incident, then secretly laughs at him for elaborately interpreting the dream, he asks Jim what the "leaves and rubbish" on the raft stand for. Jim's first action—"Jim looked at the trash, and then looked at me, and back at the trash again" (HF, 104)—prefigures the powerful association he next makes. In fact, we can almost see the metaphor being created in Jim's mind in his act of looking from Huck to the trash. Jim's speech shows the power of metaphor:

> "What do dey stan' for? I's gwyne to tell you. When I got all wore out wid work, en wid de callin' for you, en went to sleep, my heart wuz mos' broke bekase you wuz los', en I didn' k'yer no mo' what become er me en de raf'. En when I wake up en fine you back agin, all safe en soun', de tears come en I could a got down on my knees en kiss' yo' foot I's so thankful. En all you wuz thinkin 'bout wuz how you could make a fool uv ole Jim wid a lie. Dat truck dah is *trash;* en trash is what people is dat puts dirt on de head er dey fren's en makes 'em ashamed." (HF, 105)

The metaphor is all the more powerful because Jim chooses to omit "white" from the phrase "white trash," but the implication is very clear. Like Pap, Huck is considered by his society to be white trash, and to be considered so by his friend, even if the friend is himself a "nigger," affects him powerfully. Jim makes a chiasmus in the creation of the metaphor, crossing metonymically from the trash to Huck, even though the connection is erased. This is one of the most powerful moments in the novel, and metaphor has a good deal to do with that.[41]

So what are we to make of these crossovers, these metaphors and metonymies, this confusion about race on the most fundamental level of language? It is helpful to place these points in the context of what David L. Smith calls "racial discourse." In his essay in *Satire or Evasion?*, Smith claims, "Those who brand the book racist generally do so without having considered the specific form of racial discourse to which the novel responds." Smith continues:

> When I speak of "racial discourse," I mean more than simply attitudes about race or conventions of talking about race. Most importantly, I mean that race itself is a discursive formation which delimits social relations on the basis of alleged physical differences. "Race" is a strategy for relegating a segment of the population to a permanent inferior status. It functions by insisting that each "race" has specific, definitive, inherent behavioral tendencies and capacities which distinguish it from other races. . . . [T]he primary emphasis historically has been on defining "the Negro" as a deviant from Euro-American norms. "Race" in America means white supremacy and black inferiority, and "the Negro," a socially constituted fiction, is a generalized, one-dimensional surrogate for the historical reality of Afro-American people. It is this reified fiction that Twain attacks in *Huckleberry Finn.*

Race becomes a metaphorical vision, and most of us are victims of that metaphor. In any case, the confusion over racial metaphor corroborates Smith's point, the questioning of race occurring at such a fundamental level of language. In Genette's terms, metaphor "is the stylistic equivalent of the psychological experience of involuntary memory," so Twain's use of metaphor reveals to us what he wants to say about the confused status of racial identity, whether or not he recognized this confusion as he wrote these scenes, a process we have seen before. Even at the level of metaphor, the categories of race are unstable and shifting, signaling to us the larger point Twain is trying to make about the fictional construction of race. The stakes here are high, not only for our understanding of Mark Twain, but also for literary study, and even more widely, for our ongoing national debate. After her examination of *Huckleberry Finn* in *Playing in the Dark*, Toni Morrison reaches this conclusion: "Race has become metaphorical—a way of referring to and disguising forces, events, classes, and expressions of social decay and economic division far more threatening to the body politic than biological 'race' ever was. . . . I remain convinced that the metaphorical and metaphysical uses of race occupy definitive places in American literature, in the 'national character,' and ought to be a major concern of the literary scholarship that tries to know it."[42]

Analyzing the way metaphor destabilizes our assumptions about race is an important step in this ongoing process and debate. As one final illustrative point, we might recall the moment near the end of the novel when Huck says of Jim, "I knowed he was white inside" (*HF*, 341). Here is another moment of metaphor-making for Huck. On the outside, Jim is literally black, but Huck makes the judgment that he is metaphorically "white inside." Exactly how are we to read that? Up to now, I have always read that statement as an ironic but ultimately positive comment. Now, the very idea of race, of whiteness and blackness, is so destabilized that I am not sure at all what it means. I am made very, very uneasy by these words. That uneasiness may have been exactly what Mark Twain intended.

3

Figuring Metaphor

Style may be likened to an army, the author to its general, the book to the campaign.

—Mark Twain, "Cooper's Further Literary Offenses"

In his introduction to *Selected Shorter Writings of Mark Twain,* Walter Blair makes this important point: "To trace Twain's development as a writer from its start to its conclusion, therefore, one must study his shorter creations. Any account of Twain's changing philosophy—or, if that seems too pretentious a term, his evolving opinions and prejudices—also depends upon a scrutiny of short works. For his ideas about literary craftsmanship, about the drives determining men's actions, about the damned and doomed human race, often appear first and last and are most clearly set forth in shorter writings" (*SSWMT,* vii). To Blair's list we can add metaphor. Twain used metaphor, of course, but rarely mentioned it, and even more rarely discussed it. When he did either, as Blair says, it was most often in some of his short works. His most notable expression is one that I will refer to more than once in this chapter: the remark in "Baker's Blue-jay Yarn" that those birds are just "bristling with metaphor" (*SSWMT,* 172).

Twain's comments on metaphor are usually part of a joke, as in a memorable exchange in a piece from 1870, "How I Edited an Agricultural Paper Once." The narrator, presumably "Mark Twain," recounts how he was the temporary editor of an agricultural paper, though he had never had any agricultural experience. He is berated by an old man who quotes from the paper—"Turnips should never be pulled—it injures them. It is much better to send a boy up and let him shake the tree" (*CTSS1*, 413)—and then asks Twain what he thinks of that. The exchange culminates in a rare mention of figurative language:

> "Think of it? Why, I think it is very good. I think it is sense. I have no doubt that, every year, millions and millions of bushels of turnips are spoiled in this township alone by being pulled in half-ripe condition, when, if they had sent a boy up to shake the tree—"
>
> "Shake your grandmother! Turnips don't grow on trees!"
>
> "Oh, they don't, don't they? Well, who said they did? The language was intended to be figurative, wholly figurative. Anybody, that knows anything, will know that I meant that the boy should shake the vine." (*CTSS1*, 413)

The whole piece turns on such comic substitutions; the narrator understands metaphor about as well as he does agriculture.

In a piece from 1882, "The McWilliamses and the Burglar Alarm," McWilliams tells Twain why he does not like burglar alarms, beginning with his story of finding a burglar smoking a pipe in his house in the middle of the night. He asks the burglar, "What business have you to be entering this house in this furtive and clandestine way, without ringing the burglar alarm?" (*CTSS1*, 837–38). The burglar's answer is a good example of Twain's penchant for parodying inflated language: "He looked confused and ashamed, and said, with embarrassment: 'I beg a thousand pardons. I did not know you had a burglar alarm, else I would have rung it. I beg you will not mention it where my parents may hear of it, for they are old and feeble, and such a seemingly wanton breach of the hallowed conventionalities of our Christian civilization might all too rudely sunder the frail bridge which hangs darkling between the pale and evanescent present and the solemn great deeps of the eternities. May I trouble you for a match?'" (*CTSS1*, 838). McWilliams's answer provides an apt comment on such absurdity: "Your sentiments do you honor, but if you will allow me to say it, metaphor is not your best hold" (*CTSS1*, 838). Twain's "best hold" is undoubtedly humor, but metaphor proves time and again to be a very good hold for him, and his control and understanding of it certainly have a great deal to do with the quality and success of his humor, as I will discuss in my last chapter. For now, I would like to highlight a few excellent metaphors and other uses of figurative language, ones that may not be familiar because they appear in short works that are not as often read or discussed. For example, later in "The McWilliamses and the Burglar

Alarm," McWilliams returns to his house after having been away for the summer: "When we returned in the fall, the house was as empty as a beer closet in premises where painters have been at work" (*CTSS1*, 842). In "Riley—Newspaper Correspondent" (1870), Twain describes the subject of his piece with this memorable simile, one that also aptly describes Twain's own usual comic stance: "Riley has a ready wit, a quickness and aptness at selecting and applying quotations, and a countenance that is as solemn and as blank as the back side of a tombstone when he is delivering a particularly exasperating joke" (*CTSS1*, 479). In "The Canvasser's Tale" (1876), an echo, absurdly, must be repaired by an architect, who bungles the job, with this result: "Before he meddled with it, it used to talk back like a mother-in-law, but now it was only fit for the deaf and dumb asylum" (*CTSS1*, 669).

I conclude this introduction to my chapter on figuring metaphor with some of Twain's more explicit comments about figurative language in a piece from 1870, "The Noble Red Man." It is a polemic about Native Americans, but also about romanticism and realism, as much an attack on writers like James Fenimore Cooper as it is on a race of people, although by the end, its rampant racism hits on the mind harder. The piece opens with the words "In books," describing the "noble red man" in the way a nineteenth-century reader would recognize him. But by the third paragraph, the reader may have forgotten the first two words and make the mistake of thinking that Twain is talking straight, until his irony begins to show: "His language is intensely figurative. He never speaks of the moon, but always of 'the eye of the night;' nor of the wind *as* the wind, but as 'the whisper of the Great Spirit;' and so forth and so on. His power of condensation is marvellous. In some publications he seldom says anything but 'Waugh!' and this, with a page of explanation by the author, reveals a whole world of thought and wisdom that before lay concealed in that one little word" (*CTSS1*, 442). Figurative language as used by certain writers comes under a veiled attack here, but in the middle of the piece, the veil is removed and his vitriol becomes overt: "Such is the Noble Red Man in print. But out on the plains and in the mountains, not being on dress parade, not being gotten up to see company, he is under no obligation to be other than his natural self" (*CTSS1*, 443). Twain then turns to what he implies is his real, and literal, vision of the Indian: "He is little, and scrawny, and black, and dirty; and, judged by even the most charitable of our canons of human excellence, is thoroughly pitiful and contemptible" (*CTSS1*, 443). After a page more of such physical description, he returns to his point about language: "There is nothing figurative, or moonshiny, or sentimental about his language. It is very simple and unostentatious, and consists of plain, straightforward lies. His 'wisdom' conferred upon an idiot would leave that idiot helpless indeed" (*CTSS1*, 444). This is not the late dark and angry Twain, but the Twain of 1870, just barely embarked upon his literary career. The words are hard to take, and his racism cannot be winked at or explained away. We can see, though, how deeply held were his concepts about the uses, and abuses, of figurative language. It is just another piece of the puzzle in figuring metaphor, in figuring Mark Twain.

In this chapter, I further examine some of Twain's short works, first to show what metaphor can reveal about two very different works, and then to see the way Twain composed metaphor in some important pieces, leading to a look at the composition of metaphor in the first half of *Huckleberry Finn*. The chapter concludes with an examination of the metaphors of writing in the correspondence between Twain and his close friend and fellow writer, William Dean Howells. Even with such seemingly disparate elements, this chapter provides the most focused look at how Mark Twain viewed and handled metaphor over the course of his career.

I. Metaphors of North and South, East and West in "The Private History of a Campaign That Failed"

Mark Twain's semiautobiographical narrative of his aborted Civil War experience seems on first reading to be very straightforward—so straightforward, in fact, that some readers have taken it as memoir and missed its strong fictional element. "The Private History of a Campaign That Failed" is clearly a narrative about North and South, but it is also about the other main compass directions and regions of the country, East and West. In fact, it is about *confusion* over directions, and, on a deeper level, about confusion over war in general and war writing in particular. Despite Twain's comic tone, he was making a profound corrective statement to his predominantly northern, eastern audience. As the narrator says in the first paragraph, in a tone of apology, but also using figurative language, "Surely this kind of light must have some sort of value" (*CTSS1*, 863).

The context in which Twain wrote the piece in 1885 is important; he was asked to contribute to the *Century* magazine his war experiences, to be part of the popular series "Battles and Leaders of the Civil War," which included accounts from Generals Grant, McClellan, Longstreet, and Beauregard. Recognizing the incongruity of his narrative with the others, Twain begins with, as I say, an apology: "You have heard from a great many people who did something in the war; is it not fair and right that you listen a little moment to one who started out to do something in it, but didn't?" (*CTSS1*, 863). This introduction sets the tone, and "The Private History" has almost always been read as an apology—which it clearly is.[1] But the next paragraph serves as a kind of second introduction, and one that frames another theme, which we can see most clearly if we consider its metaphorical nature.

The second paragraph begins by highlighting direction, but also highlighting *confusion over* direction: "Out West, there was a good deal of confusion in men's minds during the first months of the great trouble" (*CTSS1*, 863). The narrator continues, "[A] good deal of unsettledness, of leaning first this way, then that, then the other way. It was hard for us to get our bearings" (*CTSS1*, 863). The phrase "out West" implies a "back East," an East that is the home of Twain's main audience, and an East that was, indeed, his home—he wrote this piece when he was living in Hartford. The rest of the paragraph sets up a sort of metaphorical map, drawing on all four compass directions, and in constantly highlighting confusion over those directions, reveals the narrative's main theme.

The narrator tells us, "I was piloting on the Mississippi when the news came that South Carolina had gone out of the Union on the 20th of December, 1860" (*CTSS1*, 863). That sentence contains all four directions—south and north explicitly, but east and west implied by the river, bisecting the country into east and west as it runs from north to south. The river is a cross over the country and a cross over the beginning of the narrative. The rest of the paragraph describes the confusion over direction this map establishes. The narrator continues, "My pilot-mate was a New Yorker. He was strong for the Union; so was I. But he would not listen to me with any patience; my loyalty was smirched, to his eye, because my father had owned slaves" (*CTSS1*, 863). The next sentence stands out with metaphorical irony: "I said, in palliation of this dark fact, that I had heard my father say, some years before he died, that slavery was a great wrong, and that he would free the solitary negro he then owned if he could think it right to give away the property of the family when he was so straitened in means" (*CTSS1*, 863). Dark fact, indeed. The strength of that image comes from its concentration as a figure. Both a metaphor and a metonymy, it contains great power. Metonymic in its association with the slave's color, metaphoric in its comparison to the darkness of slavery as an evil, the phrase "dark fact" sits ominously over the whole piece, especially when it becomes clear that there is total confusion over the direction to follow in the aftermath of the dark fact of slavery, confusion highlighted in this paragraph, then in the whole piece, just as it was before, during, and after the war. Embedded even in the word "palliation," in its Latinate root, is another figure, for cloaking—with the connotation that it is, as the dictionary says, "to cover with excuses: conceal or disguise the enormity of excuses and apologies."[2] "Palliation" is precisely what the narrator is up to.

The paragraph continues the confusion: "A month later the secession atmosphere had considerably thickened on the Lower Mississippi, and I became a rebel; so did he" (CTSS1, 863). They have literally as well as figuratively moved south, but direction is just as confused with the pair of friends: "He did his full share of the rebel shouting, but was bitterly opposed to letting me do mine. He said that I came of bad stock—of a father who had been willing to set slaves free" (CTSS1, 863–64). The phrase "bad stock" is another powerful figurative term, again both metaphorical and metonymic. By the end, they have split, the friend "piloting a Federal gunboat and shouting for the Union again" (CTSS1, 864), and the narrator in the Confederate army. The pull in this opening between North and South metaphorically maps out the confusion over direction that informs the whole piece and underscores a deeper point about the war and the cause. Just exactly what is this "great cause" everyone is fighting for, if allegiances can shift so rapidly and so totally?

Finally the militia is formed: "Several of us got together in a secret place by night and formed ourselves into a military company" (CTSS1, 864); they named their company the Marion Rangers. At this point in the narrative, an illustration of a map is introduced, "The Seat of War," in which the river points out north and south, with the "campaign" roughly mapping out east and west (see fig. 1). The primitive, hand-drawn map is surely part of Twain's satire and comment on the Century series, since all the other essays in the series include elaborate battle maps. Comparing Twain's crudely drawn map with one of the "real" maps is humorous to us, but must have been both humorous and somewhat scandalous to his contemporary readers.

The company's initiation into the cause comes with a speech from a veteran, notable for its confused metaphorical language, and also for the parallel confusion of the listeners:

We stacked our shabby old shot-guns in Colonel Ralls's barn, and then went in a body and breakfasted with that veteran of the Mexican war. Afterwards he took us to a distant meadow, and there in the shade of a tree we listened to an old-fashioned speech from him, full of gunpowder and glory, full of that adjective-piling, mixed metaphor, and windy declamation which was regarded as eloquence in that ancient time and that

Figure 1. Mark Twain's hand-drawn map, "The Seat of War," purports to lay out the location of the beginning of the Civil War in Missouri in the mind of the narrator of "The Private History of a Campaign That Failed," published in *Century* magazine in December 1885 (vol. 31, issue 2, pp. 193-204). Courtesy of Cornell University Library, Making of America Digital Collection Mark Twain, "The Private History of a Campaign That Failed."

remote region; and then he swore us on the Bible to be faithful to the State of Missouri and drive all invaders from her soil, no matter whence they might come or under what flag they might march. This mixed us considerably, and we could not make out just what service we were embarked in; but Colonel Ralls, the practiced politician and phrase-juggler, was not similarly in doubt; he knew quite clearly that he had invested us in the cause of the Southern Confederacy. (*CTSS1*, 868)

Again, so much for the glory of the war and the cause. The young soldiers are just as mixed, just as confused, as the colonel's metaphors—and that confusion reigns over the whole narrative. Examples of this kind of confusion in the men's daily life abound. No one will cook, since they all consider it beneath them. When they finally get hungry enough, they *all* do the work, and the narrator tells us: "Afterward everything was smooth for a while; then trouble broke out between the corporal and the sergeant, each claiming to rank the other. Nobody knew which was the higher office; so Lyman had to settle the matter by making the rank of both officers equal" (*CTSS1*, 870). In such an army, all is confusion, especially direction, as when they argue over which way to retreat—retreat being the only course of action they consider when they learn of an advancing enemy: "The question was which way to retreat; but all were so flurried that nobody seemed to have even a guess to offer. Except Lyman. He explained in a few calm words, that insasmuch as the enemy were approaching from over Hyde's prairie, our course was simple: all we had to do was not to retreat *toward* him; any other direction would answer our needs perfectly. Everybody saw in a moment how true this was, and how wise; so Lyman got a great many compliments" (*CTSS1*, 871). "Any . . . direction would answer our needs": that phrase becomes a metaphor for the confusion of the whole piece, and a statement in itself, about war and its purpose.

The subsequent retreat is an example of Twain's absurd, slapstick comedy:

> The route was very rough and hilly and rocky, and presently the night grew very black and rain began to fall; so we had a troublesome time of it, struggling and stumbling along in the dark; and soon some person slipped and fell, and then the next person behind stumbled over him and fell, and so did the rest, one after the other; and then Bowers came with the keg of powder in his arms, whilst the command were all mixed together, arms and legs, on the muddy slope; and so he fell, of course, with the keg, and this started the whole detachment down the hill in a body, and they landed in the brook at the bottom in a pile, and each that was undermost pulling the hair and scratching and biting the rest in their turn, and all saying they would die before they would ever go to war again if they ever got out of this brook this time, and the invader might rot for all they cared, and the country along with him—and all such talk as that, which was dismal to hear and take part in, in such smothered, low voices, and such a grisly dark place and so wet, and the enemy may be coming any moment. (*CTSS1*, 871–72)

When they finally reach Mason's farm, they are greeted by an enemy, but not the kind they expect: "[B]efore we could open our mouths to give the countersign, several dogs came bounding over the fence, with great riot and noise, and each of them took a soldier by the slack of his trousers and began to back away with him. We could not shoot the dogs without endangering the persons they were attached to; so we had to look on, helpless, at what was perhaps the most mortifying spectacle of the civil war" (*CTSS1*,

872). The narrator's tone here would certainly have had a strong effect on contemporary readers, their memories of actual mortifying spectacles still fairly fresh. But the scene then becomes even *more* absurd, a surreal cartoon: "There was light enough, and to spare, for the Masons had now run out on the porch with candles in their hands. The old man and his son came and undid the dogs without difficulty, all but Bowers's; but they couldn't undo his dog, they didn't know his combination; he was of the bull kind, and seemed to be set with a Yale time-lock; but they got him loose at last with some scalding water, of which Bowers got his share and returned thanks" (*CTSS1*, 872–73). The way Twain builds that last metaphor is equal to some of the best constructions in his work. He starts plausibly, with the metaphor muted—"couldn't undo the dog"—then more overt, but still subtle, when he mentions the combination. Audaciously, he then compares the bulldog to a time-lock, surely with the hidden extra meaning of "Yale bulldog." The map that accompanies the engagement satirizes real battle maps, with its compass directions and labels "First position of Dogs," "Second position of Dogs" (see fig. 2). Curiously, it seems to be almost a replica of the earlier map, with the road in almost the same position the river had been in in that one. Where are we? Are all maps the same, merely copies of each other?

In *Mark Twain on the Loose,* Bruce Michelson offers a cogent analysis of the satirical and comic layers of Twain's sketch "Map of Paris," and much he says about that absurd map can apply here, including its satire of maps, of a gullible reading public, and of the comic dislocations such absurdities bring. Michelson concludes his analysis with this persuasive argument: "Maps, names, words, knowing—in the 'Map of Paris' funhouse these things become for a flash preposterous, dizzying. Then the dislocated world can stop wobbling, and if we like we can proceed to read, credulously or skeptically, the rest of the daily papers, including perhaps 'real' maps on other pages, and talk glibly again about people we have never seen and violence among strangers in unknowable places."[3] Twain's maps in this narrative do some of the same things, if not as much as the in-the-looking-glass "Map of Paris"; in any case, a map of a battle does abstract all violence out of existence, even the cartoonish violence of the "Engagement at Mason's Farm."

To put a nice gloss on the whole affair, Farmer Mason comments sarcastically on the aptness of the company's name: "Marion *Rangers*! Good name, b'gosh!" The joke hinges, of course, on a slip in the metonymic meaning, with the farmer making the assessment that "we were a curious breed of soldiers, and guessed we could be depended on to end up the war in

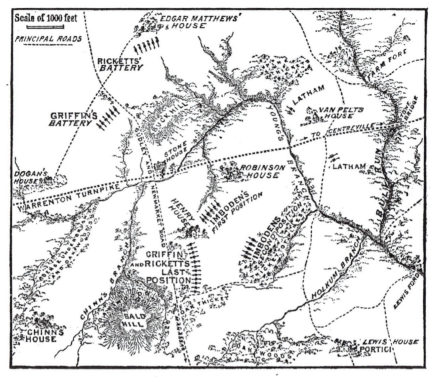

PLAN OF THE BULL RUN BATTLE-FIELD.

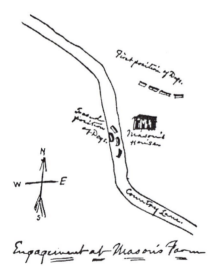

Figure 2. Compare Mark Twain's hand-drawn map entitled "Engagement at Mason's Farm" with the map "Plan of the Bull Run Battlefield," one of the real maps that appeared with essays in the *Century* magazine series "Battles and Leaders of the Civil War." "Mason's Farm" map courtesy of Cornell University Library, Making of America Digital Collection Mark Twain, "The Private History of a Campaign That Failed," *Century* 31, no. 2 (December 1885): 193-204. "Bull Run" map courtesy of Cornell University Library, Making of America Digital Collection General John D. Imboden, "Incidents of the Battle of Manassas," *Century* 31, no. 1 (May 1885): 92-99.

time, because no government could stand the expense of the shoe-leather we should cost it trying to follow us around" (*CTSS1*, 873).

The comic confusion continues, with soldiers who refuse to stand picket unless superiors will exchange rank with them, then stand watch as subordinates, and with a mock war in a corn crib, which is serving as a barracks, but finally the piece changes radically in tone as the Marion Rangers confront a lone enemy and shoot him down. The description now is very different: "When we got to him the moon revealed him distinctly. He was lying on his back, with his arms abroad; his mouth was open and his chest heaving with long gasps, and his white shirt-front was all splashed with blood. The thought shot through me that I was a murderer; that I had killed a man—a man who had never done me any harm. That was the coldest sensation that ever went through my marrow."[4] The piece now becomes as serious as it had previously been absurd and comic, as the narrator continues to ponder his act:

> The man was not in uniform, and was not armed. He was a stranger in the country; that was all we ever found out about him. The thought of him got to preying upon me every night; I could not get rid of it. I could not drive it away, the taking of that unoffending life seemed such a wanton thing. And it seemed an epitome of war; that all war must be just that—the killing of strangers against whom you feel no personal animosity; strangers whom, in other circumstances, you would help if you found them in trouble, and who would help you if you needed it. My campaign was spoiled. (*CTSS1*, 880)

"My campaign was spoiled," the narrator says, not "my campaign was ruined," or even, echoing his title, as a lesser writer might have been tempted to say, "my campaign had failed." The metaphoric overtones resonate, as does the irony: by finally doing exactly what he is supposed to be doing, he fails, which takes us to the heart of the narrative's powerful statement. "An epitome of war," he says, but he could have said "a metaphor of war"—as indeed the whole piece is. And the metaphor that underlies the whole narrative is confusion: confusion of direction, confusion of rank, confusion of cause, confusion of the meaning of war itself. Hidden in what seems a mostly comic piece is actually a stinging condemnation of war in general and of the Civil War in particular—and subversively, published in a magazine series that celebrated the battles and leaders of the war, for a national audience that took the war most seriously, North or South. One of those leaders, Grant, the narrator says near the end, he almost met, but characteristically, the narrator was "proceeding in the other direction" (*CTSS1*, 882). That other direction, of course, is retreat. "I could have become a soldier myself, if I had waited," the narrator concludes. "I had got part of it learned; I knew more about retreating than the man who invented retreating" (*CTSS1*, 882).

North and East are pitted against South and West, with South and West seemingly ludicrous, absurd, and shameful, and North and East supposedly serious, rational, and glorious. But the confusion of direction, the metaphor that underlies everything, shows that all war is insane, is as ludicrous as the Marion Rangers, is as pointless as the murder of the stranger. In a comic piece, Twain manages to make a very serious statement about war, a strong and effective statement, even if many of his readers were merely amused or thought he was apologizing. The epitome of war, the metaphor of war, all rides on the irony of war: to succeed is to be wanton, to lose some of one's humanity.

One passage near the end grimly underscores this point, with a key use of a machine metaphor at its core: "One might justly imagine that we were hopeless material for war. And so we seemed, in our ignorant state; but there were those among us who afterward learned the grim trade; learned to obey like machines; became valuable soldiers; fought all through the war, and came out at the end with excellent records" (*CTSS1*, 877). That statement is as ironic as any Mark Twain ever wrote, and highlights the irony of the whole piece, and the ultimate irony of talking about "success" in war, of celebrating it in a magazine series. As in a black comedy of the late twentieth century, the world is turned upside down: to retreat is to advance; the private history is public; an apology becomes a statement; the campaign that fails is a campaign that succeeds. Metaphor does its work again; this kind of light truly *does* have a sort of value.

II. "I did it but to clear my nether throat":
Mark Twain and the Metaphorical Psychology of Bodily Discharge

In the summer of 1876, at Quarry Farm in Elmira, Mark Twain did some of the best work of his entire career, finishing *The Adventures of Tom Sawyer* and beginning *Adventures of Huckleberry Finn*. But a short work he wrote there that summer has fascinated and puzzled readers ever since, even though Twain never published it under his own name in his lifetime. The short, bawdy sketch, *1601*[5] (subtitled *Conversation, as It Was by the Social Fireside, in the Time of the Tudors*), has often been used against its author by critics, beginning with Van Wyck Brooks, who set the terms for debate about this text in

The Ordeal of Mark Twain. His thesis, of course, is that Twain constantly wrote in rebellion against the Victorian repression of his wife, Olivia ("Livy"), and his friend William Dean Howells. Not intending the pun, I am sure, Brooks argues that Twain "let himself go" in *1601*, that he wrote it in secret as a sort of escape valve for the pressure built up by Livy and Howells, and that *1601* is further proof that Twain abdicated his role as an artist. Brooks's words, besides getting the title a bit wrong, are full of metaphorical language that seems ironically to refer to the very discharge he is condemning:

> Mark Twain's verbal obscenities were obviously the expression of that vital sap which, not permitted to inform his work, had been driven inward and left there to ferment. No wonder he was always indulging in orgies of forbidden words. Consider the famous book, *1601*, that "fireside conversation in the time of Queen Elizabeth": is there any obsolete verbal indecency in the English language that Mark Twain has not painstakingly resurrected and assembled here? He, whose blood was in constant ferment and who could not contain within the narrow bonds that had been set for him, the riotous exuberance of his nature, had to have an escape-valve, and he poured through it a fetid stream of meaningless ribaldry—the waste of a priceless psychic material!

It is as if, in 1920, a fart is the bodily discharge that dare not speak its name—but Brooks encodes it nonetheless in his figurative language, wittingly or unwittingly, in a way that seems highly comic in the midst of his outraged tirade. Brooks cannot help but metaphorize his own repression.[6]

Twain's *1601* was not published among his collected works until the 1990s, when it was included by Louis Budd in the Library of America's *Collected Tales, Sketches, Speeches, and Essays,* then by Shelley Fisher Fishkin in the Oxford Mark Twain, with an introduction by Erica Jong and an afterword by Leslie Fiedler. Jong's observations are especially noteworthy since she has written what she herself calls "pornography," the term she uses to describe *1601.* "Mark Twain was transporting himself to a world that existed before the invention of sexual hypocrisy," she argues—and he was also clearing the pipes, so to speak, to find the voice of Huck Finn. More from the author of *Fear of Flying:* "This is why the pornographic spirit is *always* related to unhampered creativity. Artists are fascinated with filth because we know that in filth everything human is born. Human beings emerge between piss and shit, and so do novels and poems." She continues:

> *1601* is deliberately lewd. It delights in stinking up the air of propriety. It delights in describing great thunder-gusts of farts that make great

stenches, and pricks that are stiff until cunts "take ye stiffness out of them" (ix). In the midst of all this ribaldry, the assembled company speaks of many things—poetry, theater, art, politics. Twain knew that the muse flies on the wings of flatus, and he was having such a good time writing this Elizabeth [sic] pastiche that the humor shines through a hundred years and twenty later. I dare you to read 1601 without giggling and guffawing.[7]

A headnote to 1601 tells us that "[t]he following is supposed to be an extract from the diary of the Pepys of that day, the same being Queen Elizabeth's cup-bearer" (CTSS1, 661).[8] The old man is of noble birth, we are told, and "he despises these literary canaille; that his soul consumes with wrath to see the queen stooping to talk with such"—but that he must stay until he is dismissed (CTSS1, 661). Much of the humor depends on the cup-bearer, as Twain himself wrote many years later in his Autobiography: "We [he and the Reverend Joseph Twichell, to whom he originally sent the piece] used to laugh ourselves lame and sore over the cupbearer's troubles" (AMT, 269). The confinement of the room and the disruption that soon fills it are part of the situation that raises the humor to another level; like "Mark Twain" in "The Jumping Frog," the cupbearer is backed into a corner—but this time, the room begins to seem even smaller and more closed in.

The supposed diary entry begins with a setting of the scene and the naming of characters: "Yesternight took her maiste ye queene a fantasie such as she sometimes hath, and had to her closet certain that doe write plays, bokes, and such like, these being my lord Bacon, his worship Sir Walter Ralegh, Mr. Ben Jonson, and ye child Francis Beaumonte, which being but sixteen, hath yet turned his hand to ye doing of ye Lattin masters into our Englishe tong, with grete discretion and much applaus. Also came with these ye famous Shaxpur" (CTSS1, 661). Mentioning Shakespeare as an afterthought is clearly a Mark Twain joke on one of his favorite targets. Then the narrator makes a comment that establishes a metaphor for the whole piece: "A righte straunge mixing of mighty blode with meane, ye more in especial since ye queenes grace was present" (CTSS1, 661). Also present are five more women, ranging in age from fifteen to seventy.[9]

"A righte straunge mixing" indeed, mixing genders and ranks, but also language, within which much of the humor resides. We see this mixture as the action begins: "In ye heat of ye talk it befel yt one did breake wind, yielding an exceding mightie and distresfull stink." What is the reaction to this outrage? "Whereat all did laugh full sore" (CTSS1, 661). That laughter from all present—except for the cupbearer—is a key, and a sort of test from Mark Twain for the reader. From here on out, no holds are barred, and the squeamish reader had best turn back.

Queen Elizabeth's reaction and her questions are interesting in that she immediately sees the matter in terms of gender: even though the action is scatological, she sees it in sexual terms. Even more revealingly, she uses a metaphor that links the bodily discharge to the act of *writing:* "Verily in mine eight and sixty yeres have I not heard the fellow to this fart. Meseemeth, by ye grete sound and clamour of it, it was male; yet ye belly it did lurk behinde should now fall lean and flat against ye spine of him yt hath bene delivered of so stately and so vaste a bulk, whereas ye guts of them yt doe quiff-splitters bear, stand comely still and rounde. Prithee let ye author confess ye offspring" (*CTSS1*, 661–62). With all the writers who are present, her quest to find the "author" of the fart is apt, but also revealing when we think about the author of the sketch and his relationship to his writing and his profession (a topic I return to later in this chapter, when I examine Twain's letters to Howells).

In fact, what chiefly interests me is Twain's subsequent writerly reaction to *1601*, his comments many years later in his *Autobiography*, and specifically his act of sending the whole thing as a letter to his friend and pastor and what he says happened afterward:

> It made a fat letter. I bundled it up and mailed it to Twichell in Hartford. And in the fall, when we returned to our home in Hartford and Twichell and I resumed the Saturday ten-mile walk to Talcott Tower and back, every Saturday, as had been our custom for years, we used to carry that letter along. There was a grove of hickory trees by the roadside, six miles out, and close by it was the only place in that whole region where the fringed gentian grew. On our return from the Tower we used to gather the gentians, then lie down on the grass upon the golden carpet of hickory leaves and get out the letter and read it by the help of these poetical surroundings. We used to laugh ourselves lame and sore over the cup-bearer's troubles. (*AMT*, 269)

If this account can be believed, it is striking in its detail and its absurdity. The picture of Mark Twain and his minister lounging in nature, reading *this* letter, impersonating *these* voices, strikes one as strange beyond credulity. Imagine Twain or Twichell answering her majesty in the voice of Lady Alice, who at the end metaphorizes the stench: "Good your grace, an' I had room for such a thundergust within mine ancient bowels, 'tis not in reason I could discharge ye same and live to thank God for yt He did choose handmaid so humble whereby to shew his power. Nay, 'tis not I yt have broughte forth this rich o'ermastering fog, this fragrant gloom, so pray you seeke ye further" (*CTSS1*, 662). Or Lady Margery's answer, again invoking religious faith, then ending her speech with a simile: "In ye good providence of God, an' *I* had contained this wonder, forsooth wolde I have gi'en ye whole evening of my sinking life to ye dribbling of it forth, with trembling and uneasy soul, not launched it sudden in its matchless might, taking mine own life with violence, rending my weak frame like rotten rags. It was not I, your maisty" (*CTSS1*, 662). The queen's embattled reply echoes the sketch itself, whose author chose to remain anonymous for many years: "O' God's name, who hath favored us? Hath it come to pass yt a fart shall fart *itself*? Not such a one as this, I trow" (*CTSS1*, 662). The answers from her authors—Jonson, Bacon, and Shakespeare—reflect the outlook and diction of each writer, with Shakespeare's being particularly eloquent, and a nice parody of his metaphorical style: "In the great hand of God I stand and so proclaim mine innocence. Though ye sinless hosts of heaven had foretold ye coming of this most desolating breath, proclaiming it a work of uninspired man, its quaking thunders, its firmament-clogging rottenness his own achievement in due course of nature, yet had I not believed it; but had said the pit itself hath furnished forth the stink, and heaven's artillery hath shook the globe in admiration of it" (*CTSS1*, 663).

No, a fart cannot fart itself, just as a story cannot write itself. There must be an author, and he must at the last claim authorship, as Raleigh finally does, pretending to be ashamed of his "weakling" offspring: "Most gracious maisty, 'twas I that did it, but indeed it was so poor and frail a note, compared with such as I am wont to furnish, yt in sooth I was ashamed to call the weakling mine in so August a presence. It was nothing—less than nothing, madam, I did it but to clear my nether throat; but had I come prepared, then had I delivered something worthy. Bear with me, please your grace, till I can make amends" (*CTSS1*, 663). And he proceeds to do just that: "Then delivered he himself of such a godless and rock-shivering blast that all were fain to stop their ears, and following it did come so dense and foul a stink that that which went before did seem a poor and trifling thing beside it" (*CTSS1*, 663).

What do these bodily discharges mean, for the piece and for the reader? In a 1978 book, *Metaphor: A Psychoanalytic View*, Robert Rogers traces the effect of figurative language on reader-response. In a section distinguishing levels of diction, he differentiates between what he terms technical, obscene, and poetic language. His example is drawn from the poem "On a Fart Let in the House of Commons," which Rogers says is incorrectly attributed to Matthew Prior. The first two lines allow him to differentiate the three terms: "Reader I was born, and cry'd / I cracked, I smelt, and so I dy'd." The technical term, according to Rogers, would be "flatus," the obscene term "fart," and the poetic term "die." In Twain's *1601*, the poetic term might be Lady Alice's "rich o'ermastering fog" or Shakespeare's "this most desolating breath" (*CTSS1*, 662, 663). Technical terms are "low-voltage," Rogers says; "[o]bscene terms," he continues, "possess shock value, but their strong immediate impact has little cumulative energy." "In contrast," he concludes, "poetic metaphors generate a subtle interplay of forces in our minds that builds toward greatness in a quantitative way that has qualitative consequences."[10] The experience of reading *1601* is heightened by the contrast between the obscene and the poetic: the "righte straunge mixing" the cupbearer talks about. That kind of incongruity, of course, lies at the heart of most humor, and in the case of *1601*, the conflict between the obscene and the poetic fuels our laughter.

But the humor of *1601* lies even deeper, in a psychological process Rogers points out, drawing on Freud's ideas of the primary and secondary processes. Primary mentation, Rogers says, is "concrete, pictorial, perceptual, emotional, intuitional, and more imaginative," while secondary mentation is "abstract, conceptual, less emotional, analytical, more controlled, and less spontaneous." While poetic language appeals to both primary and secondary processes, obscene language causes only primary mentation—and in a very powerful, direct way, Rogers maintains. Using the example of Sandor Firenczi's patient who "reduced resistance to further analysis once he was able to utter the word 'fart,'" Rogers argues that "[t]he force behind obscenity must be roughly equivalent to the strength of repression in any given case." He further cites Firenczi: "[O]bscene words have the capacity of forcing the listener 'to revive memory pictures in a regressive and hallucinatory manner.'" As Rogers concludes, "This sounds like a description of the primary process." What obscene language thus gains in immediacy, it loses in ultimate power: "only poetic language," Rogers says, "has the potential for more or less simultaneously inducing both mentational modes to a significant degree." He goes on to compare the ambiguity of poetic language to other modes that generate both processes: "Play, jokes, parapraxes, dreams, neurotic symptoms, and symbolism generally."[11] The fact that *1601* draws not only on obscenity, but also on poetic language, play, and jokes (if not neurotic symptoms) may explain its power and complexity, a power the reader feels but cannot quite explain.

Following Freud's idea that "[t]he ego is first and foremost a bodily ego," Rogers convincingly argues for the centrality of body imagery and metaphor in poetic language. As he puts it, "Poet and reader experience their bodily needs in words." Fundamental to psychoanalysis is the idea that "[w]e have bodies first, minds afterwards." In an argument that echoes Jong's statement about birth, although less graphically, he notes, "We are made by bodies, born with bodies, and we bear these bodies with us to the grave. The body is basic." And citing Ella Freeman Sharpe, he notes the "subterranean passage between mind and body underlying all analogy." "Speech," he says, "can be a symbolic substitute for other forms of bodily discharge." Now we begin to approach the mystery at the heart of *1601:* "The main function of libidinalized speech is discharge, getting outside what is bottled up inside." This seems literally (and crudely) to describe exactly what Raleigh has done, and what Twain has done in writing the piece—it seems so literal that we might fail to see the metaphorical act, and its importance. The result, both for the writer and for the reader, is a direct appeal to the primary process, and a powerful discharge of psychic energy.[12]

The concept of libidinalized speech can be applied to *Huckleberry Finn,* which Twain was beginning at the time he wrote *1601.* In the opening chapter, Huck says of the widow, "She put me in them new clothes again, and I couldn't do nothing but sweat and sweat, and feel all cramped up" (*HF,* 2). This is literal sweat, but soon after, he is metaphorically "all in a sweat" to learn about Moses (*HF,* 2). The second chapter opens with the need to scratch spreading all over his body, until he is, in a memorable phrase, "itching in eleven different places now" (*HF,* 7). In the next chapter, he takes a lamp and an iron ring and "rubbed and rubbed until I sweat like an Injun" (*HF,* 17). All that "sweat" in the opening of the novel seems very suggestive in the context of libidinalized speech, a bodily discharge that gets out what is bottled up inside Huck—as he himself is so bottled up in the beginning chapters.

Also suggestive are the implications of some of Twain's other comments about *1601,* specifically his repeated references to Rabelais. He calls the words he puts into the characters' mouths "grossnesses not to be found outside Rabelais, perhaps" (*AMT,* 268). He tells us that he sent it to an editor who was calling for "the new Rabelais," only to have it returned, along with much abuse for its author (*AMT,* 268). The most noted twentieth-century study of Rabelais, of course, is Mikhail Bakhtin's *Rabelais and His World.* His analysis sheds more light on Twain's *1601:* "Wherever men laugh and curse, particularly in a familiar environment, their speech is filled with bodily images. The body copulates, defecates, overeats, and men's speech is flooded with genitals, bellies, defecations, urine, disease, noses, mouths, and dismembered parts." What strikes me about *1601* is its mixture of men *and* women talking this way. Twain intended this coarse talk for a strictly male audience, but he looks back to a time when men and women shared that kind of speech and humor—and looks ahead to a time when men and women can do the same if they choose. One of Bakhtin's key perceptions in his study of Rabelais is the change between fifteenth-century and sixteenth-century France, a change from freedom to restriction, and the same can be said, perhaps, for Twain's *1601*. His entitling the piece with the date "1601" must mean that Twain was marking a cusp in time.[13]

But more interesting than comments on the past is what Twain was saying about the future, what he was projecting for us. Bakhtin argues that Rabelais's focus on the body, particularly on the lower body, is a projection toward the future: "This lower stratum is mankind's real future," he declares. Rabelais, according to Bakhtin, saw that "the hierarchical world of the Middle Ages was crumbling," and that a new world was being born. The same is happening in *1601*. One hundred years after the Declaration of Independence, Mark Twain wrote about a coming new order—even when he was in the midst of, and himself very much a part of, a repressive old order. In 1876, there was definitely a fear of the body. Bakhtin points out that "[i]n the sphere of imagery cosmic fear (as any other fear) is defeated by laughter. Terror is conquered by laughter."[14] "Against the assault of laughter, nothing can stand," he might have said.

III. Composing Metaphor in Mark Twain's Short Fiction

If Mark Twain was, in Aristotle's terms, a "master of metaphor," we can learn more about his skill with figurative language by examining his composing process, that in the white heat of composition and then that in the cooler heat of revision. In the composition of four of his short works—"A True Story," "The Invalid's Story," "Baker's Blue-jay Yarn," and "The Man That Corrupted Hadleyburg"—Twain's handling of metaphor is different each time, ranging from minimal to brilliant to what might seem at first downright clumsy and clichéd. I have chosen these pieces because they are so well known, because they are all excellent stories, and because they span three decades of Twain's career. I looked at the manuscripts for clues about the way Twain composed metaphorical language: exactly what was original to the moment of composition, and what was a revision? How much of his metaphorical language came to him from the beginning, and how much was added later? Knowing his habits of quick composition and his dread of revision, I assumed that most of his metaphors had been achieved on the first draft; but I was surprised to see an almost even split between original metaphor and metaphor added in revision. Seeing the way Twain handles metaphor in these works will enhance my subsequent examination of the first half of the manuscript of *Huckleberry Finn*, an opportunity that opened up only recently.

The subtitle of "A True Story" (1874) is "Repeated Word for Word as I Heard It." As William Gibson declares in *The Art of Mark Twain*, "[T]his can scarcely be literally true." Gibson continues: "The intent of the subtitle is plainly to claim the status of history rather than fiction for the story, and perhaps to warn the reader not to expect humor as its central theme."[15] Yet the narrative presents itself as a verbatim narrative, including the title and the unusual move of having the narrator addressed as "Misto C," and despite the apparent contradiction of Twain's explanation to Howells in a letter that he had "amend[ed] dialect stuff by talking & talking & *talking* it till it seems right" (*MTHL*, 1:26), suggesting creative intervention on his part. The clear biographical connection between the story's Aunt Rachel and the real-life former slave Mary Ann Cord, the cook at Quarry Farm, further underscores the apparent verbatim nature of the story. The story contains very little of the kind of metaphorical language we might expect in the best Twain works, either in the original composition or in subsequent revision, but an examination of the manuscript shows a few changes, several of them involving metaphorical language, usually to make Aunt Rachel's speech more colorful or to heighten her characterization. For example, at a key moment, the narrator tells us that "Aunt Rachel had gradually risen, while she warmed to her subject, and now she towered above us, black against the stars" (*CTSS1*, 579). The original is "bright against the stars," but the substitution of "black" for "bright" is effective and powerful. Besides probably being more accurate literally—that she would be silhouetted rather than illuminated as she stood above them—"black" also has clear thematic and symbolic resonance.

The most significant change in the revisions is to her repeated saying, or her "word," as she calls it, "I wa'nt bawn in de mash to be fool' by trash! I's one o' de ole Blue Hen's Chickens, *I* is!" (*CTSS1*, 579). This saying, she says, she learned from her mother, and now she uses it herself when she is "riled." The saying is what triggers the scene of recognition and reunion with her son, and is clearly a message to Misto C and to the reader, as well as to the other black characters within the frame of the story. Arguably, this is the most important phrase in the story, and certainly the phrase most closely identified with Aunt Rachel, and it is highly figurative. But half of it is an *addition* in the manuscript. Because of the way Twain canceled its subsequent repetition, the original saying is clearly legible only on its first appearance; it reads, "I ain't no houn'-dog mash, to be trod on by common trash! I's one o' de ole Blue Hen's Chickens, *I* is!" The first part is lined out, with "I wa'nt bawn in de mash to be fool' by trash!" written above in a smaller hand (see fig. 3). Each subsequent time the saying occurs in the manuscript, the "houn'-dog mash" phrase is crossed out and the new phrase inserted. It seems clear that Twain wrote "houn'-dog mash" throughout and was satisfied with it, then changed his mind and inserted the phrase we now know. Interestingly, he was not content merely to cross out the original phrase; after the first lining out, in its other appearances it is X'ed out and crosshatched, then a rectangular box is drawn around it, then the lines are heavily inked out, as if he wants to cover the words indelibly. It is a plausible guess that "I ain't no houn'-dog mash, to be trod on by common trash!" were Aunt Rachel's (or more accurately, Mary Ann Cord's) original words, and that therefore, at least here, this is not "repeated word for word" as Mark Twain heard it. The heavy deletions, unlike the kind of deletions seen elsewhere in his manuscripts, suggest that he was trying to obliterate something from his own imagination.[16]

Why did Twain make this significant change, and what part does his handling of figurative language play in it? If we consider the original phrase— "I ain't no houn'-dog mash, to be trod on by common trash! I's one o' de ole Blue Hen's Chickens, *I* is!"—we see a succession of three metaphors: houn'-dog mash, common trash, and Blue Hen's Chickens. The change to "bawn in de mash" shifts the metaphorical emphasis; our attention would be arrested by "houn'-dog mash," but now we pay more attention to "fool' by trash," which is also made more metaphorical by the deletion of "common," and then we pay even *more* attention to the highly metaphorical "Blue Hen's Chickens." By erasing one colorful animal reference, Twain shifts our attention to the second. Despite claiming to repeat his story word for word, he is clearly manipulating the language for maximum effect. The phrase holds so much power for the reader not only because of its repetition and emphasis (Aunt Rachel digs her fists into her hips when she says this, as her mother before her did), but also because of Twain's careful handling of literal and figurative language. Aunt Rachel's characteristic "word" is not word for word, but rather an example of Twain's use of metaphorical language.

Why, though, is there so little metaphorical language in the piece? I think it is because Twain really was trying to write this "true story," if not exactly word for word as he had heard it, at least very close and true to the spirit of the original. Even though he makes a key change in Aunt Rachel's most important phrase, the lack of many changes in the rest of the manuscript

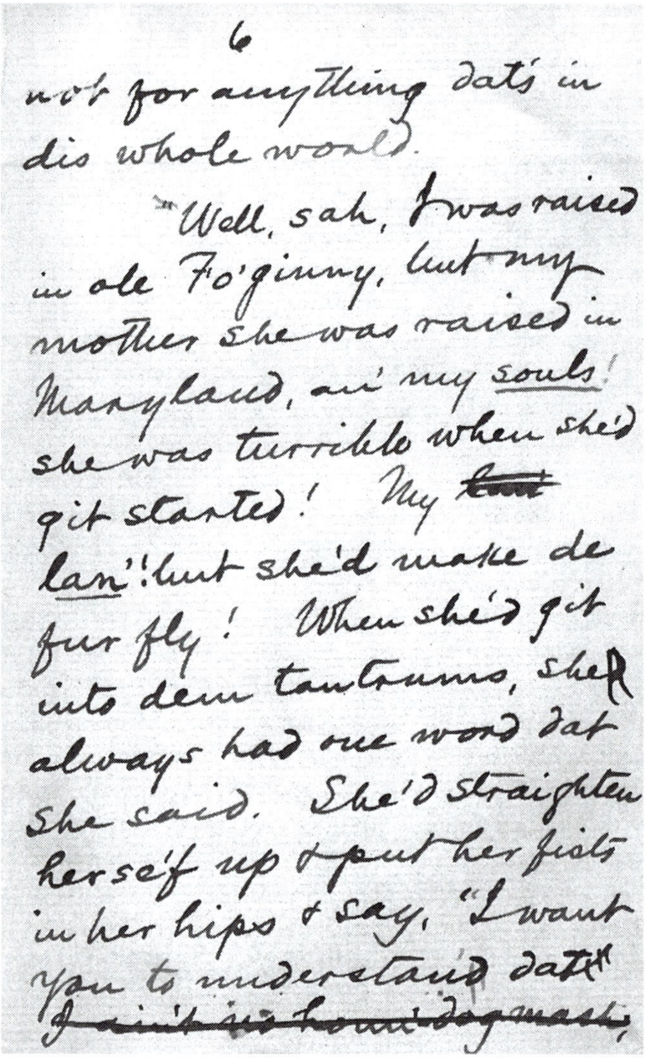
6

not for anything dat's in
dis whole worl'.

"Well, sah, I was raised
in ole Fo'ginny, but my
mother she was raised in
Marylan', an' my souls!
she was turrible when she'd
git started! My ~~lan~~
lan'! but she'd make de
fur fly! When she'd git
into dem tantrums, she
always had one word dat
she said. She'd straighten
herse'f up & put her fists
in her hips & say, "I want
you to understan' dat
~~I ain't no houn' dog mash,~~

Figure 3. Manuscript pages 6-8 of "A True Story," showing Mark Twain's initial revision of the repeated saying on pp. 6-7 and his heavy cross-hatching over the saying on p. 8. Reproduced by permission: "A True Story" 6314, Clifton Waller Barrett Library of American Literature, Special Collections, University of Virginia Library.

I wa'nt bawn up de mash to be fool' by trash!
~~to be trod on by common trash~~ I's one o' de ole
Blue Hen's Chickens, I
is!" — 'case you see dat's
what folks dat's bawn
in Maryland ... dey-
selves, an' d...
it. Well da...
word. I [becase]
yit it, she
an' becase...
day when...
tone. his...
most b...
right a...
forehe...

8
didn't fly aroun' fas'
enough to 'tend to him.
An' when dey talkin' back
at her, she up an' she
says, "Look-a-heah!"
she says, "I want you niggers to understan'
~~...~~
dat I wa'nt bawn up de mash to be fool' by
trash! — I's one o' de
ole Blue Hen's Chickens,
I is!" an' den she clar'
dat kitchen an bandage [says dat word too, when I's riled.]
up de chile herse'f. So I
"Well, byme-by my ole

suggests that he was trying to remain true to his source. That the story gives the reader such an impression without Twain's characteristic metaphorical touches stands as testimony to the power of Aunt Rachel's character, to Twain's characterization of her, to the power of her words, and to the thematic and symbolic power of the subject. Even though he was restraining his artistic impulse, Twain couldn't resist making changes at the structural and thematic heart of the story, and tellingly, those changes involve manipulation of figurative language.

"The Invalid's Story" was written in 1877 and was intended for publication in the *Atlantic*, where "A True Story" was printed.[17] It was to have been part of the series "Some Rambling Notes of an Idle Excursion," but the magazine's editor and Twain's friend, William Dean Howells, found the story unsuitable for his publication because of the subject matter: horrible smells coming from a pine box containing guns, with a package of Limburger cheese on top, but which the characters in the story think is the decomposing corpse of the title character's friend (*MTHL*, 1:251). As a writer, Twain's task is to make the scene vivid enough for humor, yet not overstep the bounds of taste too far, which he achieves through the use of euphemism and metaphor (although not to Howells's standards). The manuscript reveals that much of the euphemism and the metaphor were included from the very start, underscoring the centrality of figurative language to the story's humorous effect.

The first important revision comes as the smells begin. The original reads, "Presently I began to detect a most evil and searching odor stealing about on the frozen air. This depressed my spirits still more, because of course I attributed it to my dear departed friend. There was something infinitely saddening about his calling himself to my remembrance in this dumb pathetic way" (*CTSS1*, 689). Twain began to write "attention," pausing in mid-word and without canceling to choose "remembrance," a bit more apt, since the invalid has made much of his grief. The change also heightens the humor and incongruity, the formal "remembrance" an irreverent way of saying he had begun to smell the corpse. Another insert begins a few lines later, as the narrator is grateful that the expressman does not seem to notice the smell. "Grateful, yes," he says, "but still uneasy; and soon I began to feel more uneasy every minute, for every minute that went by," and then an "over," and this insert completes the sentence: "that odor thickened up the more, and got to be more and more gamey and hard to stand." This crucial point in the story shifts the level of diction from the formal tone of the opening to an increasing reliance on such words as "gamey." The humor of the piece depends not only on the incongruity of the situation, of mistaking smelly cheese for a rotting corpse, but also on these conflicting levels of language.

The mixed dignity and indignity of the situation gives the piece its comic tension, which finally bursts out in a moment original in the manuscript, and for me the highlight of the sketch. The invalid continues to worry that the expressman, Thompson, notices the smell, and finally we see that he does in this climactic scene:

> After a contemplative pause, he said, indicating the box with a gesture,—
>   "Friend of yourn?"
>   "Yes," I said with a sigh.
>   "He's pretty ripe, *ain't* he?" (*CTSS1*, 690)

The eruption of the vernacular metaphor into what has been more formal diction recalls the Scotty Briggs episode in *Roughing It*, but this time, the characters understand each other, and Thompson's figurative and earthy statement of the obvious provides comic release for the reader, as well as a kind of release for the characters, as they can now discuss their awful situation more openly. The rest of the piece consists largely of dialogue, with Thompson's speech quoted directly, and the inner narrator's mostly given indirectly. After one more insertion, the manuscript shows very few revisions. Twain seems to find his tone, and then he is able to sustain that level in the heat of composition, a performance that we can often see in his manuscripts, as comic moments appear to flow from his pen with ease. Thompson's next speech, which he delivers "in a low, awed voice" (*CTSS1*, 690), contains a long insertion that seems to mark the place where Twain found the mixture of high and low that makes the piece work: "'Sometimes it's uncertain whether they're really gone or not,—*seem* gone, you know—body warm, joints limber—and so, although you *think* they're gone, you don't really know. I've had cases in my car. It's perfectly awful, becuz *you* don't know what minute they'll rise right up and look at you!' Then, after a pause, and slightly lifting his elbow toward the box,—'But *he* ain't in no trance! No, sir, I go bail for *him!*'" (*CTSS1*, 690). Like the vernacular metaphor "ripe," "go bail" punctuates the humor of the situation. Twain has found his tone with this insertion, and now he can deliver long passages without revision, as in the next speech by Thompson, a mixture of conventional high metaphor, filtered through Thompson's dialect, interspersed with exposition that underscores the uncomfortable comedy of the scene. Twain's proficiency at these levels shows in a manuscript passage that contains no revisions:

"Well-a-well, we've all got to go, ain't no getting around it. Man that is born of woman is of few days and far between, as Scriptur' says. Yes, you look at it any way you want to, it's awful solemn and cur'us: they ain't *nobody* can get around it; *all's* got to go—just *everybody*, as you may say. One day you're hearty and strong"—here he scrambled to his feet and broke a pane and stretched his nose out at it a moment or two, then sat down again while I struggled up and thrust my nose out at the same place, and this we kept on doing every now and then—"and next day he's cut down like the grass, and the places which knowed him then knows him no more forever, as Scriptur' says. Yes-'ndeedy, it's awful solemn and cur'us; but we've all got to go, one time or another; they ain't no getting around it." (*CTSS1*, 690–91)

Solemn and curious indeed! Though the word "strong" is literal as Thompson uses it, the pause focuses our attention and makes us see it, or smell it, as a figurative reference to the corpse. The mixture of Thompson's high/low biblical metaphor and the frantic actions of the two characters is among the best moments of Twain's low humor. Unfortunately, this coarse humor was too much for the readers of the *Atlantic*.

Much of the humor of the piece depends on metaphorical euphemisms for the smell supposed to be coming from the corpse. When Thompson first shows that he is smelling it too, he says, in language original in the manuscript: "Pfew! I reckon it ain't no cinnamon 't I've loaded up thish-yer stove with!" Later, we get a long passage of description, again punctuated by one of Thompson's colorful comparisons:

Thompson sat down and buried his face in his red silk handkerchief, and began to slowly sway and rock his body like one who is doing his best to endure the almost unendurable. By this time the fragrance—if you may call it fragrance—was just about suffocating, as near as you can come at it. Thompson's face was turning gray; I knew mine had n't any color left in it. By and by Thompson rested his forehead in his left hand, with his elbow on his knee, and sort of waved his red handkerchief towards the box with his other hand, and said,—

"I've carried many a one of 'em,—some of 'em considerable overdue, too,—but, lordy, he just lays over 'em all!—and does it *easy*. Cap., they was heliotrope to *him*!" (*CTSS1*, 691)

The trope on heliotrope, like the rest of the passage, is all original in the manuscript.

The other significant metaphors in the piece are original, too, as are most of those used in Thompson's metaphorical ranking of the rank smell after the two try to "modify" it by smoking cigars. When that doesn't work, the narrator tells us that Thompson "got to referring to my poor friend by various titles,—sometimes military ones, sometimes civil ones; and I noticed that as fast as my poor friend's effectiveness grew, Thompson promoted him accordingly,—gave him a bigger title" (CTSS1, 692). Thus begins a comic extended metaphor: "Suppos'n' we buckle down to it and give the Colonel a bit of a shove towards t' other end of the car?—about ten foot, say. He wouldn't have so much influence, then, don't you reckon?" (CTSS1, 692). After that fails, and after another desperate gasp for air, Thompson asks, "Do you reckon we started the Gen'rul any?" (CTSS1, 692). Near the end, Twain makes a small but telling revision to this sequence. Thompson gives up: "We got to stay out here, Cap. We got to do it. They ain't no other way. The Governor wants to travel alone, and he's fixed so he can outvote us" (CTSS1, 694). In the manuscript, the corpse is here called "the judge," which is crossed out and "Governor" inserted. The subtle change makes sense in the metaphorical terms of "outvote" and, in the next speech, "we're elected."

What leads Thompson to give up provides the comic highlight of the piece, an interesting mixture of the literal and the metaphorical, of metonymy and metaphor, ending with a richness that the narrator speaks of, although he is of course talking about quite another kind of richness:

> He had brought a lot of chicken feathers, and dried apples, and leaf tobacco, and rags, and old shoes, and sulphur, and assafoetida, and one thing or another; and he piled them on a breadth of sheet iron in the middle of the floor, and set fire to them. When they got well started, I could n't see, myself, how even the corpse could stand them. All that went before was just simply poetry to that smell,—but mind you, the original smell stood up just as sublime as ever,—fact is, these other smells just seemed to give it a better hold; and my, how rich it was! I did n't make these reflections there—there was n't time—made them on the platform. (CTSS1, 694)

Twain has a page of going in for blankets and buffalo hides that he crosses out, realizing rightly that he has finished his piece. The manuscript of "The Invalid's Story" contains very little revision after the original insertions, the ones that helped him find his metaphorical pitch, and stands as a fine example of Twain's artistry and craftsmanship coming to him in the heat of composition.

Twain seems to have focused on mastering language and metaphor in a piece that is often reprinted alone as a short story, "Baker's Blue-jay Yarn," published in 1880 in *A Tramp Abroad*.[18] Its narrator tells us, "According to

Jim Baker, some animals have only a limited education, and use only very simple words, and scarcely ever a comparison or a flowery figure; whereas, certain other animals have a large vocabulary, a fine command of language and a ready and fluent delivery; consequently these latter talk a great deal; they like it; they are conscious of their talent, and they enjoy 'showing off'" (*SSWMT*, 172). Twain seems to be speaking of himself here, and indeed "Baker's Blue-jay Yarn" is a tour de force of showing off. Much of that linguistic showing off involves metaphorical language; as Jim Baker says of blue jays' talk, the story is "bristling with metaphor . . . —just bristling!" (*SSWMT*, 172), and it is interesting to examine the manuscript to see which metaphors were written at the time of composition and which ones were added in revision—about half and half, as it turns out. A simile in the original has the jay looking into the hole "like a 'possum looking down a jug" (*SSWMT*, 173), which is so visually striking that the reader may not at first realize that the narrator is clarifying an implausible image—the blue jay looking down a hole—by comparing it to something that is probably even more absurd—a possum looking down a jug. We usually expect the vehicle of a metaphorical expression to clear up and explain the tenor, not to extend its absurdity. Twain did not revise this simile.

As the jay gets increasingly perturbed with the hole, the narrator says, "that smile faded gradually out of his countenance"; then, in the manuscript, Twain inserts, in a different ink and hand, this simile: "like breath off'n a razor" (*SSWMT*, 173). Here he relies on a concrete image familiar to his audience, a concrete vehicle that clarifies the original vehicle, as well as using dialect that suits and characterizes Jim Baker. The simile is an afterthought, but seems effortless and seamless with the original. A simile original to the manuscript comes when the narrator describes the jay at work: "You never see a bird work so since you was born. He laid into his work like a nigger, and the way he hove acorns into that hole for about two hours and a half was one of the most exciting and astonishing spectacles I ever struck" (*SSWMT*, 174). Such a racial simile was probably so common in the 1880s that the reader, and even Mark Twain, may have seen it as at least a cliché, and perhaps even as a dead metaphor. The intervening years and events have resuscitated the metaphor, giving the modern reader a different sense from what Twain's white audience would have experienced at the time. A few sentences later, the exhausted jay "comes a-drooping down, once more," and Twain inserts above the line, "sweating like an ice-pitcher" (*SSWMT*, 174). Here, the image is again familiar, as well as vivid, but again absurd—to think of a blue jay sweating. So close to the "nigger" simile, and given the common racial slur of "sweating like a nigger," the similes begin to cluster, making us see the jay as human, which is after all one of the explicit points of the story: "a jay is everything that a man is" (*SSWMT,* 173). And that itself is a kind of metaphor.

The climax of the piece involves more figurative language. In the manuscript, the gathering of jays is first written this way: "They called in more jays; then more and more, till pretty soon this whole region was blue with them." He revises to say, "till pretty soon this whole region 'peared to have a blue flush about it" (*SSWMT,* 175). Later in the paragraph, he describes the birds examining the house: "They all came a-swooping down," then in an insert is the memorable simile "like a blue cloud." This beast fable is about human nature, as Jim Baker's comments make clear: "Yes sir, a jay is everything that a man is. A jay can cry, a jay can laugh, a jay can feel shame, a jay can reason and plan and discuss, a jay likes gossip and scandal, a jay has got a sense of humor, a jay knows when he is an ass just as well as you do—maybe better. If a jay ain't human, he better take in his sign, that's all" (*SSWMT,* 173). One of the main ways the story makes this point is by making a metaphorical comparison between a jay and a human, a metaphor that Twain repeats so much that it finally transcends metaphor and becomes symbolic. Bernard DeVoto sees the use of language here as one of Twain's finest achievements: "His speech has been caught so cunningly that its rhythms produce complete conviction. Fantasy is thus an instrument of realism and the humor of Mark Twain merges into the fiction that is his highest reach."[19] In addition to speech and rhythms and memorable fantasy, the piece owes much of its power to its figurative language. Jays are "just bristling with metaphor," as is so much of Twain's best work.

In contrast with the metaphorically rich "Baker's Blue-jay Yarn," "The Man That Corrupted Hadleyburg," first published in 1899, is metaphorically poor.[20] The result is a comparative matter-of-factness that may well have been intentional. Many of the metaphors and similes original to the manuscript could only be called dead metaphors: "weak as water," "like a house of cards," "easy game," "apple of your eye," and "chilled to the bone," for example. Twain often has *characters* who overuse such dead figurative language, but his *narrators* usually do not (except, as I have argued, in the case of *Tom Sawyer*). Further, the metaphorical language he adds in this manuscript during revision is also not particularly memorable. For example, as Edward Richards tries to remember the service he made to the stranger, the narrator says in the original that "it would be the most glaring relic in his own memory." "Be the most glaring relic" is canceled, and "glare like a limelight" is inserted. The change is an improvement, it seems to me, but only a slight one. There are no similes to compare with the ones in "Baker's Blue-jay Yarn." In fact, Twain in several instances early on *removes* metaphorical language from the manuscript. The original says, "Then his wife eagerly sprung the great secret upon him," but that is revised to read, "Then his wife told him the secret." Similarly, "It will make all the other towns green with jealousy" is truncated to the flat "It will make all the other towns jealous." The way Twain crosses out the words "green with" and the single letter "y" in jealousy rather than crossing out the whole phrase and inserting the new one (his more common practice) shows the care with which he was toning down metaphorical language.

Clearly, Twain is up to something with this story. He uncharacteristically uses dead metaphors and clichés, he adds unremarkable figurative language, and he takes some pains to tone down what little metaphorical language he originally used. Why would he do this, when we know he was so capable of writing a story rich in metaphorical language? In "A True Story," he was constrained by the limits of his nonfictional model, but in "Hadleyburg," he has no such constraints. He could have written a story that was "bristling with metaphor," but he seems to have chosen not to. The comparative absence of metaphor results in a linguistic flatness that throws the story's pervasive irony into sharper relief. Rich metaphorical language would perhaps obscure the story's stark irony. Whether or not that was Twain's intention, it is surely the result, an effect that Kenneth Burke outlines in "Four Master Tropes." His comments on irony seem to me to apply very well to "The Man That Corrupted Hadleyburg":

> Irony, as approached through either drama or dialectic, moves us into the area of "law" and "justice" (the "necessity" or "inevitability" of the *lex talionis*) that involves matters of form in art (as form affects anticipation and fulfilment) and matters of prophecy and prediction in history. There is a level of generalization at which predictions about "inevitable" developments are quite justified. We may state with confidence, for instance, that what arose in time must fall in time (hence, that any given structure of society must "inevitably" perish). We may make such prophecy more precise, with the help of irony, in saying that the developments that led to the rise will, by the further course of their development, "inevitably" lead to the fall (true irony always, we hold, thus involving an "internal fatality," a principle operating from within, though its logic may also be grounded in the nature of the extrinsic scene, whose properties contribute to the same development).[21]

This observation seems to me to be as clear a theoretical explanation of what Twain is up to as any direct commentary on the story I have seen: the pervasive, inevitable, ironic downfall of a whole town, and by extension, perhaps a whole society. By flattening metaphor, and even removing it, Twain throws an intensified light on his subject.

So these four stories, spanning the major phase of Twain's writing career, are very different in their use of metaphorical language. They show the high degree with which Twain manipulated metaphor—sometimes heightening it, sometimes flattening it, for valid artistic reasons. The rediscovery of the first half of the manuscript of *Huckleberry Finn* allows us to examine the composition of metaphor in Twain's greatest work, where we will again see his use of metaphor, a tool and a matter of style, but also a way of thinking, a kind of vision.

IV. (De)composing Metaphor in Huckleberry Finn

The great literary discovery of the twentieth century for Mark Twain studies, and perhaps for American literature in general, was the unexpected recovery of the long-lost first half of the manuscript of *Adventures of Huckleberry Finn*. To find that literary treasure in an attic in Los Angeles, of all places, over one hundred years after its composition, was to recover not only a critical missing piece of Mark Twain's greatest work, but also to give us a glimpse into his creative process, a glimpse that seemed to have been blocked from us forever. As the millennium turned to the twenty-first century, the publication of the manuscript in a new technology gave scholars and general readers access to the manuscript in ways that would have been unimaginable when the recovery came in the early 1990s. *"Huck Finn" CD-ROM: The Complete Buffalo and Erie County Public Library Manuscript—Teaching and Research Digital Edition* reunites the two halves of the manuscript and lets us see for the first time the changes Twain made in the first half of the manuscript.[22]

As I noted in the last chapter, *Huckleberry Finn* is among the least metaphorical of Twain's works, a fact I had always attributed to the way he imagined the voice of the literal-minded narrator. Although an astonishing amount of the manuscript seems to have come out of his pen with very few changes, a good number of the substantial changes he did make involve figurative language. And those changes mainly involve deleting figurative language, what I am calling "(de)composing metaphor." A look at the manuscript shows that the bulk of Twain's revisions in the early part of *Huckleberry Finn*, when he was establishing the voice and character of Huck, and thus the tone of the novel, involve moving away from Twain's natural tendency toward colorful and vivid metaphor, a kind of flattening of the metaphorical vision and a movement toward the more literal vision that we are familiar with in the novel. We have just seen this kind of flattening in the composition of "The Man That Corrupted Hadleyburg," but the changes in *Huckleberry Finn* are even more substantive and more significant, especially since the words of his great novel are so firmly implanted in the reader's mind. A close examination of the revisions will give us a greater appreciation for Twain's craftsmanship and help us better understand a novel we thought we knew so well.

Several of the metaphors and similes that remain in the novel were original in the manuscript, composed in the moment without revision. In chapter 1, Huck's comment "she called me a poor lost lamb" is original, as is Huck's response about Moses, "I don't take no stock in dead people."[23] Huck's memorable comparison at the end of the first chapter—"the house was all still as death"—not only fits his melancholy mood, but sets up an important theme for the whole novel, a theme that resonates throughout. In chapter 2, Tom talks about being "polite as pie" to the women captives, and Huck tells us that he "sweat like an Injun" as he rubs the lamp at the end of chapter 3. When Pap appears, his comment about "hand of a hog" is original, setting up an extended metaphor associating Pap with that animal. His being "drunk as a fiddler" was already a cliché, perhaps even a dead metaphor in the nineteenth century, although it may strike twenty-first-century readers as much fresher (at least to those who have not spent much time around backcountry fiddlers).

Huck's description of Jackson's Island is impressive in its figurative power: "big and dark and solemn, like a steamboat without any lights." The storm that breaks out has always struck me as a strong piece of writing, including onomatopoeia, metaphor, personification, and a vivid simile at the end, a simile that becomes extended by Huck's homely explanation. All of this sentence is original to the manuscript: "And now you'd hear the thunder let go with an awful crash and then go rumbling, grumbling, tumbling down the sky towards the under side of the world, like rolling empty barrels down stairs, where it's long stairs and they bounce a good deal, you know." We might expect such a sentence to have come after much revision and polish, but it seems to have fairly flowed from Twain's pen.

What might be called Huck's "poetic passages" are also mostly original, with few if any revisions. His description of the lonesome night at the end of chapter 1, his description of the sleeping town and twinkling lights in chapter 2, and his description of waking on Jackson's Island contain very

few substantive deletions or additions, and offer proof that from the start
Twain had a good sense of Huck's voice and vision. These poetic passages,
as we might expect, contain more metaphorical language than other parts
of the novel, and with the lack of metaphor elsewhere, they stand out even
more starkly for the reader. The cluster of black-and-white imagery discussed in the last chapter—Jim's hair-ball prophecy, Huck's vivid description of Pap, and Pap's speech on "govment"—are also substantially
unchanged in the manuscript, again showing his immediate perception of
Huck's voice. Overall, it is interesting to note how much of the figurative
language that we know so well came to Twain in the first moments of composition.

However, Twain did make many deletions, many of them involving figurative language. In change after change, we can see the way he first characteristically wrote using colorful metaphor, then, either immediately or
after some passage of time, deleted the metaphors, in effect dampening
down the metaphorical voice and achieving the flatter effect that we have
come to know as Huck's voice. As the evidence of original metaphor shows,
he had from the start a good idea of what Huck's voice should sound like,
but what the manuscript shows is that he first conceived of Huck as a more
colorful, metaphorical speaker and thinker than the very literal-minded
Huck he finally created. An examination of the changes involving figurative language in the first eight chapters, where he made the bulk of these
revisions, will show the pattern very clearly (see table 1). I use the traditional markings of textual criticism to show deletions (< >) and insertions
(^ ^).

Five changes in chapter 1 introduce us to the way Twain was working
with figurative language. He changes Huck's comments about eating at the
widow's from "When you got to the table you couldn't <sail in>" to "When
you got to the table you couldn't ^go right to eating,^" the first glimpse
we have of the way he substitutes literal language for the metaphorical.
Miss Watson's torture with a spelling book is toned down, the figurative
and slangy "She <made me hump myself> for about an hour" replaced by
"She ^worked me middling hard^ for about an hour." In an especially noteworthy change, we can see the extreme flattening effect Twain achieves by
changing Huck's first decision about going to hell: "Well, I couldn't see no
advantage in going where she was going, so I made up my mind <to lay
low + keep dark + go for the other place>." The deletion of that string of
metaphor changes the sentence dramatically: "Well, I couldn't see no
advantage in going where she was going, so I made up my mind ^I
wouldn't try for it.^" When Huck continues thinking about the hereafter,

and asks if Tom Sawyer will be going to heaven, Twain first writes these sentences, beginning with metaphor, then ending with what would have been a very good piece of humor: "I was glad about that. <So I guessed my head was level about steering for the other place. I didn't want to go to a place where I warn't acquainted, anyway.>" That passage is temporarily changed, becoming more literal, but still quite discursive, and also containing another joke: "I was glad about that. ^cause I knowed I would be lonesome with angels, not being used to them, + they not being used to my kind, but I could get along anywheres with Tom Sawyer.^" That second passage is also deleted, and Twain's final decision is astonishing when we have seen the progression: "I was glad about that ^because I wanted him + me to be together.^" Any of the three would have been memorable, and the first two would actually have been really funny statements that introduce us to the narrator. The third achieves not only a flatness of tone and an economy of words, but is actually more humorous, I think, partly because it is so compact, but also because it is more characteristic of Huck's voice and vision. In all three, Huck is characteristically unaware of the incongruity and absurdity of his statements, but the extreme flatness and concision of the final version show a brilliant efficiency, which we can only fully see by knowing the choices Twain made as he wrote. The other deletion in the first chapter involves avoiding a repetition of the metaphorical phrase Huck has already used about dead people. Originally, he was to have said the same about playing a harp in heaven forever: "So I didn't <take no stock in it>." In the revised version, he says, "So I didn't ^think much of it.^" The deletion gives the Moses remark more force, even though we do not realize it without knowing the composition history.

The rewriting of chapter 2 also contains four significant changes to this kind of language, the first three in the passage where Huck is yearning to scratch himself. The manuscript has Huck saying, "There was a place on my ancle that got to itching <like sin;> but I darsn't scratch it;" the revision deletes the simile: "There was a place on my ancle that got to itching^;^ but I darsn't scratch it." Even such a small deletion has an effect, especially when it is combined with so many other changes. We see a subtle effect in the next change, a move from a metaphor to a metonymy: "If you are <in a starchy company,>" revised to "If you are ^with the quality^." As Huck makes the decision to scratch himself before that act is revised out, Twain moves from being relatively metaphorical—"+ then <I turned my self loose, + I don't think I ever had such a good time in my life>."—to, uncharacteristically, more graphically metaphorical in this change: "+ then <I turned my ^claws^ loose, + I don't think I ever had such a good time in

my life>." The image of "claws" was perhaps too vivid and "low"; Twain changes the passage again to its final form, "+ then ^I was pretty soon comfortable again.^" We can see now just how much activity lies behind that seemingly innocuous final phrase. Perhaps these changes and deletions are examples of the kind of changes Livy Clemens is supposed to have called for—one likes to imagine the scene of the nightly manuscript readings at Quarry Farm when such a passage was first heard. Much—perhaps too much—has been made of the revisions Twain made for propriety's sake. Given the violent reaction to the novel as "trash," we can only surmise how virulent the calls for banning and censorship would have been if such passages had been left intact.

The final change in chapter 2 is interesting. In the discussion about ransoming, Ben Harper originally says this colorful phrase: "We will keep them till they're ransomed <deader'n a smelt—>." Such a phrase would leap off the page in its figurative power, but compare the revision: "We will keep them till they're ransomed ^to death—^." Here, Twain not only achieves the flattening of tone that he seemed to be aiming for, but also makes the joke even better.

The first two instances in chapter 3 are small but telling; talking about his attempts at prayer, Huck at first says, "I tried for the hooks three or four times, but some-how I couldn't make <the trip>," which is changed to "I tried for the hooks three or four times, but some-how I couldn't make ^it work.^" Similar is the revision from "I wouldn't worry about it no more, but <tackle something else>" to the flatter "I wouldn't worry about it no more, but ^just let it go.^" Comparing Huck's comments about Providence shows clearly the direction Twain was working toward in revising to establish Huck's voice. The original ends with two slangy metaphors: "there was two Providences, + a poor chap would stand considerable show with the widow's, but if Miss Watson's <took him into camp he was a goner.>" The revision flattens the ending, putting all the metaphorical emphasis on "show": "^I could see that^ there was two Providences, + a poor chap would stand considerable show with the widow's<,> ^Providence,^ but if Miss Watson's ^got him there warn't no help for him any more.^" A Huck who says "took him into camp" and "he was a goner" is a quite different Huck from the one we know so well.

The next series of revisions in this chapter revolve around the after effects of Tom Sawyer's Gang. Once again toning down his initial impulse toward slangy metaphor, Twain changes Huck's statement from "We played robber now + then about a month, + then I <shook the Gang.>" to the much more straightforward "We played robber now + then about a month, + then

I ^resigned.^" It would have been believable for a character like Huck to use phrases like "shook the Gang," but he would not have been the same Huck if he did. In these revisions, we can see his transformation, almost from the start, from what would have been a predictably slangy vernacular Huck to a more subtle character, a more subtle voice. Figurative language is excised from other characters' speeches, too; Tom's comment about genies is changed, with a simile revised in such a way that it is hardly a simile anymore: "'Why,' said he, 'a magician could call up a lot of genies, + they would hash you up like <smoke>, before you could say Jack Robinson'" becomes "'Why,' said he, 'a magician could call up a lot of genies, + they would hash you up like ^nothing^, before you could say Jack Robinson.'"

In a rare example, we can see Twain not merely removing a metaphor, but searching for exactly the right one, as Huck argues with Tom over the genies. At first, he has Huck say this: "'Well,' says I, 'I think they are a pack of <chuckle-heads,> for not keeping the palaces themselves 'stead of fooling them away like that.'" "Chuckle-heads" is deleted and replaced by "softies," then *that* is deleted and replaced by the metaphorical expression we are familiar with in this passage: "flatheads." Any of the three would have served, although it was certainly best to save "chuckle-heads" as an expression for Jim to use. "Pack of flatheads" has a better ring to it than "pack of softies," and it is certainly a more colorful expression, rare for Huck, thus all the more memorable.

There is only one such revision to figurative language in chapter 4, the deletion of a simile, a change that certainly fits the pattern we have seen developing: "At first I hated the school <like sin>, but by + by I got so I could stand it." Without these kinds of intensifications, Huck's voice acquires the flat level we think of as his natural voice, but that flatness was something Twain had to fine-tune as he composed. In the next chapter, a cluster of revisions involve the way Pap names Huck. These three revisions are not on the manuscript, but must have happened sometime later, either as the book was typewritten, when it was set into type, or during revision of the proofs. Pap originally says to Huck, "Starchy clothes—very. You think you're a good deal of a swell, don't you?" A better metaphorical term is inserted by the time of the first edition: "Starchy clothes—very. You think you're a good deal of a ^big-bug^, don't you?" "Swell" must have suited Twain for a time, but he then consistently deleted it: first here; in the next instance, where it was used twice, then deleted altogether (again in the first edition); and in the last, where he changed "swell" to "dandy." These are rare changes to the figurative language, coming as they do so much later in the composing process, suggesting that Twain was still fine-tuning the metaphorical levels of language even as late as the typesetting stage.[24]

When Huck describes life at the widow's in chapter 6, we see a return to the toning down of colorful metaphor. Huck says, "you had to wash, + eat on a plate, + comb up, + go to bed + get up regular, + be forever <bully ragging> a book," and the end of that is changed to "+ be forever ^bothering over^ a book." Such changes, though small in themselves, are a look into Twain's composing process, and we can imagine him running through the manuscript, his eye and ear attuned to figurative language, systematically making the changes he is seeing and hearing.

In the next revision, he actually adds a metaphor, and a graphic one. Huck is describing Pap's cabin, saying, "There warn't a window to it;" then Twain adds to that phrase "^big enough for a dog to get through.^" This is the first instance I find of metaphor that he adds to what he originally wrote, where there had been none before; the exception stands out, showing us how extensive his operations were in the other direction. The last example in the chapter is a change from one level of metaphor to another, from a vivid image to one that is more subtle and understated (and arguably more powerful). Describing Pap after a bender, Huck first says, "A body would a thought he <had been whitewashed with mud.>" In the revision, Twain comes up with an amazing expression, especially amazing for Huck: "A body would a thought he ^was Adam, he was just all mud.^" Here, Twain retains the meaning of the original, but adds a powerful, biblical/mythic image. The original is probably more characteristic of Huck, but the revision adds layers of meaning.

In chapter 8, the last chapter I offer as evidence, we have first another rare addition of metaphorical language, this time a single word inserted in the description of waking up on Jackson's Island, a word that intensifies the scene: "There was ^freckled^ places on the ground where the light sifted down through the leaves." As Huck watches the search for his supposedly drowned body, we see Twain first use a bit of slangy metaphor, a burst of figurative language that is surprising to see: "Says I, you started out <for to roust out> this corpse, + you've filled your contract to a dot; <you've come to the right place;> you couldn't done better under no circumstances." In the kind of toning down that we have come to expect, he makes this change: "Says I, you started out ^to look up^ this corpse, + you've filled your contract to a dot; you couldn't done better under no circumstances." The sentence stays that way in the manuscript, but in the first edition, it has all been deleted. My last example could stand as a statement on metaphor in the manuscript: Huck first says, "I judged I was <a

goner>," and Twain changes it to the much flatter "I judged I was ^gone^."
So is much of the metaphor, and I stop after chapter 8 because this kind of
revision largely stops.

Numerous manuscript pages go by and we do not find these kinds of
changes, so prevalent in the first chapters, suggesting that Twain had found
the voice and the level he was seeking, and further (although there is no
way to prove this), that he made many of the revisions I have been discussing before he moved on. I would suggest that he wrote in the kind of
haste he tells us, then made a pass (or several passes) through the manuscript, with a keen eye focused on and a keen ear attuned to the level and
nature of the figurative language. The voice and tone we are so familiar
with came to him mostly but not totally from the very start, but needed
some careful attention, no matter what he said about hating to revise or
proofread. As I said before, it is impressive how much of the manuscript
seemed to come to him on the spot, but it is also impressive to see the revisions he made, especially these revisions of metaphor, and to recognize the
effect they have on the novel. The Huck that he originally came up with
would have been startling and original, but the toned-down Huck that he
fashioned in the end is a true mark of his achievement.

One last look at an extended passage will give further evidence of
Twain's skill in handling language. The opening of chapter 19, the description of the river, is justly famous, and has been cited by many commentators on Mark Twain's style, beginning with Leo Marx and his excellent
analysis in "The Pilot and the Passenger." Marx's point about the unity of
Huck's vision and the way it resolves the conflict between romance and
realism that Twain describes in "Old Times on the Mississippi" is an excellent one. "It was impossible," Marx asserts, "to do justice to American experience by treating nature, in the conventional manner, as benign and
beautiful. Clemens knew better, and his continuing impulse was to parody the existing mode. To him the landscape, no matter how lovely, concealed a dangerous antagonist." Marx goes on to argue that Twain had
found the solution in "the incomplete manuscript of *Huckleberry Finn*." His
argument is important enough to quote at length:

> Here was a tale told by a boy who—granted his age, his education, and
> the time he lived—could not possibly feel the anxiety Clemens felt. To
> Huck nature was neither an object of beauty nor the raw material of
> progress. Or, rather, it was both. He was as tough and practical as the
> pilot, and as sensitive to color and line as an artist; he kept his eye on
> dangerous snags, but he did not lose his sense of the river's loveliness.

Table 1. Mark Twain's Revision of Metaphor in *Adventures of Huckleberry Finn*

	<Deletions>	^Insertions^
Chap. 1	When you got to the table you couldn't <sail in>	When you got to the table you couldn't ^go right to eating,^
	She <made me hump myself> for about an hour	She ^worked me middling hard^ for about an hour
	Well, I couldn't see no advantage in going where she was going, so I made up my mind <to lay low + keep dark + go for the other place>.	Well, I couldn't see no advantage in going where she was going, so I made up my mind ^I wouldn't try for it.^
	So I didn't <take no stock in it>.	So I didn't ^think much of it.^
	I was glad about that. <So I guessed my head was level about steering for the other place. I didn't want to go to a place where I warn't acquainted, anyway.>	I was glad about that. ^cause I knowed I would be lonesome with angels, not being used to them, + they not being used to my kind, but I could get along anywheres with Tom Sawyer.^
		I was glad about that ^ because I wanted him + me to be together.^
Chap. 2	There was a place on my ancle that got to itching <like sin;> but I darsn't scratch it;	There was a place on my ancle that got to itching^;^ but I darsn't scratch it;
	If you are <in a starchy company,>	If you are ^with the quality,^
	+ then <I turned my self loose, + I don't think I ever had such a good time in my life>.	+ then <I turned my ^claws^ loose, + I I don't think I ever had such a good time in my life>.
		+ then <I was pretty soon comfortable again.>
	We will keep them till they're ransomed <deader'n a smelt —>	We will keep them till they're ransomed ^to death —^
Chap. 3	I tried for the hooks three or four times, but somehow I couldn't make <the trip>.	I tried for the hooks three or four times, but somehow I couldn't make ^it work.^

	<Deletions>	^Insertions^
Chap. 3	I wouldn't worry about it no more, but <tackle something else>.	I wouldn't worry about it no more, but ^just let it go.^
	there was two Providences, + a poor chap would stand consider-able show with the widow's, but if Miss Watson's <took him into camp he was a goner.>	^I could see that^ there was two Providences, + a poor chap would stand considerable show with the widow's<,> ^Providence,^ but if Miss Watson's ^got him there warn't no help for him any more.^
	We played robber now + then about a month, + then I <shook the Gang.>	We played robber now + then about a month, + then I ^re-signed.^
	"Why," said he, "a magician could call up a lot of genies, + they would hash you up like <smoke>, before you could say Jack Robinson."	"Why," said he, "a magician could call up a lot of genies, + they would hash you up like ^nothing,^ before you could say Jack Robinson."
	"Well," says I, "I think they are a pack of <chuckleheads,><^softies, ^> for not keeping the palaces themselves 'stead of fooling them away like that.	"Well," says I, "I think they are a pack of ^flatheads^ for not keep-ing the palaces themselves 'stead of fooling them away like that.
Chap. 4	At first I hated the school <like sin>, but by + by I got so I could stand it.	At first I hated the school, but by + by I got so I could stand it.
Chap. 5	"Starchy clothes —very. You think you're a good deal of a swell, don't you?"	First edition: "Starchy clothes — very. You think you're a good deal of a ^big-bug^, don't you?"
	"Yes, a nice swell — a mighty nice swell. You're putting on considerable many frills since I been away."	First edition: "You're putting on considerable many frills since I been away."
	"Ain't you a sweet-scented swell, though?	First edition: "Ain't you a sweet-scented dandy, though?

	<Deletions>	^Insertions^
Chap. 6	you had to wash, + eat on a plate, + comb up, + go to bed + get up regular, + be forever <bully ragging> a book	you had to wash, + eat on a plate, + comb up, + go to bed + get up regular, + be forever ^bothering over^ a book
	There warn't a window to it;	There warn't a window to it ^big enough for a dog to get through.^
	A body would a thought he <had been whitewashed with mud.>	A body would a thought he ^was Adam, he was just all mud.^
Chap. 7	The sky looks <powerful> deep when you lay down on your back in the moon-<light>;	The sky looks ^ever so^ deep when you lay down on your back in the moon-^shine^;
Chap. 8	There was places on the ground where the light sifted down through the leaves,	There was ^freckled^ places on the ground where the light sifted down through the leaves,
	Says I, you started out <for to roust out> this corpse, + you've filled your contract to a dot; <you've come to the right place;> you couldn't done better under no circumstances.	Says I, you started out ^to look up^ this corpse, + you've filled your contract to a dot; you couldn't done better under no circumstances. First edition: all deleted
	I judged I was <a goner.>	I judged I was ^gone.^

Source: "Huck Finn" CD-ROM: The Complete Buffalo and Erie County Public Library Manuscript—Teaching and Research Digital Edition, ed. Victor A. Doyno and Robert Berthoff (Buffalo and Erie County Foundation Board, 2003).

Moreover, he spoke a language completely unlike the stilted vocabulary of the cult of nature. His speech, never before used in a sustained work of fiction, was as fresh and as supple as his point of view. The interaction of narrative technique and the heightened emotion to which that technique lent expression helps account for the singular power of the sunrise passage. Behind the mask of Huck Finn, Clemens regained that unity of thought and feeling he felt himself, along with his contemporaries, to be losing.[25]

What Marx had no way of knowing, and what no one had been able to see until the recovery of the first half of the manuscript, is that this "unity of thought and feeling" did not occur in the original draft.

Huck's "poetic mode" is in full operation in this long passage. It begins with an apt and perhaps the most beautiful metaphor in the entire novel, the tenor and vehicle perfectly matched, well-suited to Huck's character and voice: "Two or three nights went by; I might say they swum by, they slid along so quiet and smooth and lovely." In the manuscript, Twain inserts the sentence "Here is the way we put in the time," making the description not a particular day, but a generalized one. What is really striking about the passage is Twain's addition of three things, not in the manuscript itself, but sometime before the first edition. To highlight the additions: Huck says, "Not a sound, anywheres—perfectly still, just as if the whole world was dead asleep," but Twain later deletes "dead" and adds the phrase "only sometimes the bull-frogs a-cluttering, maybe" after "asleep." In the second change, after describing "a log cabin in the edge of the woods," he adds by the time of the first edition, "being a wood-yard, likely, and piled up by them cheats so you can throw a dog through it anywheres." The third revision is the most telling of all; Huck says in the manuscript, "then the nice breeze springs up, and comes fanning you from over there, so cool and fresh, and sweet to smell, on account of the woods and the flowers." His memorable further comment was added at, it seems, a much later time: "but sometimes not that way, because they've left dead fish laying around, gars, and such, and they do get pretty rank. . . ."

We must somewhat revise our understanding of Marx's point in "The Pilot and the Passenger": in Huck's unified voice, Twain was indeed able to solve the impasse between realism and romanticism that he had outlined in "Old Times on the Mississippi"—but we now know that Twain arrived at that solution after a good bit of work. Marx had no way of knowing the inaccuracy of a statement such as this: "The discovery came to him not conceptually, but spontaneously, in the practice of his art."[26] The discovery did come "in the practice of his art," but not spontaneously, at least not in the original burst of composition, in what has always appeared to us to be a unified vision. Twain had let the original passage stand for several years, but at a late point in the book's composition, he amended Huck's original vision. His early decomposing of metaphor must have shown him that Huck's figurative description needed to be toned down, and thus he inserted the realistic, even distasteful, phrases that deflate the poetic quality of the passage. The result is still a tour de force, but by seeing behind the scenes into the composing process, we get a clearer view of Twain as an artist. He reached the vision that Marx rightly points out, but it took him quite a bit of time and work to get there.

To sum up, the manuscript of the first part of *Huckleberry Finn* shows us that, while the novel as it was revised does not have the amount of metaphor as in other works of the same period, there was more metaphor in the original burst of composition, metaphor that was revised away, much of it relatively soon, some of it later. At a certain point in the manuscript—after chapter 8—it seems clear that Twain had found the metaphorical voice and vision he was seeking, the voice that revolutionized American literature and helped forge a national style.

V. Writing Metaphor in the Twain–Howells Letters

Unlike many writers, Mark Twain was never one to write much explicitly about writing. His few pieces about writing—including "How To Tell a Story" and "The Art of Authorship"—are short and nontechnical, especially when compared to the kind of writing about writing that his contemporaries Henry James and William Dean Howells, for example, engaged in. Why, then, would Howells, the preeminent critic of his day, write to his sister Aurelia in 1906 that Mark Twain "is really a great literary critic, so that his praise is better worth having now than any other man's" (*MTHL*, 2:814n2)? The answer, I think, lies in the forty-year correspondence between the two friends and writers. Perhaps because he needed to maintain his persona as a rough-edged, vernacular artist and humorist, Twain refrained from much public comment about the act of writing and the profession of authorship, but in his letters with Howells, he was able to open up and, as he says, "talk shop." Thus, Howells's judgment no doubt stemmed from this view of the artist Mark Twain that no other contemporary had.

Even so, the letters are not as full of shop talk and criticism and writing about writing as one might expect—or hope. Their great appeal has been more to biographers of the two than to critics, recording as they do their daily life and friendship in a way that no other resource can. As the letters' editors, Henry Nash Smith and William M. Gibson, describe them, "The abundant, richly allusive letters of Howells and Mark Twain, both humorists, are filled with laughter, gentle or raucous, shallow or profound, which may rise from a state of euphoria, or a vivid satirical impulse, or an inner motion of despair, or even the frustration of a too hot desire to tell in Howells's phrase the 'black heart's truth.' The letters also embody on occasion the extremity of grief. They tell, in fact, a full story of almost forty years, episodic, not very dramatic, yet rarely dull, and always human" (*MTHL*, 1:xiii). Though Kenneth Eble, in a book-length study of the friendship, notes that "[a]ttention to the details of their writing was a part of the link between Howells and Mark Twain during the early years, years in which each had the primary task of developing his literary skills," he also says that "Mark Twain rarely enunciates any literary principles except the fundamental ones of being true to experience and of finding the exact language for conveying the writer's truth." From where, then, does Howells derive his opinion of Mark Twain as "a great literary critic"? The answer, as I say, lies in the letters, but not so much in their literal as in their metaphoric content. As René Wellek and Austin Warren point out, "We metaphorize . . . what we love, what we want to linger over and contemplate, to see from every angle and under every lighting, mirrored in specialized focus by all kinds of like things."[27] Like most writers, Twain metaphorized writing, he lingered over and contemplated it, and although he surely loved it, his metaphors for it are sometimes surprising, even a bit shocking.

Metaphor, by its very structure, is revealing, always showing more than a writer would realize, more than a casual reader would notice. I quote Gérard Genette again: "[M]etaphor is not an ornament, but the necessary instrument for a recovery, through style, of the vision of essences. . . ." When we say one thing in terms of another, as we do when we use metaphor, we always say more than we mean literally, and often something quite different from what a quick translation into literal language seems to say. In Genette's terms again, "Every figure is translatable, and bears its translation, transparently visible, like a watermark, or a palimpsest, beneath its apparent text."[28] I have examined these two volumes of letters with special attention to their metaphorical language, specifically metaphorical language about writing, with the goal of uncovering subtle aspects of Twain's attitude about writing, about the writing process, and about his estimation of himself and other writers. The bulk of the metaphorical comments about writing in the letters breaks into three general categories: comments about writing subjects and material; comments about the act of writing and the writing process; and comments about the writer, both himself and others.

Twain's comments about material have two general threads: his attitude about material and his perceptions of it. As one might expect of any writer, but particularly of Mark Twain, the attitude toward material, especially during the act of composition, is generally negative, and even when positive, is tinged with the negative. For example, while in the process of writing *A Tramp Abroad*, he calls it "[t]hat most infernally troublesome book"

(*MTHL*, 1:290); he compares two possible chapters of *A Tramp Abroad* to "having a life-preserver handy in a ship which *might* go down though nobody is expecting such a thing" (*MTHL*, 1:248); and he refers to his brother Orion, whom Twain proposes as the subject for a play he and Howells might collaborate on, as "a field which grows richer and richer the more he manures it with each new top-dressing of religion or other guano" (*MTHL*, 1:269).[29] This last metaphor reveals a common theme in the vehicles of many of his metaphors about material: perception of the material of writing in terms of the organic. He says, for example, "There are few stories that have anything superlatively good in them except the *idea,*—& that is always bettered by transplanting" (*MTHL*, 1:153).

Twain nearly always views his material as something living, as in this comment about writing "Old Times on the Mississippi": "The piloting material has been uncovering itself by degrees, until it has exposed such a hoard to my view that a whole book will be required to contain it if I use it" (*MTHL*, 1:62). If he does not see it as specifically organic, it is still natural, as in another comment about "Old Times": "There is a world of river stuff to write about, but I find it won't cut up into chapters, worth a cent. It needs to run right along, with no breaks but imaginary ones" (*MTHL*, 1:85). In other words, he sees the material for writing about the river in terms of the river itself, and its structure must be like the river itself. Thus, the tenor and vehicle of the metaphor are so closely allied that each enhances the other.

Twain's organic metaphors are sometimes as grotesque as nature, as in an 1875 letter referring to a novel in progress that cannot now be identified. Twain writes about a "rattling good character for my novel! That great work is mulling itself into shape gradually" (*MTHL*, 1:105); then follows a half-page cancellation, of which these words can be deciphered: "Those graded foetuses one sees in bottles of alcohol in anatomical museums. . . . I can look back over my row of bottles, now, & discover that it has already developed from a rather inferior frog into a perceptible though rather libelous suggestion of a child. I hope to add a bottle a day, now, right along" (*MTHL*, 1:105n8). The cancellation is followed by a parenthetical remark: "(All of the above ruthlessly condemned by the Head Chief of the Clemens tribe)" (*MTHL*, 1:105). Livy's censorship notwithstanding, we can still see (as could Howells) the thrust of the extended metaphor. Such gestation and birth metaphors are especially common in this early period, as we shall see better when we turn to an examination of his metaphors about the act of writing, but it would seem obvious that these metaphorical connections came so readily to hand because the Clemenses were in the midst of their child-bearing and child-rearing years. Thus, in writing about his profession, he chooses his metaphorical field from an intensely personal association.

His metaphorical comments about the act of writing are even more revealing, but also break into the general categories of attitude and perception. A quick catalog of some of his metaphorical references to the writing process shows his attitude clearly. Of prewriting, he promises to "rattle off a *good* one" and to "bang away again" (*MTHL*, 1:74, 71), suggesting the blind confidence of a writer in the beginning. Of actual writing, he will "trim up & finish . . . & then buckle in"; or he is "yoked down to the grinding out" of a long book (*A Tramp Abroad*); or he is "almost at a dead standstill with my new story"; or, most ominously, he is "fighting a life-&-death battle with this infernal book" (*A Tramp Abroad* again) (*MTHL*, 1:67, 248, 113, 286). Of revision, he will "lick it into shape"; or he tells Howells to "slash away"; or, after his own "altering, amending, rewriting, cutting down," he "would stick to it while the interest was hot," for he knows that "[a] week from now it will be frozen—then, revising would be drudgery" (*MTHL*, 1:52, 376, 189). We can see again the emphasis on the organic, on the living; for Twain, the writing process had a life of its own. But revision did not end the process; always for Twain, the worst part of the process was reading proof. In the case of *Huckleberry Finn*, he comments angrily on typesetters: "They don't make a very many great mistakes; but those that do occur are of a nature to make a man curse his teeth loose"; a few days later, he is driven even further: "My hair turns white with rage, at sight of the mere outside of the package" (*MTHL*, 2:493, 497).

As with his comments about material, he often closely links tenor and vehicle in his metaphorical expressions about writing. For example, he uses the phrase "trim up" when he is writing about steamboating, he writes "sail right in & sail right on, the whole day long" (*MTHL*, 2:435) when describing the composition of Huck and Jim's raft journey down the river, and he promises Howells he will "try to remedy the play, but I'd rather take a dose of medicine" (*MTHL*, 2:486). When he takes a break from the writing of *Life on the Mississippi*, a travel book that among other things contrasts the North and the South, to the detriment of the South, he declares that he has "been an utterly free person for a month or two; and I do not believe I ever so greatly appreciated and enjoyed and realized the absence of the chains of slavery as I do this time. . . . I have ceased from being a slave" (*MTHL*, 1:427). Such comments show not only his absolute immersion and identification with his subject and the writing process, but also his underlying attitude about writing itself. Slavery consumes him here in both subject and attitude.

His metaphorical comments about the act of writing are also often organic in the ground of the vehicle. And again, these are often related to birth, as in the comment above about "lick[ing] into shape." These metaphors can be arresting, especially coming from a male writer. Speaking again of *A Tramp Abroad*, he begs off a visit to Howells until "my confinement with this book is over & I'm able to be around again" (*MTHL*, 1:280). Here, "confinement" could mean any kind of shutting in, or even institutional confinement (and clearly the book was driving him crazy), but I prefer to read this in the nineteenth-century sense of "lying-in," especially since he makes the comment in a long letter about his speech "The Babies." More disturbing is his reference to revising *A Connecticut Yankee*, specifically to removing what he says Livy called "coarsenesses" and "blasts of opinion which are so strongly worded as to repel instead of persuade"; he explains, "I dug out many darlings of these sorts, & throttled them, with grief; then Steadman went through the book & marked for the grave all that *he* could find, & I sacrificed them, every one" (*MTHL*, 2:609). The statement is disturbing because he writes this to Howells five months after Howells's daughter Winifred died from a mysterious, undiagnosed illness, a death that Howells in his grief blamed partly on himself, and, three months after, Howells had written to Twain a description of a visit to Winnie's grave, "beside which I stretched myself the other day, and experienced what anguish a man can live through" (*MTHL*, 2:603). That Mark Twain could write so soon after his friend's tragedy of "digging out darlings" and "throttling them, with grief," and "marking them for the grave," seems macabre, perhaps cruel, and at the least insensitive, even if the comments are only metaphorical. It makes one rethink Howells's comment about his friend's letters in *My Mark Twain*, a comment usually read as proof of Twain's robust humor: " . . . I was often hiding away in discreet holes and corners the letter in which he had loosed his bold fancy to stoop on rank suggestion; I could not bear to burn them, and I could not, after the first reading, quite bear to look at them." I am not suggesting that Twain was not sympathetic; he went through many family deaths himself, of course, and although there are no extant letters in which he consoles Howells on the occasion of Winifred's death, Howells's memory of his sympathy, recorded in *My Mark Twain* and in letter 524, is very touching (*MTHL*, 2:604, 661–62). In any case, though, Twain was prone to misstatement and verbal blunders, and if nothing else, the language in this letter shows how deeply he got involved in his own work and in his own metaphor.[30] Metaphor, indeed, does uncover much, even if it is not always pleasant.

Finally, we have Mark Twain's metaphorical comments about writers, first about others, then about himself. In his critical comments about other writers, especially his comments about Howells, he shows the kind of perception that may have moved Howells to his remark about Twain's critical acumen. He recognizes early on (in 1879) what Howells is up to with realism when he declares in praise of *The Lady of the Aroostook*, "It is all such truth—truth to the life; everywhere your pen falls it leaves a photograph" (*MTHL*, 1:245), using as his ground of comparison a then-new invention, much heralded for its move toward verisimilitude. In the same letter, he metaphorically predicts Howells's literary legacy: "You ain't a weed, but an oak; you ain't a summer-house, but a cathedral" (*MTHL*, 1:246). Much later, in 1902, he writes perceptively and appreciatively of Howells's essay on Frank Norris in the *North American Review*: " . . . I found in it, (with envy & animosity,) what I always find in your examination of books: a microscope's vision, a chemist's mastery of analysis & proportion, & a precision all your own in setting down the details & the accumulated result of the inquisition in English which no man can misunderstand" (*MTHL*, 2:756). Even when he is critical of Howells, as he almost always was about what he felt was Howells's inability to read his own work aloud, he recognizes and praises his friend's strengths, again in metaphor. His mention here of "figures," by the way, is one of the very few times in the letters that he refers specifically to metaphorical language: "Well, *I* don't care how much you read your truck to me, you can't permanently damage it for me that way. It is always perfectly fresh & dazzling when I come on it in the magazine. Of course I recognize the *form* of it as being familiar—but that is all. That is, I remember it as pyrotechnic figures which you set up before me, dead and cold, but ready for the match—& *now* I see them touched off & all ablaze with blinding fires. You *can* read, if you want to, but you *don't* read worth a damn" (*MTHL*, 2:407). This impressive piece of reader-response criticism centers on the metaphorical language at its heart, a series of metaphors that build upon each other, culminating in a blaze of language, punctuated at the end with what would otherwise be savage criticism.

As much as Twain praised Howells, he damned other writers, in language that is memorable in large part because it is so highly metaphorical. He calls Bret Harte, in one of his milder comments about his former friend, "the worst literary shoe-maker, I know" (*MTHL*, 2:397). Of George Washington Cable, he makes this observation: "He is intellectually great—very great, *I* think—but in order to find room for this greatness in his pygmy carcase, God had to cramp his other qualities more than was judicious, it seems to me" (*MTHL*, 2:528). And in an outburst that begins in literal outrage but increasingly becomes more metaphorical (and scatological), he attacks a South Carolina lawyer and poet, Belton O'Neall Townsend, who without authorization quoted out of context a letter from Howells, then dedicated to Howells his book of very bad poetry. Try to imagine receiving a letter that contains these paragraphs:

> If you *did* write what he says you did, you richly deserve hanging; & if you didn't, *he* deserves hanging.—But he deserves hanging any-way & in any & all cases—no, boiling, gutting, brazing in a mortar—no, no, there *is* no death that can meet his case. Now think of this literary louse dedicating his garbage to you, & quoting encourageing compliments from you & poor dead Longfellow. Let us hope there is a hell, for this poets sake, who carries his bowels in his skull, & when they operate works the discharge into rhyme & prints it.
>
> Ah, if he had only dedicated this diarrhea to Aldrich, I could just howl with delight; but the joke is lost on you—just about wasted. (*MTHL*, 2:488)

One presumes Livy never got a chance to read this particular letter, and also that this letter is surely an example of one Howells would "hid[e] away in discreet holes and corners." Again, writing was associated in Twain's mind with the organic, and we can see what metaphor he applies to particularly bad writing (yet another example of the psychology of bodily discharge).

If Twain criticizes other writers, he does not spare himself. We are familiar with his comments that show his perception of himself as a writer, comments that may gain some fuller resonance when we recognize their metaphorical nature: calling himself "God's fool" or complaining that a humorist must "paint himself stripèd & stand on his head every fifteen minutes" (*MTHL*, 1:215, 49). We must always be on guard for tone, hyperbole, and irony in Mark Twain's letters: if we take either comment solely at face value, without recognizing the element of play and humor in his words, we risk misunderstanding and underestimating him. But his constant figuring of himself as a writer in such terms is revealing.

One of the very first letters between Twain and Howells shows again his irreverent use of metaphor, the famous 1872 letter in which he thanks Howells for his review of *Roughing It* in the *Atlantic:* " . . . I am as uplifted and reassured by it as a mother who has given birth to a white baby when she was awfully afraid it was going to be a mulatto" (*MTHL*, 1:10–11). Once again, he uses a birth metaphor, and once again, both the tenor and vehicle are shocking. After Twain's death, Howells writes in *My Mark Twain* of his new friend's response, unwilling then to lay the words before the reader: "I forget what I said in praise of it, and it does not matter; it is enough that I praised it enough to satisfy the author. He now signified as much, and he stamped his gratitude into my memory with a story wonderfully allegorizing the situation which the mock modesty of print forbids my repeating here. Throughout my long acquaintance with him his graphic touch was always allowing itself a freedom which I cannot bring my fainter pencil to illustrate."[31] Howells's euphemistic phrase—"wonderfully allegorizing the situation"—is quite interesting when we know the full quotation. No wonder Howells euphemizes; a white mother fearing she might be giving birth to a "mulatto" raises a shocking catalog for Victorian sensibilities: sexual promiscuity, fornication, miscegenation. The racist and sexist overtones are troubling enough, but when we shift our focus to the tenor and consider how Twain views himself as a writer at this early point in his career, the metaphor becomes all the more troubling, especially if, unlike Howells, we do not hide behind euphemism: metaphorically, he is calling himself a whore who has slept with, as he might or might not say at that point in his life, niggers as well as white men. This, only his third letter to Howells, sets quite a tone for the entire correspondence.

As a bookend, I quote a late letter, from 1904, concerning the dictation of his *Autobiography:* "[A]n Autobiography is the truest of all books; for while it inevitably consists mainly of extinctions of the truth, shirkings of the truth, partial revealments of the truth, with hardly an instance of plain straight truth, the remorseless truth *is* there, between the lines, where the author-cat is raking dust upon it which hides from the disinterested spectator neither it nor its smell (though I didn't use that figure)—the result being that the reader knows the author in spite of his wily diligences" (*MTHL,* 2:782). Mark Twain, himself a great lover of cats, surely knew the literal truth of his metaphor. I would propose, as conclusion, that he is talking here not only of autobiography, but of metaphoric language itself. The author-cat rakes his dust, but we see what he is trying to cover up, even smell it, and because of the power of metaphor, it is indeed true that "the reader knows the author in spite of his wily diligences." As metaphor critic Weller Embler describes it, "The author uses the materials of experience to fashion an image of what is going on within himself, and what he creates is an allegory of his own soul."[32] Through metaphor, we can better read that allegory, no matter how much the author tries to cover it up.

4

Figuring the End

In the majority of these journey metaphors, the journey is seldom regarded as a good thing in itself. It is undertaken because it must be: if the journey is a metaphor for life, life has to be followed to the end, but the end is the point of the journey, or at least the quality of the end is.

—Northrop Frye, *Myth and Metaphor*

Metaphor is the dreamwork of language and, like all dreamwork, its interpretation reflects as much on the interpreter as on the originator. The interpretation of dreams requires collaboration between a dreamer and a waker even if they be the same person; and the act of interpretation is itself a work of the imagination. So too understanding a metaphor is as much a creative endeavor as making a metaphor, and as little guided by rules.

—Donald Davidson, "What Metaphor Means"

Since the 1960s, with the publication of Mark Twain's late, often fragmentary and unfinished works, the metaphor of a "dark" Twain has been a matter of critical contention. These last works—bitter, sarcastic, polemical, often nihilistic—brought about a change in the way we think of Mark Twain. The genial humorist, cracker-box sage, and chronicler of nostalgic boyhood became, for many readers, a darker, more brooding figure. As we near a half century of such interpretations, the critical pendulum has begun to swing somewhat, with a reassessment of the "failures" of the late Twain revealing for a growing number of critics an experimental and creative side that may have been underappreciated in an age that valued whole works and organic unity, one that looked on fragments as failures. Metaphor provides an excellent lens for such a reexamination of the end of Mark Twain's career.

Just where "the end" begins is a kind of metaphor itself. It seems to me that the 1890s is the most obvious starting point, but I will move back one year, to 1889, to take another look at a novel that has been seen as both a triumph and a failure, then at the novel from the 1890s that has probably become Twain's second-most-studied work, and itself a source of much confusion and controversy. Thinking about *A Connecticut Yankee in King Arthur's Court* and *Pudd'nhead Wilson* in light of metaphor will help to see both novels in some new ways. A final look at Twain's humor, specifically his jokes, leads through psychology and metaphor to dreams—which is, of course, where Mark Twain has been leading us all along on this metaphorical journey.

I. Mixed Metaphor in A Connecticut Yankee in King Arthur's Court

A Connecticut Yankee in King Arthur's Court has had a mixed reaction from readers and critics since its publication in 1889. William Dean Howells considered it Mark Twain's masterpiece, although many contemporary reviewers saw it as a scandalous libel on the King Arthur myth and on England. Critics in the last half century or so have been similarly mixed, with many calling it an overall failure, a judgment shared by two of the best critics of Twain's work: Henry Nash Smith and James M. Cox. Even though they were written more than forty years ago, Smith's and Cox's serious charges against the novel have set the tone for much subsequent criticism. Metaphor answers their charges and might help reclaim for the novel something of the triumph Howells saw.[1] Hank Morgan starts his story by introducing himself to Mark Twain: "I am an American. I was born and reared in Hartford, in the State of Connecticut—anyway, just over the river, in the country. So I am a Yankee of the Yankees—and practical; yes—and nearly barren of sentiment, I suppose—or poetry, in other words" (*CY*, 50). Hank may be barren of poetry, but, like Baker's blue jays, he is "just bristling with metaphor," perhaps more so than any other of Twain's fictional narrators. The comparison with *Huckleberry Finn* is telling: while Twain certainly restrained himself with Huck's use of figurative language, in his next novel, he seems to have let himself go with Hank Morgan. Figurative language teems on every page of his narrative, especially in the first half of the novel. Hank's earthy and colorful metaphors are interesting in themselves, worthy of study, and an important reason the novel remains so vibrant.

At some point in the book, the narrative changes, with a different voice emerging, a change that has often been analyzed by critics, usually in disparaging terms. This shift forms the crux of Henry Nash Smith's objections. He says of the novel, "It is undoubtedly his most ambitious undertaking, brilliant in conception and sometimes outrageously funny. . . . But under critical analysis the book now seems on the whole a failure." Smith goes on to blame that failure on a problem with language and narration: "The mixture of farce and social criticism is further confused by impulses of doubt and despair from some obscure level of the writer's mind that contradict his original intention. In fact, the conflict between manifest and latent meanings in the novel denotes a crisis in Mark Twain's career. He was subjecting the vernacular perspective developed so variously in his earlier work to a test that destroyed it." In *Mark Twain: The Fate of Humor*, James M. Cox sees even deeper problems, also stemming from the narrator and his language:

> For Hank Morgan's collapse, more than being a prevision of coming disasters, is a disaster itself. Doubting his burlesque impulse, Mark Twain had tried to make his book serious; determining to write a satire, he had destroyed his humorous genius; seeking for truth and ideology, he had deserted the pleasure principle. His Hank Morgan—who embodies so much of the inventive, speculative, and performing aspects of Mark Twain's humorous genius—is trapped and destroyed in his effort to be a serious revolutionary. He is the unconverted indignation, and he proves that vernacular is no more proof of genuine protest that it is an assurance of an escape from gentility.[2]

Clearly, much is at stake with this novel, with this narrator, and with his language. By focusing on his language, specifically on his use of figurative language, we can learn much about the mixture that this novel is, and perhaps even salvage it somewhat from these claims of failure and disaster.

As I have argued at several junctures, figurative language can often identify a character as particularly as a fingerprint. I will establish first, then, the figurative identity of the early Hank Morgan, then mark the shift, the change, to a narrator so much more sophisticated that he is clearly someone else, clearly not the Connecticut Yankee of the opening. Since these two narrators both use metaphor, and since they coexist as the novel progresses, I am calling the result "mixed metaphor"—but I propose that, rather than this mixture constituting a flaw or a loss of control, it actually reveals an emerging complexity of thought, of theme, and of meaning. In short, it prefigures a kind of freeing up for Mark Twain, and it is the proof of his attainment of a new level as an artist. Where the mixed narration of *The Adventures of Tom Sawyer* showed Twain experimenting near the beginning of his novelistic career with what Bakhtin called the novel's dialogic voice, the mixed narration here at the beginning of the end signals a new phase in Twain's career and in his thinking.

Both Smith and Cox arrive at their critical judgments about the novel by comparing it to *Huckleberry Finn,* specifically comparing the two first-person narrators, Huck and Hank, a contest Hank Morgan is sure to lose. In Cox's case, his analysis is even more unfair, as he bases his entire argument on one passage. He quotes Hank's description of a young girl in Camelot:

> Presently a fair slip of a girl, about ten years old, with a cataract of golden hair streaming down over her shoulders, came along. Around her head she wore a hoop of flame-red poppies. It was as sweet an outfit as I ever saw, what there was of it. She walked indolently along, with a mind at rest, its peace reflected in her innocent face. The circus man paid no attention to her; didn't even seem to see her. And she—she was no more startled at his fantastic make-up than if she was used to his like every day of her life. She was going by as indifferently as she might have gone by a couple of cows; but when she happened to notice me, *then* there was a change! Up went her hands, and she was turned to stone; her mouth dropped open, her eyes stared wide and timorously, she was the picture of astonished curiosity touched with fear. That she should be startled at me instead of at the other man, was too many for me; I couldn't make head or tail of it. (*CY,* 56–57)

"This passage," Cox writes, "is as representative as it is revealing." He finds a lack of vernacular, and in its place, he says, "a certain exaggeration of metaphor and figure, as illustrated by the 'cataract of golden hair streaming down over her shoulders,' and 'hoop of flame-red poppies.'" After also pointing out the reliance on literary clichés, he concludes: "The entire passage illustrates the essential rhythm and feature of Morgan's language. Grounded in clichés and conventional syntax, its character emerges by means of exaggeration and calculated vulgarity. The exaggeration is achieved largely by relying on clichés which generalize images and impersonate Arthurian gentility; the slang is the means of dissociating from and exposing the overelaborate impersonation."[3] But a wider look at Hank's language, specifically his figurative language, will show whether or not this passage is representative, as Cox claims, and even more importantly, will help to establish Hank's figurative identity.

I present a list of metaphors, similes, and other figurative language as counterargument. For example, Hank's first description of Clarence: "This was an airy slim boy in shrimp-colored tights that made him look like a forked carrot" (CY, 61). In a joke that depends for its incongruity upon metaphor, to Clarence's claim that he is "a page," Hank says, "Go 'long. . . . you ain't more than a paragraph" (CY, 61). He describes a kind of "scale armor whose scales are represented by round holes—so that the man's coat looks as if it had been done with a biscuit punch" (CY, 65). The Round Table, he says, "was as large as a circus ring" (CY, 65). Of the inhabitants of Camelot, he says, "There did not seem to be brains enough in the entire nursery, so to speak, to bait a fish-hook with; but you didn't seem to mind that, after a little, because you soon saw that brains were not needed in a society like that, and, indeed, would have marred it, hindered it, spoiled its symmetry—perhaps rendered its existence impossible" (CY, 69). Different readers will respond differently to such language, of course, but I find it, on the whole, arresting, humorous, inventive, and, quite often, very perceptive. I would propose that these early metaphors are more representative of Hank's style than the passage Cox quotes.

But perhaps Cox still has a valid point, even if his evidence is skimpy or unrepresentative. He argues that Hank's rebellion is not a real rebellion, a fact revealed by his style. Cox argues: "For Hank's supposed vernacular is not really vernacular at all but indulged colloquialism. It is, in a word, slang, which is to say that it is simply put-on vernacular. Mark Twain, in *A Connecticut Yankee*, succumbed to the lure of mere lingo, which so many writers since his time have done." Cox defines slang explicitly in terms of metaphor: "Slang is a patronizing indulgence of metaphor by someone consciously taking imaginative flights for purposes of mystification, in-group solidarity, or protective, secret communication."[4] I know exactly the kind of writing Cox means; the first that comes to mind, and rankles me the most, are the Hollywood attempts at southern or hillbilly speech, a Jed Clampett "Whew doggies! I'm feeling lower than a hound dog's belly in a possum swamp!"—"a patronizing indulgence of metaphor" for sure, and an exaggeration of language that clangs false to anyone with even a passing familiarity with the region and the people. This constitutes a kind of paint-by-numbers regionalism, and it is all too common in books, in movies, and on television. Much bad writing aimed at and depicting youth and minority groups is guilty of precisely what Cox is talking about.

Hank's figurative language often does draw on his personal domains of knowledge, and thus he might be guilty of the charge Cox makes against him (and against Twain). Again, the reader must decide. Many of his similes and metaphors are drawn from the domains of firearms, machinery, gambling, and, for the first time ever in literature, from baseball—domains absolutely suitable to a character who is supposed to be foreman of the Colt Arms Factory, a practical man, and "a Yankee of the Yankees" (*CY*, 50). Sandy has talk "as steady as a mill"; Sir Kay "got up and played his hand like a major—and took every trick"; Hank says of his changes to society that he is "turning on my light one candle-power at a time"; of Sandy, he says, "it may be that this girl had a fact in her somewhere, but I don't believe you could have sluiced it out with a hydraulic; nor got it with the earlier forms of blasting, even; it was a case for dynamite" (*CY*, 149, 69, 129, 139); characters are told repeatedly it is "their innings" or they are "up to bat." His constant metaphorical comparison of the people of Camelot to various animals—they are called "mollusks," "clams," "swine," "rabbits," and so on—dramatizes the supposed superiority The Boss feels. Hank's grim comment on the Battle of the Sand Belt is in character for the foreman of the Colt Arms Factory, and provides the ending of the novel with a heft of tone that makes it resonate into the bloody twentieth and twenty-first centuries: "No living creature was in sight! We now perceived that additions had been made to our defences. The dynamite had dug a ditch more than a hundred feet wide, all around us, and cast up an embankment some twenty-five feet high on both borders of it. As to destruction of life, it was amazing. Moreover, it was beyond estimate. Of course, we could not count the dead, because they did not exist as individuals, but merely as homogeneous protoplasm, with alloys of iron and buttons" (*CY*, 478).

It seems to me that Twain not only characterizes the Yankee well with these metaphorical fingerprints, but also plays up the contrast between the sixth and the nineteenth centuries, all with figurative language that strikes at least my ear and eye as being fresh, precise, and accurate. In fact, he uses the same kind of conflict in language that he exploits so well elsewhere, as in the Scotty Briggs episode of *Roughing It,* an episode widely recognized as a triumph for the vernacular voice, an episode I examined at length in my first chapter. For example, this extended interchange between Hank and Sandy highlights their perceptual differences by highlighting their confusion over language:

> "And so I'm proprietor of some knights," said I, as we rode off. "Who would ever have supposed that I should live to list up assets of that sort.

I shan't know what to do with them; unless I raffle them off. How many of them are there, Sandy?"

"Seven, please you, sir, and their squires."

"It's a good haul. Who are they? Where do they hang out?"

"Where do they hang out?"

"Yes, where do they live?"

"Ah, I understand thee not. That I will tell eftsoons." Then she said musingly, and softly, turning the words daintily over her tongue: "Hang they out—hang they out—where hang—where do they hang out; eh, right so; where do they hang out. Of a truth the phrase hath a fair and winsome grace, and is prettily worded withal. I will repeat it anon and anon in mine idlesse, whereby I may peradventure learn it. Where do they hang out. Even so! Already it falleth trippingly from my tongue, and forasmuch as—"

"Don't forget the cow-boys, Sandy."

"Cow-boys?"

"Yes, the knights, you know. You were going to tell me about them. A while back, you remember. Figuratively speaking, game's called."

"Game?"

"Yes, yes, yes. Go to the bat. I mean, get to work on your statistics, and don't burn so much kindling getting your fire started. Tell me about the knights." (*CY*, 172–73)

"Figuratively speaking, game's called"—at least I think it is in my argument with James Cox. A fuller look than Cox's at the novel's metaphors shows Twain's accomplishment, and how much it goes beyond what Cox disparages as mere slang.

Henry Nash Smith includes more evidence from the novel in his objection than does Cox. In *Mark Twain: The Development of a Writer*, more than forty years after its publication still one of the best critical studies of Twain's work, Smith makes this argument: "When he does mount an attack, the force of his indignation leads him into moralizing that destroys the fictive world of the story. The Yankee's purchase of the hogs, for example, reminds Mark Twain that he is out to demolish the Established Church as well as the nobility, and he stops the action in order to insert a bit of polemic embroidery." Smith quotes this passage from the novel:

I was just in time; for the Church, the lord of the manor, and the rest of the tax gatherers would have been along next day and swept off pretty much all the stock, leaving the swineherds very short of hogs and Sandy out of princesses. But now the tax people could be paid in cash, and there would be a stake left besides. One of the men had ten children; and he said that last year when a priest came and of his ten pigs took the fattest one for tithes, the wife burst upon him, and offered him a child and said:

"Thou beast without bowels of mercy, why leave me my child, yet rob me of the wherewithal to feed it?"

How curious. The same thing had happened in the Wales of my day, under this same old Established Church, which was supposed by many to have changed its nature when it changed its disguise. (CY, 231)

Smith continues:

> When Hank Morgan speaks in this fashion he has ceased being the pro-tagonist of a comic burlesque and has become a mouthpiece for the author. His language retains some colloquial color (in such phrases as "pretty much all the stock" and "leaving . . . Sandy out of princesses") but is for the most part Mark Twain's workmanlike prose: "supposed by many to have changed its nature when it changed its disguise" is not colloquial in either diction or syntax. The identification of author with narrator destroys the kind of fictional integrity Mark Twain had been able to confer on Huck Finn and thus rules out the kind of ironic effect that is so powerful in the earlier novel. In the Yankee's harangues addressed directly to the reader he resembles instead the narrator of the second part of *Life on the Mississippi*, who is not identified, but enters it as an observer from a distance endowed with absolute moral authority.

I would argue here with Smith's phrase "for the most part": the phrase he quotes is decidedly not "for the most part," but a very small part of the passage. Smith's ear is characteristically good, though; the phrase truly is different from Hank's usual voice, though Hank's voice still predominates. But Smith is right: another voice does begin to appear as the novel progresses. Smith, again, judges this other voice to be a grave defect: "Something like this happens to Mark Twain's style almost invariably when he assumes the stance of righteous indignation." Smith quotes this next example from the novel: "It is enough to make a body ashamed of his race to think of the sort of froth that has always occupied its thrones without shadow of right or reason, and the seventh-rate people that have always figured as its aristocracies" (CY, 110). "'Without shadow of right or reason' is unworthy of Mark Twain and not characteristic of the Hartford mechanic," Smith argues, and although the diction does seem out of character for the narrator of the novel, why is it "unworthy" of Mark Twain? In fact, it sounds characteristic of his late style—which is precisely my point about mixed metaphorical styles. When Smith highlights that phrase out of the whole passage, he fails to comment on phrases like "enough to make a body ashamed of his race," "the sort of froth," and "the seventh-rate people," phrasing that fits the metaphorical fingerprint of Hank Morgan, and, it seems clear to me, phrasing that still predominates in the novel. That other metaphorical fingerprint destroys the style of the novel for Smith, arguing as he is for a unified vernacular vision, and seeing anything else as a falling away and thus a failure. He concludes: "Translated into fictional terms, the ideas and emotion that govern this kind of rhetoric become melodrama. Many pages of *A Connecticut Yankee* are given over to incidents that have no relation to comedy or to the vernacular perspective, but are simply exempla illustrating the injustices and cruelties visited on the common people by the kind of despotism Mark Twain imagines to have existed in the Middle Ages."[5] If the goal is for a unified vernacular vision, Mark Twain truly does fail—*A Connecticut Yankee* is clearly not *Adventures of Huckleberry Finn*. But what if the goal is quite different?

Smith is right about another voice emerging, but I would highlight the change in metaphoric vision rather than the fall from the vernacular. What we have here is another set of metaphorical fingerprints, a voice that Mark Twain was to continue to develop in his last years. Rather than the flaw Smith finds in such a mixture of metaphorical narrators, I think we can see the kind of richness and multiple voicings that Bakhtin argues exist in all novels. *A Connecticut Yankee* is, in Bakhtinian terms, dialogic. "The novel," Bakhtin says, "always includes in itself the activity of coming to know another's word, a coming to knowledge whose process is represented in the novel." He casts this argument in terms of a metaphor: "Within the arena of almost every utterance an intense interaction and struggle between one's own and another's word is being waged, a process in which they oppose or dialogically interanimate each other."[6] Smith sees in this novel a crisis for Mark Twain as a writer, and I think he is right. I merely disagree that he failed in that crisis; in fact, I think he found a way to move to a different level of expression, and the mixed nature of this novel's narration is just an indicator of that development.

In a famous letter to Howells after he had finished writing the novel, Twain dramatizes in a vivid metaphor just what is at stake: "Well, my book is written—let it go. But if it were to write over again there wouldn't be so many things left out. They burn in me; & they keep multiplying and multiplying; but now they can't ever be said. And besides, they would require a library—& a pen warmed up in hell" (*MTHL*, 2:301).

Rather than a fall from vernacular grace, in this strange mixture of a novel, we see the beginnings of Twain's late-career discovery of a new voice, the discovery of a renewed self. That discovery required Twain to delve into the frightening world of his own unconscious, a world of dream and nightmare and disillusion and despair. That discovery set Mark Twain free in a way, free to use his "pen warmed up in hell." Where Smith and Cox and a whole generation of Twain scholars have seen in the writer's last years a descent into failure, many now see a renewed creativity and a heroic artistic quest. Before moving on to the dream worlds that mark the achievement of that quest, we must examine another troubled—and troubling—novel, another crucial step in Twain's late career.

II. Killing Half a Dog, Half a Novel:
The Trouble with Pudd'nhead Wilson and Those Extraordinary Twins

From the beginning, Mark Twain's novel *Pudd'nhead Wilson* (1894) has been trouble. It troubled the author, who tells us that he delivered it by a kind of "literary Caesarean operation" from a quite different novel. It troubled the contemporary audience, who seemed puzzled at this strange new novel from Mark Twain. It troubled a generation of New Critics, who quibbled endlessly over a puzzle set up very near the beginning of the text, as well as, and more importantly, over the apparent lack of unity in the finished novel. It puzzled cultural critics of the late twentieth century, who struggled to make sense of the novel's troubling statements about race. And it troubled one important textual critic, who pronounced the novel not only a "flawed text," but finally, an unreadable one.[7]

Metaphor provides one possible solution to much of this trouble. By applying metaphor theory and using metaphor as a way to read the novel, we can figure out and solve some of these puzzles. I begin by using again the opposition between metaphor and metonymy to read *Pudd'nhead Wilson*, then move to a plea for reading the *whole* text Mark Twain published in 1894, including as part of it *Those Extraordinary Twins*, the "half a novel" that is often ignored in critical appraisals of *Pudd'nhead Wilson*. That examination will allow me to address the "half a dog" controversy, as well as the controversy over the novel's apparent lack of unity, and in the most extreme charge leveled against the novel, the question of a flawed, unreadable text.

Almost all readers have agreed that Mark Twain's troubled novel turns on identity. John C. Gerber sums up the issue well: "Probably because he was so unsure of his own identity as a person or as a writer, Mark Twain kept coming back to the subject of identity in book after book. Characters are forever playing roles or altering identities by changing clothes. *Pudd'nhead Wilson* is the first work, however, in which Twain attacks identity as a universal, ongoing problem. There is no major character in *Pudd'nhead Wilson* without a problem of identity."[8] After Roxy switches her black slave baby with the white master's baby, the plot revolves around figuring out the true identity of the children. By the time Pudd'nhead Wilson has used fingerprints to resolve the issue, the reader, rather than feeling satisfaction at the resolution of the problem, feels only frustration and confusion over the troubling implications of Twain's narrative. Not surprisingly, much of the critical comment on the novel concerns itself with this issue of problematic identity and the frustration it engenders. An earlier generation of New Critics either searched for or decried a lack of structural unity in the text, while more recent cultural critics find the problems of identity and structure to be marks of illumination. Consider this from the introduction to Susan Gillman and Forrest G. Robinson's collection of essays from a number of cultural critics, *Mark Twain's "Pudd'nhead Wilson": Race, Conflict, and Culture:*

> What are now regarded as its leading critical features were once dismissed as the signs of its failure: we read the incoherence in Twain's narrative not as aesthetic failure but as political symptom, the irruption into this narrative about mistaken racial identity of materials from the nineteenth-century political unconscious. Instead of searching for a hidden unifying structure, as did a previous generation of New Critics, the scholars in this volume are after what Myra Jehlen calls "the novel's most basic and unacknowledged issues." We do thus share the earlier critical passion for detection, although we are not similarly inclined to dismiss evidence of authorial intention.[9]

Metaphor provides a bridge between these two approaches, allowing us to focus *both* on the text as an object *and* on the wider political and cultural implications of the text and its language. Reading the novel as I have read "Old Times on the Mississippi" and *Huckleberry Finn*, in terms of metaphor and metonymy, helps us recover a middle ground between formalist and cultural approaches. The opening paragraphs of *Pudd'nhead Wilson* seem at first to be nothing more than a description of the town of Dawson's Landing, a conventional enough opening for a novel. But if we read them with an eye toward the metaphor/metonymy opposition that Jakobson says underlies all discourse, we will see beyond the convention to other meanings and to an underlying but obscured pattern of the text. The opening is predominantly metonymic, as we should expect, since, according to

Jakobson, fiction is based predominantly on a succession of contiguities, but as we should also expect, it includes metaphor, since both poles of language are always present. It helps as we read the passage to imagine that we are watching a film, which Jakobson also claims is predominantly metonymic, generally composed of a selection of contiguous images, parts for the whole, one after the other. Reading the novel's second paragraph this way will make the metaphors, when they appear in the midst of a metonymic string, more significant:

> In 1830 it was a snug little collection of modest one- and two-storey frame dwellings whose white-washed exteriors were almost concealed from sight by climbing tangles of rose-vines, honeysuckles, and morning-glories. Each of these pretty homes had a garden in front, fenced with white palings and opulently stocked with hollyhocks, marigolds, touch-me-nots, prince's-feathers and other old-fashioned flowers; while on the window-sills of the houses stood wooden boxes containing mossrose plants and terra-cotta pots in which grew a breed of geranium whose spread of intensely red blossoms accented the prevailing pink tint of the rose-clad house-front like an explosion of flame. When there was room for a cat, the cat was there—in sunny weather—stretched at full length, asleep and blissful, with her furry belly to the sun and a paw curved over her nose. Then that house was complete, and its contentment and peace were made manifest to the world by this symbol, whose testimony is infallible. A home without a cat—and a well-fed, well-petted, and properly revered cat—may be a perfect home, perhaps, but how can it prove title? (*PWET,* 3)

The images in succession—the "modest one- and two-storey frame dwellings," the "white-washed exteriors," the images of flowers and window boxes—are all metonymic in the sense that they are related to each other by contiguity or that they are parts for the whole. When we reach the geranium, Twain introduces his first metaphoric image, the simile that pictures the red blossoms "like an explosion of flame." David Lodge makes the point that any metaphor brings "disruption" to the realistic text, which is why the realistic writer must make sure the context of tenor and vehicle are relatively close to each other, that the vehicle must come from the descriptive context of the tenor.[10] But in this case, we can see how far apart flowers and explosions of flame are—which, in Lodge's terms, brings disruption in the text, disruption that clearly foreshadows the explosions to come.

The passage then moves to another metonymic detail—the cat—but something is different now. A contented, sleeping, and blissful cat so soon after a metaphoric explosion of flame strikes the reader as somewhat odd.

The cat becomes something more; indeed, the narrator openly calls it a "symbol." Lodge discusses the way "the realistic writer can, by selection (or deletion) and repetition within a field of contiguities, construct a metonymic metaphor, or symbol, without disturbing the illusion of reality."[11] That, I would propose, is exactly what Twain has set up in the novel: a seemingly beautiful scene, with a potential for violent explosion, but in a town that sleeps contentedly. What has happened here is a chiasmus, a crossover from metonymy to metaphor, and this opening is a rehearsal for the crossovers of metaphor and metonymy that the text will enact. That confusion of metaphor and metonymy is what I now trace.

The opening action of the novel involves a series of identity switches, switches in a number of categories: names, clothes, race, and class. Underlying all these switches are crossovers between metaphor and metonymy. For example, because of his offhand remark about killing half a dog, newcomer to town David Wilson is renamed metaphorically as a "pudd'nhead," a fool. For the rest of the text, he is in opposition to the metonymical "town," and one of the plots is his attempt to change his metaphorical status. Roxy switches the babies by changing their names and their clothes, both metonymies. The narrator's emphasis is on the metaphoric change in the white baby rather than on Roxy's child:

> She undressed Thomas à Becket, stripping him of everything, and put the tow-linen shirt on him. She put his coral necklace on her own child's neck. Then she placed the children side by side, and after earnest inspection she muttered—
> "Now who would b'lieve clo'es could do de like o' dat?" (*PWET*, 14)

Names are metonymies for our identities, but in this case, both children's names—Thomas à Becket and Valet de Chambre—are also highly metaphoric and suggestive of the owner's social class. The slave becomes the master and the master becomes the servant. Significantly, though, when both names are shortened, "Tom" loses his metaphoric status, but "Chambers" retains his.

Roxy fears only one person, Pudd'nhead Wilson, and she recognizes his true, non-metaphoric identity: "Dey calls him a pudd'nhead, en says he's a fool. My lan', dat man ain't no mo' fool den I is! He's de smartes' man in town . . ." (*PWET*, 16). She fears him because of his use of a metonymy: fingerprints. But when even he can't tell the babies apart, she knows she is safe.

The switch of the babies also makes other identity changes. One we might not fully recognize is the switch in Roxy, who changes her relation to her son from being his mother to being his slave. "Mother" is a metonymic relationship, "slave" a metaphoric one, and the text reveals by its language the crossover from metonymy to metaphor:

> With all her splendid common sense and practical everyday ability, Roxy was a doting fool of a mother. She was this toward her child—and she was also more than this: by the fiction created by herself, he was become her master; the necessity of recognizing this relation outwardly and of perfecting herself in the forms required to express the recognition, had moved her to such diligence and faithfulness in practicing these forms that this exercise soon concreted itself into habit; it became automatic and unconscious; then a natural result followed: deceptions intended solely for others gradually grew practically into self-deceptions as well; the mock reverence became real reverence, the mock obsequiousness real obsequiousness, the mock homage real homage; the little counterfeit rift of separation between imitation-slave and imitation-master widened and widened, and became an abyss, and a very real one—and on one side of it stood Roxy, the dupe of her own deceptions, and on the other stood her child, no longer a usurper to her, but her accepted and recognized master. He was her darling, her master, and her deity all in one, and in her worship of him she forgot who she was and what she had been. (*PWET*, 19)

The heavily metaphorical phrase "her darling, her master, and her deity" underscores Roxy's loss of identity, a loss she herself engineers, then deceives herself into believing. A passage a few pages later makes this point even more clearly, pointing up her figuratively underpinned loss of identity, ending with yet another packed metaphoric phrase:

> Tom had long ago taught Roxy "her place." It had been many a day now since she had ventured a caress or a fondling epithet in his quarter. Such things, from a "nigger," were repulsive to him, and she had been warned to keep her distance and remember who she was. She saw her darling gradually cease from being her son, she saw *that* detail perish utterly; all that was left was master—master, pure and simple, and it was not a gentle mastership either. She saw herself sink from the sublime height of motherhood to the sombre deeps of unmodified slavery. The abyss of separation between her and her boy was complete. She was merely his chattel now, his convenience, his dog, his cringing and helpless slave, the humble and unresisting victim of his capricious temper and vicious nature. (*PWET*, 21)

As before, the passage ends with a series of metaphors that seals the point.

The identity switches, then, are all fully set, and all based on crossovers between metaphor and metonymy. The rest of the plot turns on having those crossovers reversed. The first step is for Roxy to reveal to Tom his true identity. In this powerful passage, a constant switch between metaphor and metonymy underlies Tom and Roxy's dialogue, which begins with Roxy taking a metaphorical position above her son:

> She rose, and gloomed above him like a Fate. [metaphor]
>
> "I mean dis—en its de Lord's truth. You ain't no more kin to ole Marse Driscoll den I is!—*dat's* what I means!" and her eyes flamed with triumph.
>
> "What?"
>
> "Yassir, en *dat* ain't all! You's a *nigger!*—*bawn* a nigger en a *slave!* [metaphor]—en you's a nigger en a slave dis minute; en if I opens my mouf ole Marse Driscoll'll sell you down de river befo' you is two days older den what you is now."
>
> "It's a thundering lie, you miserable old blatherskite." [metaphor]
>
> "It ain't no lie, nuther. It's jes de truth, en nothin' *but* de truth, so he'p me. Yassir—you's my son—" [metonymy]
>
> "You devil!" [metaphor]
>
> "En dat po' boy dat you's be'n a-kickin' en a'cuffing to-day is Percy Driscoll's son en yo' *marster*—" [metaphor]
>
> "You beast!" [metaphor]
>
> "En *his* name's Tom Driscoll [metonymy], en *yo'* name's Valet de Chambers [metaphoric metonymy], en you ain't *got* no fambly name, beca'se niggers don't *have* 'em!" (*PWET,* 41)

The dizzying switch between metaphor and metonymy underscores the text's figural confusion at this point, and thus reveals to the reader Tom's extreme identity confusion. A recognition of the roles metaphor and metonymy play helps us see this confusion in a way that we would overlook in a conventional reading of the scenes.

Now to move to the revelation of true identity that follows. One key scene is the murder scene, where all the clues are dropped. This passage also unfolds as if it were a film, with a succession of partial images related contiguously as metonymies, punctuated by metaphor at key moments:

> Tom set his candle on the stairs, and began to make his way toward the pile of notes, stooping low as he went. When he was passing his uncle, the old man stirred in his sleep, and Tom stopped instantly—stopped, and softly drew the knife from its sheath, with his heart thumping and

his eyes fastened upon his benefactor's face. After a moment or two he ventured forward again—one step—reached for his prize and seized it, dropping the knife-sheath. Then he felt the old man's strong grip upon him, and a wild cry of "Help! help!" rang in his ear. Without hesitation he drove the knife home—and was free. Some of the notes escaped from his left hand and fell in the blood on the floor. He dropped the knife and snatched them up and started to fly; transferred them to his left hand and seized the knife again, in his fright and confusion, but remembered himself and flung it from him, as being a dangerous witness to carry away with him. (*PWET,* 94)

The metonymic emphases on "hand" and "blood" become very important as the plot unravels, and both become increasingly metaphoric, as foreshadowed by this scene. In one of the novel's many dramatic ironies, public prosecutor Pembroke Howard says the murder "was conceived by the blackest of hearts and consummated by the cowardliest of hands" (*PWET,* 100), thinking he is accusing the twins, but actually making metonymic metaphors that refer to Tom. In the form of fingerprints, hands play the central role when Pudd'nhead Wilson finally reveals the identity switch, setting all matters right at last. David Wilson loses his metaphorical name, and the metonymic town takes it on:

> "And this is the man the likes of us has called a pudd'nhead for more than twenty years. He has resigned from that position, friends."
> "Yes, but it isn't vacant—we're elected." (*PWET,* 114)

The twins are exonerated, Roxy retires to the solace of the church, and the switched children are restored to their rightful places. All the figurative switches have been set right.

Why, then, does the reader leave this novel so disturbed? Much has been written about Mark Twain's highly ironic and problematic ending, but I suggest that one explanation for the reader's uneasiness is yet another unresolved figurative switch, involving a deeper sense of identity: the identity of race.

Society says that race is like fingerprints, a part of a person's identity, or as Pudd'nhead says of fingerprints, they are a "natal autograph," "from birth to death a sure identifier" (*PWET,* 109). And also like fingerprints, race is metonymic. It is established through two synecdoches: skin color and blood. The problem with this society is that the metonymic relationship, this "sure identifier," has been broken down by generations of miscegenation, until the one-sixteenth black Roxy and her one-thirty-second black baby can barely be called black by either blood or skin color. As the narrator says of Roxy, "Only one-sixteenth of her was black, and that sixteenth did not show" (*PWET*, 8).[12] Her baby can be switched with a white child and no one, not even the child's father, can tell. Rather than recognize the tenuousness of this metonymic identity, society chooses to make the relationship metaphorical, as witnessed by the terms "nigger" and "slave," both originally metonymic, both made by society to be highly metaphorical. To make matters worse, society does exactly what Roxy does after she has made her switch: "deceptions intended solely for others gradually grew practically into self-deceptions as well" (*PWET*, 19). Pudd'nhead solves one set of figurative switches, but he does nothing to undo this deeper one. Hand exposes blood, but blood is a fiction, a disguised metaphor, a metaphor all of society, white and black, has accepted, just as Roxy has done earlier. Rather than setting this right, the ending merely underscores the confusion. Pudd'nhead Wilson, Roxy, Tom, Chambers, Dawson's Landing, and American society have become what Murray Krieger calls "stricken by metaphor," "so that the literary works in which they function serve as warnings against an unrelieved metaphorical enclosure." "An unrelieved metaphorical enclosure" is precisely what entraps these characters, and it is a metaphorical enclosure of their own making. In Krieger's view, such a condition has dire consequences:

> For a protagonist to be stricken by metaphor is for him or her to feel an identity, an identity both ominous and dangerous, with another character from whom the difference, a quite evident difference, is required for self-preservation. More than a return to the mirror-phase, it is to feel one's adult self trapped within a hall of mirrors in which one looks outward and sees only oneself, losing all awareness of distinctions that would permit moral judgment, and hence the moral life—a life of distinction-making—to be pursued. If the tragic existents, as protagonists, are stricken by metaphor, those who chronicle their stories see duplicitously, at once through them and beyond them, and so find themselves indulging both metaphor and counter-metaphor.[13]

The burden rests with Mark Twain and with us to see "at once through them and beyond them," and America must be judged by the way it has indulged the "metaphor and counter-metaphor" of race in the one hundred years since this troubling text was published.

Beyond this indulgence, however, other problems remain with the novel. To help solve them, we need to turn to the novel as it was published in 1894, and also to think about the novel that might have been.

More than fifty years ago, in 1955, a year before F. R. Leavis called attention to *Pudd'nhead Wilson* as "Mark Twain's neglected classic," Leslie Fiedler made this perceptive comment: "The most extraordinary book in American literature unfortunately has not survived as a whole. . . . What a book the original might have been, before *Those Extraordinary Twins* was detached and Pudd'nhead's *Calendar* expurgated—a rollicking atrocious melange of bad taste and half understood intentions and nearly intolerable insights into evil, translated into a nightmare worthy of America." Fiedler goes on:

> All that the surrealists were later to yearn for and in their learned way simulate, Twain had stumbled on without quite knowing it. And as always (except in *Huckleberry Finn*) he paid the price for his lack of self-awareness; he fumbled the really great and monstrous poem on duplicity that was within his grasp. The principle of analogy which suggested to him linking the story of Siamese Twins, one a teetotaler, the other a drunk; Jekyll and Hyde inside a single burlesque skin—to a tale of a Negro and white baby switched in the cradle finally seemed to him insufficient. He began to worry about broken plot lines and abandoned characters, about the too steep contrast between farce and horror; and he lost his nerve—that colossal gall which was his essential strength as well as his curse. Down the well went the burlesque supernumeraries and finally out of the story; and the poor separated twins remain to haunt a novel which is no longer theirs.[14]

As astute as Fiedler is here, I disagree that Twain "lost his nerve." The composition is complicated and convoluted: the story that he began as *Those Extraordinary Twins* in 1892 was radically cut and changed to *Pudd'nhead Wilson*, and he could have hidden the earlier story. But by publishing *Those Extraordinary Twins* along with *Pudd'nhead Wilson*, he was able to have and eat his cake; he did not lose his courage, but found a way to present his strange story in the only way an audience of his time could have accepted it. But that can only work if we actually read both stories, which people often do not. *Those Extraordinary Twins*, textually joined to *Pudd'nhead Wilson* (the novel that most critics and readers now rank second only to *Huckleberry Finn*), is assuredly among the overlooked works of Mark Twain. Critics of *Pudd'nhead Wilson* rarely mention *Those Extraordinary Twins*, and when they do, it is disparagingly, dismissively, and in passing; or they see it only as a way for Twain to pad what would have been a slim novel into a larger volume (which is indeed somewhat true).[15] I suspect, moreover, that teachers of *Pudd'nhead Wilson* usually do not require their students to read *Those Extraordinary Twins* (and I was once such a teacher). Yet I have become convinced that the two are one story, that Mark Twain intended for us to read them (it) as one story, and that we cannot understand the main novel without its twin. Just as you can't kill "half a dog," you can't kill "half a novel." *Those Extraordinary Twins*, while often ignored, overlooked, or seen merely as an interesting appendage to *Pudd'nhead Wilson*, is actually an integral part of its brother novel, and illuminates not only that paired text, but also Mark Twain as a man and artist, revealing as well our own fragmented identities.

The first question deals with the thorny problem of authorial intention. Very uncharacteristically, Twain comments extensively (if not always accurately) about the composition of this novel, interrupting the story with explanatory comments. "A man who is not born with the novel-writing gift has a troublesome time of it when he tries to build a novel," he begins (*PWET*, 119). He tells how what he was writing "changed itself from a farce to a tragedy," that he found that "it was not one story, but two stories tangled together," and then, in an arresting and revealing metaphor, he says, "I pulled one of the stories out by the roots, and left the other one—a kind of literary Caesarean operation" (*PWET*, 119). As James M. Cox argues in *Mark Twain: The Fate of Humor*, "The terms of the account deserve emphasis—not because the account is necessarily accurate, but because it discloses how Mark Twain was dramatizing the act of writing at this juncture of his career." Cox continues: "[T]he novel is curiously and strikingly figured not as the child of the farce but as the *mother* from whom the child—the farce—is forcibly extracted." Cox is, as usual, quite perceptive, but if we carry the metaphor to its logical conclusion, we can see that, rather than a "literary Caesarean operation," the operation is actually a "literary abortion." The writer is not delivering a story, but disposing of one—then tacking it on at the end of what most readers have taken to be the primary text.[16]

But this assertion too easily dismisses the result of his operation. Most readers, as I say, ignore the cast-off story. It exists metaphorically half-alive, with an elaborate (and funny) introduction and with Twain's interspersed comments along the way, making the text an early precursor to metafiction. In these comments, Twain presents himself, misleadingly, as a "jackleg novelist" (*PWET*, 119), a judgment many readers and critics have taken too seriously. "I took those twins apart and made two separate men of them," he says. "They had no occasion to have foreign names now, but it was too much trouble to remove them all through, so I left them christened as they were and made no explanation" (*PWET*, 122). Even so, instead of making a clean break between the two stories, he leaves some puzzling reminders of the Siamese twins in *Pudd'nhead Wilson*. They sit down to play a four-handed piece at the piano, and the villagers are "astonished" (*PWET*, 30); they say they were their parents' "only child" (*PWET*, 27); their story is that their "parents could have made themselves comfortable by exhibiting us as a show" and that after their parents' death, they "were seized for the debts occasioned by their illness and their funerals, and placed among the attractions of a cheap museum in Berlin to earn the liquidation money" (*PWET*, 28). None of these comments make any sense if the brothers are merely twins, and as easy as it would have been to erase the references, Twain leaves them in, even though he extensively revised the rest of the novel. Most curious is Tom's comment at a crucial moment in the plot when he refers to the twins as a "human philopena"—a comparison to two nuts in a shell—after which the narrator says, "The descriptive aptness of the phrase caught the house, and a mighty burst of laughter followed" (*PWET*, 56). The phrase, of course, is not nearly so apt if the twins are not Siamese twins.

Robert A. Wiggins finds it "surprising to find Twain remiss in matters of detail," and I agree. Wiggins, however, goes on to call Twain here "a butcher rather than a surgeon in performing his 'literary Caesarean operation.'" "Twain," he contends, "was simply careless in reworking his manuscript to remove these traces of his surgery."[17] Whether a butcher or merely careless, neither seems characteristic of Twain, no matter how much he hated revision in general. If he had disposed of *Those Extraordinary Twins* after the revision, I might agree—but he went to the trouble of revising that story too, then included it with *Pudd'nhead Wilson*, calling great attention to his actions. I submit, then, that rather than being guilty of carelessness or shoddy craftsmanship, he intentionally left these few vestiges of the Siamese-twin story embedded in *Pudd'nhead Wilson* as a sign to us of their true linkage. He cuts the twins apart but leaves enough evidence to point us to the story in which they are still joined. Only after reading *Those Extraordinary Twins* do these passages in *Pudd'nhead Wilson* make sense. And even more importantly, only by reading both stories do we fully get Twain's point. One story remains at least partly embedded in the other because they can't really be separated—you can't kill "half a novel."

If one influential textual critic is right, however, the troubling compositional history could kill the *whole* novel. In *Flawed Texts and Verbal Icons*, Hershel Parker devotes a long chapter to *Pudd'nhead Wilson*, painstakingly unraveling the compositional process that Mark Twain followed first in writing *Those Extraordinary Twins*, then in revising that manuscript into what we know as *Pudd'nhead Wilson*. His explanation is helpful, but his conclusion is arguable. Parker argues that because Twain wrote certain passages after he had written later ones, after he had decided to focus on the slave twins switched in the cradle, "the published *Pudd'nhead Wilson* is thus patently unreadable," a viewpoint that goes against the experience of many thousands of readers. Parker then goes on, at great length and with not a little venom and sarcasm, to excoriate and satirize critics who have made critical comments based on the novel as published in 1894. Any passage Twain revised or inserted after his original manuscript is invalid, in Parker's terms, because earlier or later passages do not have the same authorial intention as when Twain originally wrote them. Parker makes valid arguments against New Critical attempts to find unity in a fractured text, but his conclusion that *Pudd'nhead Wilson* is "patently unreadable" strikes me as excessive. Reading *Pudd'nhead Wilson* alongside *Those Extraordinary Twins*, Peter Messent reaches what I find to be a more satisfactory conclusion: "The peculiar quality of the narratives lies in the lack of formal unity, the sense of incompletion and deferral, that results from their twinning. To suggest this is to see Twain on the verge of the type of artistic understanding which would only become commonplace in later, post-structuralist, times: that our representation of reality can only end in deferral and incompletion."[18] In the case of *Pudd'nhead Wilson* and *Those Extraordinary Twins*, having *the two* texts presented to us as one heightens the reading pleasure. It seems to me that in presenting the two texts as one, Twain actually made stronger art. But as I say, only if we read them both, as twinned units.

What, then, does *Those Extraordinary Twins* reveal to us about the other novel? Much critical comment—perhaps too much—has been devoted to the "killing half a dog" comment in *Pudd'nhead Wilson* that seals the title character's fate and earns him his nickname.[19] Some parallel scenes in *Those Extraordinary Twins* underscore the comment and help us to understand Twain's point. When the Siamese twins are put on trial for kicking Tom Driscoll, Pudd'nhead Wilson's absurd cross-examination centers on which twin kicked Tom:

"Mr. Rogers, you say you saw these accused gentlemen kick the plaintiff."
"Yes, sir."
"Which of them kicked him first?"
"Why—they—they both kicked him at the same time."
"Are you perfectly sure of that?"
"Yes, sir."
"What makes you sure of it?"

"Why, I stood right behind them, and *saw* them do it."

"How many kicks were delivered?"

"Only one."

"If two men kick, the result should be two kicks, shouldn't it?"

"Why—why—yes, as a rule."

"Then what do you think went with the other kick?"

"I—well—the fact is, I wasn't thinking of two being necessary, this time."

"What do you think now?"

"Well, I—I'm sure I don't quite know what to think, but I reckon that one of them did half of the kick and the other one did the other half."

Somebody in the crowd sung out:

"It's the first sane thing that any of them has said." (*PWET*, 146–47)

The statement resonates clearly with the "half a dog" comment. Curiously, here the crowd quickly recognizes the absurdity and irony of "half a kick," while in *Pudd'nhead Wilson*, they take the "half a dog" comment and subject it to what amounts to a public cross-examination:

"Said he wished he owned *half* of the dog, the idiot," said a third. "What did he reckon would become of the other half if he killed his half? Do you reckon he thought it would live?"

"Why, he must have thought it, unless he *is* the downrightest fool in the world; because if he hadn't thought that, he would have wanted to own the whole dog, knowing that if he had killed his half and the other half died, he would be responsible for that half, just the same as if he had killed that half instead of his own. Don't it look that way to you, gents?"

"Yes, it does. If he owned one half of the general dog, it would be so; if he owned one end of the dog and another person owned the other end, it would be so, just the same; particularly in the first case, because if you kill one half of a general dog, there ain't any man that can tell whose half it was, but if he owned one end of the dog, maybe he could kill his end of it. . . ." (*PWET*, 5–6)

At the end of *Those Extraordinary Twins*, the twins have run against each other for the board of aldermen, with Luigi winning over Angelo in a bitter contest. But Luigi can't be sworn in, because Angelo will not be allowed to sit in on the meetings, and Luigi can't sit there without him. So the government is at a standstill—until they come up with the idea of lynching Luigi. When some protest that Angelo is innocent and shouldn't be hanged, the answer comes: "Who said anything about hanging him? We are only going to hang the other one." And the reply to that: "Then that is all right—

there is no objection to that." The narrator concludes: "So they hanged Luigi. And so ends the history of 'Those Extraordinary Twins'" (*PWET*, 169). And so we end with another killing of half a being—a motif that we can see even more clearly if we read both narratives instead of ignoring the half that Twain has pretended to kill. "Irony was not for those people," the narrator has told us earlier, in *Pudd'nhead Wilson* (*PWET*, 25), and Twain's irony becomes more intense if we read the "whole" story.

As a number of critics have pointed out, the "half a dog" scene sheds light on the situation of Tom and Chambers, and by reading *Those Extraordinary Twins* alongside *Pudd'nhead Wilson*, we can see that situation more clearly too. In *Pudd'nhead Wilson*, the twins function as relatively weak foils for Tom and Chambers, but as Siamese twins, they highlight the splits in identity even more clearly. As absurd and ludicrous as the story is, it makes some telling comments about duality. These are supposedly identical Siamese twins, two heads and bodies joined with a single pair of legs, but one is light and one is dark, an absurdity that points out the absurdity of racial identity, where Roxy is one-sixteenth black, and that one-sixteenth does not show, and where a white baby and a black baby, born on the same day to a slave woman and her white mistress, look identical enough to be switched in the cradle. The identity confusion that rules *Pudd'nhead Wilson* is heightened when we read its companion text, where Angelo is a teetotaler, but Luigi likes to drink; where Angelo is prone to illness, but Luigi is the picture of health; where Angelo is very religious, but Luigi is a freethinker; where Angelo is a Whig, but Luigi is a Democrat. They take turns being in control of the body, one week at a time, and as Luigi says, "So exactly to the instant does the change come, that during our stay in many of the great cities of the world, the public clocks were regulated by it; and as hundreds of thousands of private clocks and watches were set and corrected in accordance with the public clocks, we really furnished the standard time for the entire city" (*PWET*, 139). They are one being, and supposedly twins, but they are as different from each other as they can be, and in the end, turn out to be adversaries.

In *Pudd'nhead Wilson*, where Tom is really Chambers, and Chambers really Tom, so much so that the narrator has to call them by the wrong names or the story will lapse into utter confusion, the two separate beings are so interchangeable that white can become black, and black white. The society of *Pudd'nhead Wilson* sees race as the biggest difference between two individuals, but the individuals are such identical twins that the society can't tell them apart. And in *Those Extraordinary Twins*, the identical twins are so different that, even before they appear on the scene, Rowena wonders which one is tallest, which one is the best looking (*PWET*, 123). Their world is so topsy-turvy that Luigi actually convinces Patsy Cooper and Aunt Betsy that he is six months older than his own Siamese twin. His evidence takes in the two old women, two women who also swallow the "logic" of a slave-holding society:

> "It is very simple, and I assure you it is true. I was born with a full crop of hair, he was as bald as an egg for six months. I could walk six months before he could make a step. I finished teething six months ahead of him. I began to take solids six months before he left the breast. I began to talk six months before he could say a word. Last, and absolutely unassailable proof, *the sutures in my skull closed six months ahead of his.* Always just six months difference to a day. Was that accident? Nobody is going to claim that, I'm sure. It was ordained—it was law—it had its meaning, and we know what that meaning was. Now what does this overwhelming body of evidence establish? It establishes just one thing, and that thing it establishes beyond any peradventure whatever. Friends, we would not have it known for the world, and I must beg you to keep it strictly to yourselves, but the truth is, *we are no more twins than you are.*" (*PWET*, 140–41)

Even though he is putting these women on, his words cut both ways, and point to a deeper truth that lies at the heart of *Pudd'nhead Wilson*, a truth that depends on a metaphorical relation. If Siamese twins are no more twins than we are, then either *they are not* twins, or *we are*. Tom and Chambers are twins, yet they are not. Tom himself is split, in a way that brings him, no matter how despicable he is, great agony. Roxy is white, Roxy is black. Pudd'nhead Wilson is the biggest fool in town and its wisest man. The jury's finding in the twins' trial is that Luigi's "identity is so merged in his brother's that we have not been able to tell which was him" (*PWET*, 153). This is the lesson of both novels, with all their ironies, with all their characters, with all their lessons about race and duality: we cannot tell which is which, which is him or her. We can extend that to say the same about Mark Twain: we cannot tell which is him. And perhaps that is even the case with us. What pudd'nhead can produce fingerprints to unravel the confusion of our own split identities? Who is brave or foolish enough to try to kill half a dog?

A description near the beginning of *Those Extraordinary Twins* highlights the absurdity but also the audacity of what Twain's imagination has concocted here, as the twins undress, revealing the monstrous assault on the senses that they and their narrative contains, and metaphorically, I think, telling us something about the struggles Twain went through with his own creation, as well as the risk he would take by telling the whole story:

> The Twins were wet and tired, and they proceeded to undress without any preliminary remarks. The abundance of sleeves made the partnership coat hard to get off, for it was like skinning a tarantula, but it came at last, after much tugging and perspiring. The mutual vest followed. Then the brothers stood up before the glass, and each took off his own cravat and collar. The collars were of the standing kind, and came up high under the ears, like the sides of a wheelbarrow, as required by the fashion of the day. The cravats were as broad as a bank bill, with fringed ends which stood far out to right and left like the wings of a dragon-fly, and this also was strictly in accordance with the fashion of the time. Each cravat, as to color, was in perfect taste, so far as its owner's complexion was concerned—a delicate pink, in the case of the blonde brother, a violent scarlet in the case of the brunette—but as a combination they broke all the laws of taste known to civilization. Nothing more fiendish and irreconcilable than those shrieking and blaspheming colors could have been contrived. (*PWET,* 127)

The extraordinary book Leslie Fiedler imagines and pines for would indeed have been "a combination [that] broke all the laws of taste known to civilization," and the audience then, and probably even much of the audience now, would not have been ready to take it. As "fiendish and irreconcilable" as the two stories are, Twain found a way to present them both to us, if we would only read them both, as he clearly intended. You can't kill half a dog, and you can't kill half a novel. Unless, that is, you don't read the whole thing.

Twain could have cleared up or hidden much of the trouble if he had chosen to hide *Those Extraordinary Twins,* to throw it into the discard pile as he did so many other late manuscripts. But he chose instead to show it to us, and even though that decision may have seemed to *add* to the trouble, I think it is clear that he actually succeeded in making these conjoined texts even more interesting—if still troubling. And maybe trouble was the goal all along.

III. Figuring the Joke: Mark Twain's Metaphorical Humor

To write about Mark Twain and ignore his humor seems nearly impossible, although some people do manage that feat.[20] At various points so far, I have discussed Twain's humor, but here I want to make the connection between jokes and metaphor more explicit. This examination will allow me to span Twain's career, going back to some works I have already mentioned, filling in some gaps by mentioning works I have omitted, and touching on some out-of-the-way places I would not otherwise probe. Here, I examine the metaphorical nature and structure of jokes, first establishing the similarity between jokes and metaphors, using both metaphor and humor theory, then analyzing the language of some of Twain's humor—all in an attempt to "figure the joke," as well as to lead up to my concluding sections on dreams.

Metaphor critic Ted Cohen examines the way metaphors create community and intimacy between teller and hearer, and gives us a good theoretical starting point: "In these respects metaphors are surprisingly like jokes. With a joke, too, there is first the recognition that it *is* a joke and then the understanding—what's called getting the joke." Cohen has preceded this comment with an extended look at the way metaphors achieve intimacy. Although he does not explicitly apply all of his comments about metaphors to jokes, we can see the implications of the connection in his analysis: "There is a unique way in which the maker and the appreciator of a metaphor are drawn closer to one another. Three aspects are involved: (1) the speaker issues a kind of concealed invitation; (2) the hearer expends a special effort to accept the invitation; (3) this transaction constitutes the acknowledgment of a community. All three are involved in any communication, but in ordinary literal discourse their involvement is so pervasive and routine that they go unremarked. The use of metaphor throws them into relief, and there is a point in that." Clearly, those three aspects are present in a joking situation as well. Cohen goes on to describe what the hearer of a metaphor must do, the comment that leads him to make the comparison between metaphors and jokes: "An appreciator of metaphor must do two things: he must realize that the expression is a metaphor, and he must figure out the point of the expression. His former accomplishment induces him to undertake the latter. Realizing the metaphorical character of an expression is often easy enough; it requires only the assumption that the speaker is not simply speaking absurdly or uttering a patent falsehood. But it can be a more formidable task: not every figurative expression which can survive a literal reading is a mere play on words."[21] It is fair to take as an implication of Cohen's argument that jokes as well as metaphors create a sense of intimacy and community between teller and hearer, and that is a point I will consider more fully when I turn to an examination of some of Twain's jokes. But Cohen's seemingly offhand remark about metaphors and jokes suggests that jokes and metaphors are similar in more ways than just their effects: if what they do to us is so similar, might not they be similar in their very structure? Humor theory provides an answer.

I begin with Freud's classic 1905 book, *Jokes and Their Relation to the Unconscious*, despite the objections that some readers might rightly raise. Freud has come under such fire in the last quarter century that we might think him totally discredited. Humor theory did not end with Freud, and the ideas of Bergson and Bakhtin—to mention two early-twentieth-century humor theorists—and the ideas of Bruce Michelson, Gregg Camfield, and Louis Budd—to mention three Mark Twain humor theorists—could certainly be fruitfully applied to the question instead.

I focus predominantly on Freud for several reasons. First, as a contemporary of Twain's, his ideas on humor respond to many of the same cultural and historical influences that Twain experienced. Second, Freud repeatedly cites Twain in *Jokes and Their Relation to the Unconscious*—clearly, Twain played a large part in Freud's ideas on the topic. Third, Freud's ideas about the structure of jokes are very close to theoretical ideas about the structure of metaphor, the puzzle that concerns me here. Finally, looking ahead to my upcoming examination of Twain's late dream texts, Freud's ideas on jokes and humor relate to his ideas about dreams, ideas kept current by Lacan's subsequent use of Freud. Twain's humor and his obsession with dreams are two topics central to a study of his works, and a synergy between metaphor, jokes, and dreams is made possible by using Freud on all three topics.

By their nature, jokes are often ephemeral and time-bound, and it seems fitting to me to apply the theory of Freud because he was one of Twain's contemporaries, someone who heard him speak and may have met him in Vienna, as Carl Dolmetsch argues in *"Our Famous Guest": Mark Twain in Vienna*. In this regard, I find what James M. Cox writes in the preface to *Mark Twain: The Fate of Humor* also quite applicable:

> Freud not only understood humor; he understood that Mark Twain was a master humorist and used his art as an example par excellence of the humor he was defining. This should not be surprising to any student of cultural history, since Freud's psychoanalytic theory was itself a culmination of nineteenth-century thought and sensibility, of which Mark Twain was so conspicuous a part. Indeed, if one sees the century in terms of evolution, as it often inclined to see itself, then Freud is one of its highest developments. He fulfilled the innumerable impulses and struggles of nineteenth-century writers and thinkers to develop a theory of consciousness.[22]

A century ago, Freud recognized a lack of serious examination of humor: "Anyone who has at any time had occasion to enquire from the literature of aesthetics and psychology what light can be thrown on the nature of jokes and on the position they occupy will probably have to admit that jokes have not received nearly as much philosophical consideration as they deserve in view of the part they play in our mental life."[23] Happily, the lack Freud saw in 1905 no longer exists. We now have a very full "philosophical consideration" of humor, much of it by prominent Mark Twain scholars, to which interested readers can turn.

In Freud's examination of the techniques, purposes, and motives of jokes, he often comes tantalizingly close to making an explicit connection with metaphor. Time and again, his language seems to point out the similar nature of jokes and metaphors, in structure, purpose, and effect. For example, when he asserts that "[a] favourite definition of joking has long been the ability to find similarity between dissimilar things—that is, hidden similarities," he is also giving a classic definition of metaphor. In the same early attempt to establish a definition of the joke, he quotes Friedrich Theodor Vischer, who according to Freud "defines joking as the ability to bind into a unity, with surprising rapidity, several ideas which are in fact alien to one another both in their internal content and in the nexus to which they belong." Again, the similarity to metaphor is clear. Freud's summary of all the definitions of joking he finds in other theorists' writing sounds amazingly close to a catalog of definitions of metaphor: "The criteria and characteristics of jokes brought up by these authors and collected above—activity, relation to the content of our thoughts, the characteristic of playful judgement, the coupling of dissimilar things, contrasting ideas, 'sense in nonsense,' the succession of bewilderment and enlightenment, the bringing forward of what is hidden, and the peculiar brevity of wit—all this, it is true, seems to us at first so very much to the point and so easily confirmed by instances that we cannot be in any danger of underrating such views." As a final example, when he is analyzing a particular joke, he uses a term more commonly associated with metaphor studies, decades before I. A. Richards coins the term: "Here the word that is the vehicle of the joke appears at first simply to be a wrongly constructed word. . . ."[24]

To test Cohen's assertion that "metaphors are surprisingly like jokes," I turn to some actual Mark Twain jokes, with analysis that will make explicit the connections implied by Cohen and Freud. First, I should make some disavowals. I think most Twain scholars would agree that although Mark Twain was a master of humor, perhaps *the* master of humor, his humor is not particularly based on what most people would call jokes. He is given more to comic stories, hoaxes, tall tales, and burlesques; indeed, that list nearly gives the titles of the most important studies of Mark Twain's humor. In "How to Tell a Story," Twain ranks the joke quite low, disdaining the jokester's emphasis on the "nub" or "snapper," preferring instead the "high and delicate art" of the American humorous story (*CTSS2*, 201). Still, we can find any number of jokes in his collected works, jokes worthy of a close examination.

My second disavowal is about the principle I have used in selecting these jokes for examination. On the problem of identifying jokes, I defer to Freud: "It is the case, however, that in a number of instances we are in doubt whether the particular example ought to be called a joke or not. . . . In coming to our decision we can base ourselves on nothing but a certain 'feeling,' which we may interpret as meaning that the decision is made in our judgement in accordance with particular criteria that are not yet accessible to our knowledge."[25] Despite a sense that Freud is perhaps indulging in a clever dodge, I think he accurately describes the way most of us know we are in the presence of a joke; thus, a joke is not only related to the unconscious by what it reveals after it is told, but is identified by the unconscious at the very moment of experience.

My first example comes from *The Innocents Abroad*, the shipboard celebration of the Fourth of July:

> But I digress. The thunder of our two brave cannon announced the Fourth of July, at daylight to all who were awake. But many of us got our information at a later hour, from the almanac. All the flags were sent aloft, except half a dozen that were needed to decorate portions of the ship below, and in a short time the vessel assumed a holiday appearance. During the morning, meetings were held and all manner of committees set to work on the celebration ceremonies. In the afternoon the ship's company assembled aft, on deck, under the awnings; the flute, the asthmatic melodeon, and the consumptive clarinet, crippled the "Star-Spangled Banner," the choir chased it to cover, and George came in with a peculiarly lacerating screech on the final note and slaughtered it. Nobody mourned.
>
> We carried out the corpse on three cheers (that joke was not intentional and I do not endorse it). . . . (*IA*, 92)

First, we could look, in Cohen's terms, at the sense of community this joke creates: the concealed invitation in asking the American reader to share in memories of July 4th celebrations, the acceptance of the invitation as the reader makes that connection, then the acknowledgment of a community when the reader recognizes the punch line and either laughs or groans. Metaphorical language lies at the heart of the joke, both its set-up and its punch line. We can see this especially in the metaphoric nature of the verbs: "the flute, the asthmatic melodeon, and the consumptive clarinet, *crippled* the 'Star-Spangled Banner,' the choir *chased* it to cover, and George came in with a peculiarly lacerating screech on the final note and *slaughtered* it. Nobody *mourned*" (*IA*, 92; my emphasis). These verbs function simultaneously as metaphors and jokes, and set up the progression that culminates in the punch line: "We carried out the corpse on three cheers" (*IA*, 92). The song is a corpse only metaphorically, made so by the metaphorical progression of verbs. Even the play on words that is the heart of the joke has a metaphoric element: a corpse might literally be carried out on three chairs, but to do so on three cheers is clearly figurative. The joke turns on an unexpected shift of our expectations, from the literal picture to the metaphoric pun. This is an example of what Freud would call "displacement," which he defines as "a shifting of the psychical emphasis."[26] Such displacement, such a psychical shift of emphasis, is precisely what happens in a metaphor. Joke and metaphor do indeed seem quite similar, and at times identical, indistinguishable.

The narrator, of course, claims that the joke is not intentional and refuses to endorse it, but clearly the joke is not only intentional but also carefully constructed, largely through the metaphoric build-up. To quote Freud again, we could say, "But here, as so often, a jest betrays something serious."[27] Before ever setting foot on European soil, this narrator, a champion of democratic principles, metaphorically kills off "The Star-Spangled Banner," a fact we may forget as he goes on his vandal attack on Europe and the Holy Land. That other running joke—the repeated question "Is he dead?"—is directed at Old World targets, but it has been preceded by a question directed at the New World. But part of the target is Mark Twain himself, calling attention to the (lame) joke at the same time he makes a disavowal. I do not think it is pushing things to say that this kind of disavowal reveals a certain anxiety on his part at being what he termed elsewhere "a mere humorist."

A sketch from 1876, "The Canvasser's Tale," has an extended joke about the canvasser's uncle and his collection of echoes, and this joke shows us the uses Twain could make of absurdity. In the last chapter, I briefly acknowledged the fine simile in the middle of this joke, but the whole joke, which has several parts, bears examination. The canvasser has come to Mark Twain's door and is telling him his story, which involves recounting his uncle's purchase of echoes:

His first purchase was an echo in Georgia that repeated four times; his next was a six-repeater in Maryland; his next was a thirteen-repeater in Maine; his next was a nine-repeater in Kansas; his next was a twelve-repeater in Tennessee, which he got cheap, so to speak, because it was out of repair, a portion of the crag which reflected it having tumbled down. He believed he could repair it at a cost of a few thousand dollars, and, by increasing the elevation with masonry, treble the repeating capacity; but the architect who undertook the job had never built an echo before, and so he utterly spoiled this one. Before he meddled with it, it used to talk back like a mother-in-law, but now it was only fit for the deaf and dumb asylum. (*CTSS1*, 669)

The simile that provides the interim punch line to this joke is, as I said before, a fine one, but it points up the absurdity of the whole scenario. In Cohen's terms, there is an invitation, a recognition, and a kind of community, but it is less a sharing than a being trapped. Just as Mark Twain has been trapped into hearing this man's increasingly absurd story, the reader is trapped into reading it, as is common in shaggy-dog stories like "The Canvasser's Tale." Unlike the swiftness of most jokes, the shaggy-dog variety depends for its humor on the speaker's carrying his story to great lengths, and the hearer's willingly letting the story ramble on.

The extended metaphor of echoes being compared to guns, the "six-repeater" repetition, is made evident as the canvasser continues, taking the joke to a different level: "Well, next he bought a lot of cheap little double-barreled echoes, scattered around over various States and Territories; he got them at twenty per cent. off by taking the lot. Next he bought a perfect Gatling gun of an echo in Oregon, and it cost a fortune, I can tell you" (*CTSS1*, 669). The Gatling gun reference ends that extended metaphor, and then an extended comparison to diamonds begins: "You may know, sir, that in the echo market the scale of prices is cumulative, like the carat-scale in diamonds; in fact, the same phraseology is used. A single-carat echo is worth but ten dollars over and above the value of the land it is on; a two-carat or double-barreled echo is worth thirty dollars; a five-carat is worth nine hundred and fifty; a ten-carat is worth thirteen thousand" (*CTSS1*, 669). The speaker's tedious delineation of the metaphor sets us up for the finish of the joke: "My uncle's Oregon echo, which he called the Great Pitt Echo, was a twenty-two carat gem, and cost two hundred and sixteen thousand dollars—they threw the land in, for it was four hundred miles from a settlement" (*CTSS1*, 669). The uncle is "sold," just as the hearer of such a joke always is. By the end of the tale, Mark Twain is "sold," too. He interrupts the canvasser as he tries to sell him some echoes, complaining bitterly of all the canvassers he has faced that day, ending with his own absurd comment: "I would not have one of your echoes if you were even to give it to me. I would not let it stay on the place. I always hate a man that tries to sell me echoes" (*CTSS1*, 672). By now, the reader is caught up in a totally absurd and insane world. The only conclusion to such a world can be another joke, another metaphor: "I bought two double-barreled echoes in good condition, and he threw in another, which he said was not salable because it only spoke German. He said, 'She was a perfect polyglot once, but somehow her palate got down'" (*CTSS1*, 672). The German comment would have been a good joke in itself, but the addition takes it to another level. We are all sold by the end, caught once again by the man who, to speak metaphorically, trades in echoes—and who, in his time, sold those words door to door through canvassers.

In his chapter "Pleasure and the Genesis of Jokes," Freud terms the last of three categories of jokes he examines as "conceptual jokes," giving examples of "faulty thinking, displacements, absurdity, representation by the opposite, etc." This kind of joking, Freud says, gives us pleasure because we once enjoyed putting words together randomly as children, while acquiring language, but as we grow up, rationality and the rules of logic make us give up our pleasurable childhood play. Thus, he says, "'Pleasure in nonsense,' as we may call it for short, is concealed in life to a vanishing point."[28] The kind of absurd humor Mark Twain indulges in in "The Canvasser's Tale," and in so much of his humor, especially early in his career, might therefore be seen as a kind of rebelliousness against the restraints of rationality, perhaps even of the conscious itself. The subversive power of the unconscious erupts in jokes like the absurd buying and selling of echoes, and brings pleasure to both the teller and the hearer.

In *Adventures of Huckleberry Finn*, Mark Twain is at the height of his powers, comic and otherwise, but the humor in that novel is not based primarily on what we would call jokes. Because of Huck's character and his literal vision, he is not conscious of his few jokes, such as his saying that he "could say the multiplication table up to six times seven is thirty-five," or when he tells us that "Jim said bees wouldn't sting idiots; but I didn't believe that, because I had tried them lots of times myself, and they wouldn't sting me" (*HF*, 18, 55). Freud would call the first a "naive joke," and the second an example of "the comic" rather than a joke at all. One very clear joke I have already mentioned, Buck Grangerford's riddle about where Moses was when the candle went out, has some interesting metaphoric overtones that make it worth revisiting. When Huck arrives at Buck's house, he can put on Buck's clothes, but he cannot put on Buck's boyish affinity for riddles. As I have said, Huck doesn't see that Buck is telling a riddle, and his inability to see, to recognize the joke, is more humorous than the joke itself. In Cohen's terms, he refuses to accept Buck's invitation of intimacy, of community, by not recognizing the terms of the joke, or indeed the concept of jokes in general. Buck immediately afterward asks, "Say, how long are you going to stay here? You got to stay always" (*HF*, 135). He won't and can't—and this inability to join Buck's community is first signaled by the failure of the joke. In Freud's definition, this joke again turns on a displacement, on a shift in emphasis from where in space Moses might have been to where anyone is once the candle goes out. Huck's insistence on the literal—wanting to know which candle, then wanting to know why Buck would ask a question he already knows the answer to—blinds him not only to the joke, but also to the psychical shift that gives pleasure, in Freud's terms.[29] As I said before, like Buck's Moses, Huck is "in the dark." And of course, in one of the novel's extended metaphors, Huck really is "like Moses," repeatedly compared to him, this joking reference linking Moses and the Bulrushers in the beginning to Huck's Moses-like activities in freeing Jim in the end.

Mark Twain often made himself the object of his own jokes, as in this passage from "Taming the Bicycle," written probably in 1886, but not published in his lifetime. The instructor makes this graphic comparison when checking Mark Twain's fitness to ride:

> Before taking final leave of me, my instructor inquired concerning my physical strength, and I was able to inform him I hadn't any. He said that that was a defect which would make up-hill wheeling pretty difficult for me at first; but he also said the bicycle would soon remove it. The contrast between his muscles and mine was quite marked. He wanted to test mine, so I offered my biceps—which was my best. It almost made him smile. He said, "It is pulpy, and soft, and yielding, and rounded; it evades pressure, and glides from under the fingers; in the dark a body might think it was an oyster in a rag." (*CTSS1*, 896)

This joke on his own shortcomings is a standard pose for the persona of Mark Twain, carefully constructed early on, especially in *Roughing It*. The intimacy with the reader such self-deprecation builds helps explain much of the appeal of this character called Mark Twain. As is so often the case in his supposedly autobiographical sketches, we feel that we are in the text ourselves, that, in this case, the instructor is talking about *our* "oyster in a rag." The joke of the passage continues, by the way: "Perhaps this made me look grieved, for he added, briskly: 'Oh, that 's all right; you need n't worry about that; in a little while you can't tell it from a petrified kidney. Just go along with your practice; you're all right'" (*CTSS1*, 896). One wonders: do we really want to develop our muscles into petrified kidneys?

The jokiest, and as I have argued, most metaphorical, of all Twain's narrators is Hank Morgan, whose early joking metaphor in *A Connecticut Yankee in King Arthur's Court* in reply to Clarence's assertion that he is a page—"Go 'long. . . . you ain't more than a paragraph" (*CY*, 61)—serves several functions. As with Huck and Buck, the joke is a failure in the sense that it fails to produce community between teller and hearer, since Clarence doesn't have the context to get the joke. The community established is between Hank and the reader, and serves to align us against the sixth century as Hank diminishes it—here, in a metaphoric joke that stands for his larger reduction of all that is medieval. This is an example of what Freud calls "condensation," a reduction combined with substitution and with displacement, the other central technique of jokes he identifies. These concepts hint at a tantalizing tie to metaphor studies, central as they are to Jakobson's formulation of metaphor and metonymy and to Freud's (and Lacan's) interpretation of dreams.

Hank's description of Clarence again produces community between him and the reader, as metaphorically, Hank describes Clarence in overtly feminine figures, perhaps reducing more than merely his page to a paragraph: "This was an airy slim boy in shrimp-colored tights that made him look like a forked carrot; the rest of his gear was blue silk and dainty laces and ruffles; and he had long yellow curls, and wore a plumed pink satin cap tilted complacently over his ear. By his look, he was good-natured; by his gait, he was satisfied with himself. He was pretty enough to frame" (*CY*, 22). The joke is patently hostile, but its implications are simultaneously obscured and revealed in the figurative language. Once again, in Freudian terms, "a jest betrays something serious." "A joke," Freud says, "will allow us to exploit something ridiculous in our enemy which we could not, on account of obstacles in the way, bring forward openly or consciously; once again, then, the joke *will evade restrictions and open sources of pleasure that have become inaccessible*" (Freud's emphasis).[30] At this early point in his story, Hank cannot comprehend the sixth century, much less defeat it. His first recourse is to hostile humor, and tellingly, to an embattled-male response, metaphorically relegating a male adversary to the realm of the feminine.

Perhaps it is in his maxims, those included in Pudd'nhead Wilson's two Calendars, as well as a wealth of others, that Mark Twain makes his best jokes, as William Gibson argues in a chapter on the maxims in *Mark Twain and the Art of Fiction*. Gibson looks at several of them explicitly as metaphors, noting that "[m]etaphor was one of Mark Twain's strong 'holds' as a wrestler with language." Here, Gibson is making a metaphor himself, and is no doubt silently echoing Twain's previously cited metaphorical comment in "The McWilliamses and the Burglar Alarm": "Your sentiments do you honor, but if you will allow me to say it, metaphor is not your best hold" (*CTSS1*, 838). Gibson highlights the metaphorical nature of several of the maxims:

> He hangs a long maxim on a business metaphor: "Do not undervalue the headache. While it is at its sharpest it seems a bad investment; but when relief begins, the unexpired remainder is worth $4 a minute." Or he creates metaphors with a simple, ironic comparison in "He is as modest as a maxim," or "He is as self conceited as a proverb"; or, in a sharp reversal of the anti-Semitic stereotype, "As charitable as a Jew—." But how profoundly he *could* plunge appears in the rare, wholly serious metaphorical insight in which he appears to look back to Melville and forward to O'Neill: "Every one is a moon, and has a dark side which he never shows to anybody." Later, he delivers this variant: "Men and women—even man and wife are foreigners. Each has reserves that the other cannot enter into, nor understand. These have the effect of frontiers."

I am not sure I would agree with Gibson that the remarkable "every one is a moon" maxim is wholly serious; with no pun intended, I would argue that it has a degree of dark humor. But its genius and insight are inarguable; Twain suggests with this pithy statement the psychology of the unconscious that Freud and others had not yet embarked on exploring. Twain showed us more of his dark side than almost anyone previously had, or at least he wrote about it, even if he did not allow much of it to be published during his lifetime. Jokes, as Freud argued, reveal the unconscious, and Twain was beginning late in his career to do just that, first in jokes, later, and much more fully, in his dream narratives.[31]

The metaphoric structure and function of many of these maxims is quite evident. I begin with the first one I ever heard, indeed the first way I ever heard of Mark Twain, at the dinner table, every time we ate cauliflower, a maxim quoted by my late father. The full quotation is from *Pudd'nhead Wilson*: "Training is everything. The peach was once a bitter almond; cauliflower is nothing but cabbage with a college education" (*PWET*, 23). The comparisons at the heart of this maxim are memorable because they are so original and visual. One sees the peach pit at the center of the fruit, and even more, one sees the wrinkles and folds of the white cauliflower, the developed brains of the formerly untrained "cabbage head," a common southern metaphorical insult for a fool. If Twain had written nothing else than the maxims contained in the two Pudd'nhead Wilson Calendars and published that as one slim volume, a certain literary fame would have already been won.

As is common for Twain, he makes great use of animal metaphors in the maxims. He liked this feline comparison so much that he used it in both *Pudd'nhead Wilson* and *Following the Equator:* "One of the most striking differences between a cat and a lie is that a cat only has nine lives" (*PWET,* 30; *FE,* 622). Like both a good joke and a good metaphor, the humor and the comparison hit with force, then grow upon further reflection. The comparison between animals and humans is implied here, but is explicit in a maxim about dogs: "If you pick up a starving dog and make him prosperous, he will not bite you. This is the principal difference between a dog and a man" (*PWET,* 80). In others, the connection is even more explicit: "Consider well the proportion of things. It is better to be a young June-bug than an old bird of paradise" (*PWET,* 33). Or one from *Following the Equator* that I think of sometimes during faculty meetings: "Noise proves nothing. Often a hen who has merely laid an egg cackles as if she had laid an asteroid" (*FE,* 77). As he did throughout his career, Twain used animals to hit his human target. By the end, he was nearly consumed by the metaphor of man as "the lowest animal."

Perhaps in the case of Mark Twain, to paraphrase and subvert Freud's famous saying, "humor is the royal road to the unconscious." But for Freud, although jokes were a useful road to travel to that mysterious land, it was of course dreams that provided the metaphorical "royal road." He published his book on jokes in 1905, six years after he published the first version of *The Interpretation of Dreams,* and he finds in jokes many of the same processes that he said operate in dreams. His terms "displacement" and "condensation" are key to the similarity, as he recognizes early in *Jokes and Their Relation to the Unconscious:* "We cannot doubt that in both cases we are faced by the same psychical process, which we may recognize from its identical results. Such a far-reaching analogy between the technique of jokes and the dream-work will undoubtedly increase our interest in the former and raise an expectation in us that a comparison between jokes and dreams may help to throw light on jokes." Near the end of the book, he takes up the topic again: "Let us now recall what it was during our investigation of jokes that gave us occasion to think of dreams. We found that the characteristics and effects of jokes are linked with certain forms of expression or technical methods, among which the most striking are condensation, displacement and indirect representation. Processes, however, which lead to the same results—condensation, displacement and indirect representation—have become known to us as peculiarities of the dream-work." The difference between jokes and dreams, Freud says, "lies in their social behavior." The distinction is important:

> A dream is a completely asocial mental product; it has nothing to communicate to anyone else; it arises within the subject as a compromise between the mental forces struggling in him, it remains unintelligible to the subject himself and is for that reason totally uninteresting to other people. Not only does it not need to set any store by intelligibility, it must actually avoid being understood, for otherwise it would be destroyed; it can only exist in masquerade. For that reason it can without hindrance make use of the mechanism that dominates unconscious mental processes, to the point of a distortion which can no longer be set straight.

When he discusses jokes, his point reminds us of what Cohen says about the social function of metaphor: "A joke, on the other hand, is the most social of all the mental functions that aim at a yield of pleasure. It often calls for three persons and its completion requires the participation of someone else in the mental process it starts. The condition of intelligibility is, therefore, binding on it; it may only make use of possible distortion in the unconscious through condensation and displacement up to the point at which it can be set straight by the third person's understanding."[32] Like a metaphor, a joke calls for what Cohen terms "the acknowledgment of a community." Twain's skill with both humor and metaphor might help to explain the close psychic bond he has gained with so many readers. I indulge in a personal anecdote to illustrate the point, but I am sure that many other Twain scholars share this experience: when a new acquaintance asks me what I do, and I say I am an English professor, invariably this news is met with a visible grimace, and often, with an audible groan. If the person asks me what I work on, when I say "Mark Twain," what a difference! The grimace is replaced by a smile, the groan by a laugh. Somehow, I don't think this would be the response if my answer were, for example, "Henry James."

Freud's concluding point takes his argument a step deeper, and underscores one of the reasons that jokes, seemingly so unimportant and perhaps even a waste of time, are actually so vitally important to all humans, as important in their own way as dreams:

> Moreover, jokes and dreams have grown up in quite different regions of mental life and must be allotted to points in the psychological system far

remote from each other. A dream still remains a wish, even though one that has been made unrecognizable; a joke is developed play. Dreams, in spite of all their practical nonentity, retain their connection with the major interests of life; they seek to fulfill needs by the regressive detour of hallucination, and they are permitted to occur for the sake of the one need that is active during the night—the need to sleep. Jokes, on the other hand, seek to gain a small yield of pleasure from the mere activity, untrammelled by needs, of our mental apparatus and thus arrive *secondarily* at not unimportant functions directed to the external world. Dreams serve predominantly for the avoidance of unpleasure, jokes for the attainment of pleasure; but all our mental activities converge in these two aims.[33]

For this comparison of jokes and dreams, Freud leans heavily on metaphor, without ever saying so explicitly. By a process of triangulation, I arrive at a merging of metaphor, joke, and dream.

IV. Figuring the Dream: Metaphor in Mark Twain's Dream Narratives

Both Mark Twain's career and my study of the way he used metaphor lead me inexorably to dreams. In the last ten or twelve years of his life, Twain wrote obsessively, but almost never to completion, about dreams. Freud moved from jokes to dreams in his quest to understand the unconscious, and I believe that Twain was on a similar quest, almost simultaneously with Freud. Freud's ideas on dreams are implicitly tied to metaphor, and Jakobson makes that tie explicit with his concept of the opposition of metaphor and metonymy. Jacques Lacan unites the two paired concepts and identifies figurative language as the key to understanding the unconscious. The dream narratives, then, not only provide the proper ending for an exploration of Mark Twain and metaphor, but also unite Twain with some of the most important psychological and philosophical ideas of the past century.

Dreams and metaphor have been bound together since at least the biblical Joseph, but they have been particularly bound together in our last century, first with Freud's and then with Lacan's dream theories. "The interpretation of dreams is the royal road to a knowledge of the unconscious activities of the mind," Freud said in his famous formulation. Freud's metaphor—comparing the dream to a royal road—hints at how close he came to explicitly linking metaphor and metonymy to his dream theory. Jakobson made the link explicit when he cast Freud's dream symbolism in terms of contiguity and similarity: "Thus in an inquiry into the structure of dreams, the decisive question is whether the symbols and the temporal sequences used are based on contiguity (Freud's metonymic 'displacement' and synecdochic 'condensation') or on similarity (Freud's 'identification and symbolism')." Lacan combined Freud's and Jakobson's insights, linking condensation with metaphor and displacement with metonymy. The two poles are set in opposition, with metaphor revealing symptom, and metonymy "eternally stretching forth towards the *desire for something else*." Using a metaphor himself, Lacan asserts that "the unconscious is structured in the most radical way like a language."[34] That structure is based on the opposition of metaphor and metonymy, which for Lacan is the key to "reading" dreams, to knowing and decoding the language of the unconscious.

I contend that Twain was attempting no less than a representation of the unconscious, that he had glimpsed something and was heroically trying to translate it for himself and for his audience. That is why he wrote so much, and always on the same topic; that is why he wrote in fragments. By examining the dream narratives in light of figurative language, I argue that rather than evidence of Mark Twain's failure as an artist, these late works constitute his brave attempt to solve a human mystery and communicate it to himself and others.

The translation of dream to text is problematic. As Freud points out, the extreme amount of condensation in dreams makes them difficult to work with. "Dreams are brief, meagre and laconic in comparison with the range and wealth of the dream-thoughts," Freud declares; he continues, "If a dream is written out it may perhaps fill half a page. The analysis setting out the dream-thoughts underlying it may occupy six, eight or a dozen times as much space." The dream is not a text, but we can only consciously deal with it *as* a text. Noting the confusion that always surrounds dreams, Meredith Ann Skura, in *The Literary Use of the Psychoanalytic Process*, makes this point: "Dreams always seem to mean more than the wakened dreamer can discern. In part this is because he never has the original dream before him. Dreams, if told, are always *re*told; we know about them only after we have lost them—and lost our original 'reading' of the hallucinatory experience, which we did not realize we had to interpret at all. We look back at dreams, puzzled." Skura elaborates: "The gap between dreaming and telling is only partly responsible for the confusion, however. Even if the wakened dreamer seems to describe his dream exactly, he always misreads it at first, if he takes it literally. There is always another gap as well—a gap between the commonsense interpretation of the dream and some other interpretation behind it."[35] As an artist, Mark Twain took dreams and retold them as texts—but as texts that unfold as dreams, with all the puzzles and gaps left in place before us.

The conventional view of Mark Twain's late career has been that he suffered a descent into abject pessimism along with a sharp loss of creativity.[36] The predominance of fragmentary writings and the seemingly obsessive repetition of themes, especially his nightmare narratives, have made Twain's late career appear to be a sharp falling off from his earlier work. The usual explanation for his pessimism and loss of creativity is biographical, and that evidence is certainly compelling: his business failures, especially of the Paige typesetter; his bankruptcy; his frantic around-the-world lecture tour; the deaths of his daughters and his wife; his own battles with illness and old age. But these late works, especially the dream fragments, are richly compelling, and perhaps they are not failures: if we read them as explorations of the dream state, of the unconscious, we may see them in a quite different way.

Four fragmentary dream narratives, written from 1896 to 1898, provide us with enticing glimpses into Twain's exploration of dreams. The pieces themselves are dreamlike: fragments that begin in the middle, that lack transitions, that have missing pages, that end abruptly. They share so many elements that they seem to be almost a single text, with events and images that recur in nightmarish fashion. At the heart of these dream texts—"The Passenger's Story," "The Enchanted Sea-Wilderness," "Which Was the Dream?," and "The Great Dark"—lies metaphor, at the level of figurative language, but more broadly, in the metaphoric operation and structure of dreams.[37]

In *The Interpretation of Dreams*, Freud explains that a dream often contains some elements from recent daily life, mixed with events from much earlier in our lives, as well as with repressed wishes from the unconscious, with the images in the dream condensed and displaced to disguise from our conscious minds their true, unconscious meanings. The dream is like a rebus, Freud maintained, again using metaphorical language to make his point. The key to dream interpretation is to read the rebus, solve the puzzle. In his return to Freud, Lacan also focuses on the puzzles in dreams, which he metaphorically calls "knots" or "nodes." The dream narrative is an endless metonymic chain of desires, punctuated by an irruption into the text of metaphoric symptoms. Again using metaphor, Lacan likens the metaphors to the buttons on upholstery—the metaphoric "buttons" holding the dream together and giving us the clue to its interpretation. Focusing on figurative language is the key to reading Twain's dream texts.

"It was on an American liner—couple of years ago," the first of these, "The Passenger's Story" (1896), begins flatly. The narrator is alone in the dark, "doing nothing," he says, then correcting himself: "That is, *thinking*" (*DRT*,

25). Solitary, after midnight, in the dark: the narrator is describing his situation on the upper deck of the ship, but he could well be describing the dream state. Using a metaphor, the narrator says, "Nobody stirring; the whole deck was a solitude" (*DRT,* 25). The solitude is interrupted by the appearance of "two dim figures"—he means that they are people, but they come to us out of the dream text as seemingly figurative. They are already in the midst of talk, one with a deep voice, the other with "a little hacking cough" (*DRT,* 25). To the narrator, they are both still metaphorical: "they were just shapeless blots in the gloom" (*DRT,* 25). The man with the bass voice is talking about a dog that saved his life and the lives of his crew of fourteen men. His description of the dog is dotted with metaphor and simile: "He came aboard at the dock, racing around with his nose down, hunting for somebody that had been there—his master, I reckon—and the crew captured him and shut him below, and we sailed in a hour. Well, sir, he was just a darling, that dog. Inside of a week he was the pet of the whole crew. He was brim full of play, and fun and affection and good nature. They bedded him like the *aristocracy,* and there warn't a *man* but would divide his dinner with him; and he was the lovingest creature and the *gratefulest* you ever saw" (*DRT,* 25–26). As will recur in the dream narratives, the conditions of the telling are themselves dreamlike: "it was *warm,* and *still* and *drowsy* and *lazy;* and the sails hung *idle,* and the deck-watch and the lookout and everybody *else* was sound *asleep*" (*DRT,* 26). We find ourselves in a dream within a dream within a dream—aroused to action by the dog's discovery of a fire. The man follows the dog to the fire in the hold, where he removes powder kegs that would have burned up the whole ship.

At this moment in the manuscript, a page is missing, which makes the fragment seem even more like an actual dream. As in a dream, the scene abruptly changes, and the ship is now fully ablaze and all the crew except the speaker in boats to escape. The speaker, the captain of the crew, then does the inexplicable: "I tied the dog to the foot of the *main*mast and then got in my*self* and took the *tiller* and said 'All ready—give *way*'" (*DRT,* 26). The crew protests mightily, and crying, they say, "Why he saved our lives— we *can't* leave him" (*DRT,* 26). The speaker replies in a jarring, incongruous figure, a figure that will be repeated in subsequent dream narratives: "You don't know what you're *talking* about. He'd be more in the way than a family of *children*—and he can *eat* as much as a family of children, too. Now men, *you know me*—and I pulled a *revolver*" (*DRT,* 26–27). Again a page is missing, and the dream has shifted to the dog's reaction as he is abandoned to the fire: "[the dog] tugged at his rope, and begged and moaned and yelped—why it was as plain as if he was *saying,* Oh, *don't* leave me, *please* don't leave me, *I* haven't done any harm. And then presently the fire swept down on him and he sent up two or three *awful* shrieks and it was all over" (*DRT*, 27). The crew's reaction is linked to the captain's incongruous simile: "And the men sat sobbing and crying like children" (*DRT*, 27). The other speaker, now identified as "H." (a metonymy for his "hacking cough"?) threatens the bass-voice speaker: "It was the vilest murder that was ever *done*—and I hope you will land in hell before you are an hour *older*" (*DRT*, 27). The last sentence of the narrative, of the dream, ends in mid-sentence, shifting the focus back to the passenger: "I heard a blow struck, then another and *another*; the ship gave a heavy *lurch* and the two vague forms came" (*DRT*, 27).

The reader awakes, disturbed, puzzled. What has happened? What does this all mean? The narrative makes no sense, yet it is richly suggestive, and the metaphors, especially the figurative linkage of the dog with children, remain in the mind, just below the level of understanding. Some kind of sense is trying to break through in the figures of the nightmare. This short but disturbing dream is our first step into the dream world, the nightmare world, that Twain explored so repeatedly, so obsessively, in his last years.

The dream is fleshed out more fully in "The Enchanted Sea-Wilderness," also written in 1896. This longer fragment begins with another narrator aboard a ship who describes an encounter with a "bronzed and gray sailor" who tells him stories about strange areas of the ocean "where no compass has any value" (*DRT*, 28). The narrator's opening remarks frame the tale in a figurative sense: "When the compass enters one of these bewitched domains it goes insane and whirls this way and that and settles nowhere, and is scared and distressed, and cannot be comforted" (*DRT*, 28). The metaphorical description of the compass prefigures the dream. Like the tale about to unfold, the dream "whirls this way and that and settles nowhere." Similarly, it prefigures the reader's reaction: "scared and distressed, and cannot be comforted." The great becalmed circles of the Enchanted Sea-Wilderness are given two further metaphoric names: the Devil's Race-Track and the Everlasting Sunday, an incongruous juxtaposition, the names seemingly contradictory, but the overall effect chilling.

The old sailor's story begins realistically enough, naming the time, December 1853; his ship, the *Mabel Thorpe;* and his captain, Elliot Cable. In the second paragraph of his embedded narrative, we are back to the story of the "lovely big beautiful dog" who wanders aboard and is taken up by the crew. This account is repeated almost verbatim from "The Passenger's Story," including the metaphorical language calling the dog "a darling" and the crew bedding "him like the *aristocracy*" (*DRT*, 29). An added section personifies the dog more fully than before: "He elected of his own notion to stand watch and watch with us. He was in the larboard watch, and he would turn out at eight bells without anybody having to tell him it was 'Yo-ho, the larboard watch!' And he would tug at all the ropes and help make sail or take it in, and seemed to know all about it, just like any old veteran. The crew were proud of him—well, of course they would be" (*DRT*, 29).

As the story continues, metaphorical descriptions signal the slide into dream: "It was warm that night, and still and drowsy and lazy; and the sails hung idle, and the deck-watch and the lookout and everybody else was sound asleep, including the dog, for it was his trick below and he had turned in at midnight" (*DRT*, 29). Again, the dog warns the captain of a fire below, the story repeated verbatim again, this time with the missing pages restored. (Twain may have pulled these pages from the earlier manuscript rather than copying them over, leaving them with the longer and more recently attempted story.) The effect on the reader is of a dream repeated, but amplified—as well as a sense of plunging yet again into nightmare. The crew hugs the dog, but the captain rebukes them, linking the crew figuratively with the animal: "You may well hug him, you worthless hounds! he saved my life, not you, you lazy rips. I've never cared for dogs before, but next time I hear people talking against them I'll put in a word for this one, anyway" (*DRT*, 30). Again, the powder kegs that would spell the ship's ruin are tossed overboard, this time with the dog's help—and again, the captain ties the dog to the mast before boarding the boat with the crew. The same scene replays, again with the captain's strange metaphor comparing the dog to "a family of children," and again, after seeing the St. Bernard (his breed is named this time) burned alive, "the men sat there crying like children" (*DRT*, 31). The dream has been fleshed out more fully, but the metaphoric nodes remain the same, with the same unsettling and puzzling effect on the reader.

But this time, the story continues. They encounter a ship, and, remarkably, not a strange ship. In all of the vast ocean, they have found their ship's twin, its sister: "and it happened that we knew her, and knew her crew, too; for she was sister to our ship and belonged to the same house, and was loaded at the same dock with us, and with the same kind of cargo. . . . She had left port a week or ten days ahead of us, but we could outsail her on a wind" (*DRT*, 32). This ship has lost its captain, but his widow and daughter are aboard. A family, on a ship—a situation metaphorically predicted by the captain in his renunciation of the dog. The rest of the narrative recounts their discovery of other becalmed ships with, literally, skeleton crews. The narrative ends, again, in mid-sentence.

Ships in an enchanted but devilish calm, dogs burned alive after hero-ism, a strong-willed but hard-hearted captain, a fearful and tearful crew—all of these repeated elements linked metaphorically by the repeated phrase "a family of children"—and now, as the dream/nightmare progresses, an actual child, a family, on board the ship. With these dream elements in place, Twain next turned to a quite different story, but one that would provide a bridge to the longer dream that ties all these elements together.

"Which Was the Dream?" (1897) is much longer than the two earlier dream fragments, and this time the focus *begins* with domestic life, with the family, rather than with the sea. In a diary entry from Mrs. Alison X., the details of planning for a child's birthday party mark the scene as realistic, but an odd element intrudes to give the opening an unsettling quality, the kind of illogical explanation one accepts readily in a dream but rejects in waking life: a play is being set up to be staged "in the north end of the picture gallery," with an asterisked note reading, "We call it the picture gallery because it isn't. It is the ball room" (*DRT*, 39). Alison writes of her husband, Tom; her daughters, Bessie and Jessie; Bessie's upcoming birthday on March 19; and her husband's long-delayed plans to write "a little sketch of his life for the children to have when we are gone" (*DRT*, 39). As the diary entry continues, she notes that her husband has been writing, but he is drowsing and falling asleep while smoking a cigar as he continues to write. Her opening frames the story and suggests that waking reality and dreamy unconsciousness cannot be clearly distinguished.

The abrupt switch to "Major General X.'s Story" begins the sketch of his life, with a childhood that reminds us of *Tom Sawyer* in its nostalgic tone, yet is odd and dreamlike. In the midst of a seemingly realistic autobiography, references to dreams and dreaming are constant. "Our days were a dream," he comments, explicitly making a metaphor that recurs throughout the fragment: "Every morning one or the other of us laughed and said, 'Another day gone, and it isn't a dream *yet*'" (*DRT*, 44, 46). A sense of foreboding lies over the seemingly happy story of courtship, a young wife and husband, his rise in politics and the military, the building of an expensive home in Washington on the wife's money: "For we had the same thought, and it was a natural one: that the night might rob us, some time or other, and we should wake bereaved" (*DRT*, 46). In Twain's dream world, night robs us, dreams rob us.

In a new section called "Postscript," again with an abrupt switch that departs from the conventions of autobiographical writing and marks the story as more like the unlinked fragments of dreaming, Tom switches his account to the children, Bessie and Jessie. He describes the two in metaphorical and metonymical terms:

> For Bessie is a thinker—a poet—a dreamer; a creature made up of intellect, imagination, feeling. She is an exquisite little sensitive plant, shrinking and timorous in the matter of pain, and is full of worshiping admiration of Jessie's adventurous ways and manly audacities. Privately we call Bessie "Poetry," and Jessie "Romance"—because in the one case the name fits, and in the other it doesn't. The children could not pronounce these large names in the beginning, therefore they shortened them to Potie and Romie, and so they remain. (DRT, 48)

In Jakobson's terms, Bessie is the metaphorical "poetry," and Jessie is the metonymical "adventure"—although they incongruously refer to her as "Romance," another odd misnaming detail. Bessie is explicitly linked with dreams, with nightmares: "Like most people, Bessie is pestered with recurrent dreams. Her stock dream is that she is being eaten up by bears. It is the main horror of her life" (DRT, 52). After Bessie complains that she is "never the *bear* but always the person *eaten*" (DRT, 53), Tom offers a response that is revealing about the nature of dreams and about what a writer can *do* with dreams:

> It would not occur to everybody that there might be an advantage in being the eater, now and then, seeing that it was nothing but a dream, after all, but there *is* an advantage, for while you are *in* a dream it *isn't* a dream—it is reality, and the bear-bite hurts; hurts in a perfectly real way. In the surprise which I am providing for the children to-night, Bessie will see that her persecuting dream can be turned into something quite romantically and picturesquely delightful when a person of her papa's high capacities in the way of invention puts his mind to work upon it. (DRT, 53)

This comment provides an important moment in Twain's exploration of dreams in these later years of his life: dreams are not figurative, but literal, at least during the dream state; and the creative artist can take dreams and do interesting things with them. All the comment lacks is the nightmare quality that Twain's dreams share, although that nightmare quality is provided by Bessie's very real bears.

For the purposes of examining the metaphor of Twain's dream stories, little more needs to be said about "Which Was the Dream?" The narrative is interrupted by the family's house burning down, a jarring reminder of the earlier dreams. Again, a fire, but this time without the sacrifice of a dog—the "family of children" are real, not metaphorical, and they are not harmed. The narrator repeatedly sleeps, to the point where he sleeps for eighteen months without realizing it. He awakes to the family's ruin because of his bad investments, in a turn of events that is clearly an auto-biographical reworking of Samuel Clemens's own misfortunes of the 1890s. The fragment ends before Twain can write what he projected in his notes. John Tuckey explains Twain's plan in *The Devil's Race-Track: Mark Twain's "Great Dark" Writings*:

> "Which Was the Dream?" was, as he planned it in the spring of 1897, to be a story that would begin with the burning of the family home and continue through a seventeen-year sequence of disasters, including again the voyage of a ship that would get into the Devil's Race-Track and then into the Everlasting Sunday. The narrator was at the end to find that it had all been a fifteen-second dream; yet the dream was to have been so terribly real to him that he would actually have aged by seventeen years and would upon awakening be unable to recognize his own children. (*DRT*, xii)

We can see, then, the clear linkage of this dream tale with the two previous, the ship narrative and the domestic narrative united. Twain went on to unite those two elements more fully in 1898, with his longer dream fragment, which Bernard DeVoto gave the title "The Great Dark."

DeVoto's title is apt, and it is better than Albert Bigelow Paine's title, "Statement of the Edwardses," which DeVoto calls "not only inept but misrepresentative" (*LFE*, 231). While that is true, the narrative does begin with statements from a husband and a wife, with Mrs. Edwards's statement setting up the narrative frame before the dream begins. "We were in no way prepared for this dreadful thing," she writes. "We were a happy family, we had been happy from the beginning; we did not know what trouble was, we were not thinking of it nor expecting it" (*DRT*, 80). Mrs. Edwards's narrative introduces the "happy family" and their situation—Alice and Henry Edwards, their two daughters, Jessie and Bessie, on March 19th, just before Jessie's eighth birthday party. Even though this part of the narrative is not a dream, it already feels like one to a reader of the dream fragments, the elements eerily familiar. As in "Which Was the Dream?," we begin with the wife's diary entry, then continue with the husband's story, and they have two little girls, Bessie and Jessie (this time Jessie is the birthday girl, again on March 19th). Both husbands write in shorthand, which seems curious. Both women make a point to tell us they are in the house's picture gallery, which is not a picture gallery, but a ballroom. In fact, these repetitions only set up the larger repetition of plot: over and over, a man falls asleep, then begins to realize his dream life is his real life, then wakes up to his former real life, and now can't tell which is the dream, causing extreme disillusionment and despair.

The fragments have usually been read biographically, and convincingly so, as John Tuckey notes: Mark Twain had just finished his long sea voyages as he wrote these fragments, even having twice crossed the Atlantic on the very ship he names in one of them, the *Batavia*; March 19th was Susy Clemens's birthday, and it was Susy's death at age twenty-four in 1896 that plunged Twain into deeper despair. And as Tuckey further points out, the loss of the Hartford home mirrors the loss of home that provides the central tragedy of several of the fragments (*DRT*, x). These biographical correspondences are undeniable and compelling, but merely making the biographical connection is not the end of the interpretive road. Clearly, Mark Twain's actual dreams became for him an important message from his unconscious, and his persistent attempts to transmute those dreams into fiction show us how important he felt that message to be. Beyond biography, his dream narratives show us his creative process as he delved into the mysteries of the unconscious.

In both "The Passenger's Story" and "The Enchanted Sea-Wilderness," there are references to "a family of children." But in "The Great Dark," *both* the captain of that ship and Henry Edwards have their children aboard. In a chilling moment in "The Great Dark," at the beginning of the dream, Henry nonchalantly says, "I take my family with me" (*DRT*, 83). The domestic scene repeats insistently, with not one but two families of children inappropriately aboard. Why does the captain have his family there, too? The children in "The Great Dark" seem to be a metaphoric condensation in the dream language. Their repetition, the "insistence of the letter," as Lacan called it, are the "buttons" on the fabric of the dream. Certainly one of the main messages of the dreams concerns men and their domestic identities, especially their identities as husbands and fathers. Men are on a quest, men are on an adventure, men are facing danger—but in the midst of this manly quest, they have their wives and children with them. The quest voyage is also a domestic voyage, and the mixture of those two seemingly incompatible ideas heightens the terror of the dream texts. The mixture highlights Twain's guilt over his disintegrating domestic situation, but it also stands metaphorically for the conflict between career and family.

According to Lacan, the whole interplay of the dream is really a quest for self-knowledge: "This signifying game between metonymy and metaphor, up to and including the active edge that splits my desire between a refusal of the signifier and a lack of being, and links my fate to the question of my destiny, this game, in all its inexorable subtlety, is played until the match is called, there where I am not, because I cannot situate myself there."[38] Lacan's "there where I am not" is the dream, the unconscious, structured like a language, operating in the interplay between metaphor and metonymy. The dream flows on endlessly, with metaphor appearing insistently as a clue to the interpretation of the dream.

In the story, the bridge between the wife's and the husband's narratives is provided by a description of the father amusing the children with a microscope. In Alice's narrative, Henry falls asleep and snores, then is up again, writing. When Henry begins, he is narrating what Alice has just told, but in more detail, showing us the microscopic world of the drop of water: "For a time there would be a great empty blank; then a monster would enter one horizon of this great white sea made so splendidly luminous by the reflector and go plowing across and disappear beyond the opposite horizon" (DRT, 82). At this point, Henry's narrative overlaps Alice's, at the moment where he falls asleep on the sofa. But in his version, much more apparently conscious thinking occurs: "I threw myself on the sofa profoundly impressed by what I had seen, and oppressed with thinkings. An ocean in a drop of water—and unknown, uncharted, unexplored by man! By man, who gives all his time to the Africas and the poles, with this unsearched marvelous world right at his elbow" (DRT, 82–83). Henry, of course, is already asleep, and the unknown, uncharted night land he explores is the world of the microscopic drop, which stands metaphorically for his own unconscious.

At this point, an intriguing character appears: the Superintendent of Dreams, who arranges the voyage, even as he warns Henry of the danger. Now the dream seems to begin, even though it has already begun in actuality. The voyage and the dream are comic and incongruous, which we see in the fractured nautical mixed metaphor of the sailors—or we would see if we understood enough about sailing to get the jokes, such as the phrase "mizzen foretop halyards" or a description of a sailor "bending on a scuttle-butt" (DRT, 86, 87). The comedy continues as the mate, Turner, sits in the lap of the invisible Superintendent of Dreams, who keeps drinking Turner's coffee. Why this comedy in such a tragic, terrifying tale? As Twain wrote Howells about the story, "I feel sure that all of the first half of the story—and I hope three-fourths—will be comedy; but by the former plan the whole of it (except the first 3 chapters) would have been tragedy and unendurable, almost. I think I can carry the reader a long way before he suspects that I am laying a tragedy-trap" (*MTHL*, 2:675–76). This mixture between the comic and the tragic, rather than being "a serious error in aesthetic judgment," as DeVoto argues in the editor's notes to *Letters from the Earth* (*LFE*, 237), is actually a vital part of the dream quality of the narrative: the absurd nautical talk that no one, not even the sailors, recognizes as absurd adheres precisely to dream logic, as does the blending of comedy and tragedy. That is partly because the language of the dream is different from waking language. Twain communicates that sense perfectly in all his dream narratives; what many readers have taken to be failures are actually artistic successes, if we judge him on his ability to translate the experience of dreams into a fictional narrative.

The split between comedy and tragedy is just one of a number of splits in all the stories. Just as they are repetitions, the fragments themselves are splits of each other, and split within themselves between multiple narrators, and even within the same narrator's story. In "The Great Dark," one story, "The Mad Passenger," is split apart from the main one. Jessie and Bessie are not only repetitions from story to story, but of themselves; they seem to be one daughter, split in two. We are used to splits with this writer; after all, he is Mark *Twain*. But as we have seen, we are often tricked by Twain into seeing two, when we should be seeing multiplicity.

In fact, we must expand our vision beyond dualities to see in more dimensions. Freud pointed out that in most dreams, multiple characters often stand for one character, usually the dreamer.[39] We might, then, read *all* the major male characters as Mark Twain. So when Turner, the confused but comic mate, his name perhaps a metonymic twist on "Twain," sits in the lap of the Superintendent of Dreams, who can also be seen as a part of Mark Twain, the scene helps us to understand something crucial about the fluidity of identity. The narrator tells us:

> I poured a steaming cup of coffee and handed it to Turner and told him to sit where he pleased and make himself comfortable and at home; and before I could interfere he had sat down in the Superintendent of Dreams' lap!—no, sat down *through* him. It cost me a gasp, but only that, nothing more. [The] Superintendent of Dreams' head was larger than Turner's, and *surrounded* it, and was a transparent spirit-head fronted with a transparent spirit-face; and this latter smiled at me as much as to say give myself no uneasiness, it is all right. Turner was smiling comfort and contentment at me at the same time, and the double result was very curious, but I could tell the smiles apart without trouble. The Superintendent of

Dreams' body enclosed Turner's, but I could see Turner through it, just as one sees objects through thin smoke. It was interesting and pretty. (DRT, 92)

What better metaphorical picture do we have of the Mark Twain/Samuel Clemens split than those multiple smiles coming at us through a smoky haze, smiles that we can tell apart "without trouble"? But Henry, looking at the split, is also Mark Twain, now observing his own split, hazy, smoky identity.

This moment is extremely important in Twain's exploration of dreams and, through dreams, the unconscious. Lacan's ideas about the self become crucial here. We begin our lives, Lacan says, seeing ourselves as an undifferentiated part of the mother. Sometime between the ages of six months and eighteen months, we experience what he called the "mirror stage," in which we see ourselves reflected in a mirror (or other reflective object) and, for the first time, recognize that we have a separate identity. On this realization, we first react with joy at our totality, but that feeling is soon replaced by alienation as we perceive the gap between the mirror image and our bodily experience. As Jonathan Scott Lee puts it, "From jubilation to alienation, the double movement of the mirror stage inaugurates the doubts about identity that haunt the human being throughout life." Lacan's formulation strikes at the heart of Western philosophy's concept of self, what Lee calls "the confidence that the human being is essentially a unified, autonomous subject, fully present to its own consciousness—indeed, essentially identical with this consciousness—a belief that all human knowledge can be grounded in the clear self-knowledge of this unified subject, and a conviction that the moral assessment of human actions is grounded in the human being's autonomy as a thinking, knowing subject."[40] We can begin to see here some comparisons with the Samuel Clemens/Mark Twain split. Rather than as a unified ego, this artist chose to represent himself to the world as a divided self. The Clemens/Twain split has caused us no end of controversy, but what happens if we read the supposed psychic split as a *metaphor* for the universal human condition? Twain had no knowledge of Lacan, of course, but his representation of his own "divided self" prefigures Lacan's ideas of the ego. Lacan rejected Freud's simple term "ego," substituting the French first-person personal pronouns "*moi*" and "*je*." What we think of as a "self," Lacan says, is a construction, a fiction—a fiction that we present to the world as well as to ourselves. Without going too deeply into the thicket of Lacanian theory, we can propose that the Samuel Clemens/Mark Twain split is a metaphorical image of the "*moi/je*" relationship. Psychologically, Mark Twain named himself to show us the fictional construction of his divided self—a fictional construction we all share.

Lacan's *moi* is mysterious, operating both in the conscious and the unconscious, but impossible to see fully or clearly. Ellie Ragland-Sullivan compares the *moi* to recent scientific theoretical formulations: "Akin to the Heisenberg principle in physics or the 'Compton effect' in electron microscopy (an object modifies under scrutiny), the *moi* is a dialectical project of becoming, a suspension, a set of signifying potentials, which never ceases to displace Desire along an endless chain of the incomplete story of identity." But the *moi*, Ragland-Sullivan continues, "can be intermittently grasped as repeated identity themes (signifieds)." Her list of methods for glimpsing the *moi* includes much that has been the concern of this study of Mark Twain and metaphor: "Through the mediation of another; by reading backward; by decoding language and relationships in terms of substitutions and displacements (metaphor and metonymy) for the *objet a* of Desire; by paying heed to repetitions; by reading dream texts as messages to and from the Other(A), an individual may become conscious of some of the components that went into forming the *moi*. Fragments and details can be grasped."[41] "Fragments and details can be grasped"—what better explanation can we have of Twain's process in his dream narratives? Read in this way, the dream texts are Twain's heroic attempts to confront his *moi*. The dream writings are explorations, self-explorations, the ending of a long life process that began when he named himself "Mark Twain." As we have seen, "Mark Twain" is *both* metaphor and metonymy, substitution and displacement, Symptom and Desire, flickering back and forth in an endless play of language.

But to continue with the dream: for much of the first part of "The Great Dark," Henry retains the jaunty attitude he had at the very beginning, when he speaks so boldly to the Superintendent of Dreams, not being worried about any of the dangers, about his diminished size, about the dangerous creatures to be encountered: "They have an ugly look, but I thank God I am not afraid of the ugliest that ever plowed a drop of water" (*DRT*, 83). "It is no matter; you have seen me face dangers before," he tells the Superintendent (*DRT*, 83). After all, he will only be dreaming, and he is safe in the dream. As the dream progresses, he has the attitude that we all have, even in a nightmare, once we realize that we are "only" dreaming. The mate, Turner, is increasingly upset that the water they are voyaging does not match up to the maps, that Greenland, the Gulf Stream, and even the sun have vanished. He has come to a frightening conclusion: "That the world has come to an end. Look at it yourself. Just look at the facts. Put them together and add them up, and what have you got? No Sable island; no Greenland; no Gulf Stream; no day; no proper night; weather that won't jibe with any sample known to the Bureau; animals that would start a panic in any menagerie; chart no more use than a horse-blanket, and the heavenly bodies gone to hell!" (*DRT*, 98). Still, Henry is not worried, though he does ask the Superintendent why he plays these "tricks" on the mate and the others on the ship who do not realize that the voyage is only a dream. In their long conversation that follows, Henry admits, "It is more of a voyage than I was expecting . . ." (*DRT*, 100)—and then the story takes its turn toward the tragic, when he orders the Superintendent to "stop appearing to people" and then, to end the dream: "You may like it or not, just as you choose. And moreover, if my style doesn't suit you, you can end the dream as soon as you please—right now, if you like" (*DRT*, 102). The ensuing dialogue provides another key moment in Twain's metaphorical dream explorations:

He looked at me steadily in the eye for a moment, then said, with deliberation—
"The dream? *Are you quite sure it is a dream?*"
It took my breath away.
"What do you mean? *Isn't* it a dream?"
He looked at me that same way again; and it made my blood chilly, this time. Then he said—
"You have spent your whole life in this ship. And this is *real* life. Your other life was the dream!"
It was as if he had hit me, it stunned me so. Still looking at me, his lip curled itself into a mocking smile, and he wasted away like a mist and disappeared. (*DRT*, 102–3)

The Superintendent's words shake the narrator, and Henry's response takes the narrative to a new depth, our first real clue that this dream voyage is going to take us to deeper psychological levels:

We are strangely made. We think we are wonderful creatures. Part of the time we think that, at any rate. And during that interval we consider with pride our mental equipment, with its penetration, its power of analysis, its ability to reason out clear conclusions from confused facts, and all the lordly rest of it; and then comes a rational interval and disenchants us. Disenchants us and lays us bare to ourselves, and we see that intellectually we are really no great things; that we seldom really know the thing we think we know; that our best-built certainties are but sand-houses and subject to damage from any wind of doubt that blows. (*DRT,* 103)

Our seemingly most solid "best-built certainty" is our personal identity. But Lacan tells us the way that apparently unified identity is actually split several times, fragmented, and that what we build is the illusion of a single identity. Mark Twain, who named himself in what seems like an artistic whim, who then lured his readers and critics and biographers into seeing him as a split, was, I believe, insistently and unceasingly exploring this illusion in his late, dark writings.

Life is a dream, the old unrecognized metaphor tells us, but here the metaphor becomes literal. The turns Twain makes on that idea drive the story to yet another level, as Henry and Alice discuss their prior memories of life. What he tells her makes her remember parts of their life together, as does what she tells him. Gradually he comes to realize that the supposed dream of life on the ship was actually reality, and the other reality only a succession of dreams. His confusion reaches its peak as Alice tells him of the solid details of what he has been considering a dream world: "I said to myself, are we real creatures in a real world, all of a sudden, and have we been feeding on dreams in an imaginary one since nobody knows when—or how *is* it? My head was swimming" (*DRT,* 108). In book 2, Alice agrees to try to reclaim even more of their lost domestic life, and they engage in what sounds suspiciously like psychotherapy: "By my help, and by patient probing and searching of her memory she succeeded. Gradually it all came back, and her reward was sufficient. We now had the recollections of two lives to draw upon, and the result was a double measure of happiness for us" (*DRT,* 119). Then they embark on a kind of group therapy: "We even got the children's former lives back for them—with a good deal of difficulty—next the servants'. It made a new world for us all, and an entertaining one to explore. . . . Talking over our double-past—particularly our dream-past—became our most pleasant and satisfying amusement, and the search for missing details of it our most profitable labor" (*DRT,* 119). Clearly, we can read this passage biographically, with Samuel Clemens seeking a way to restore the family that is dissolving, but from another perspective, Mark Twain the artist and thinker is seeing a positive force in dream therapy, as well as coming to terms with his emerging ideas about the unconscious.

The voyage, of course, is not pleasant and amusing, but a nightmare voyage, with huge, horrible monsters and the threat of the great white glare of the microscope's lamp. A giant, blind squid attacks. The children are lost, then found again. The ship's crew threatens to mutiny, and just as the captain is making a heroic speech to rally the crew onward, the narrative abruptly ends: "*I* don't know where the ship is, but she's in the hands of God, and that's enough for me, it's enough for you, and it's enough for anybody but a carpenter. If it is God's will that we pull through, we pull through—otherwise not. We haven't had an observation for four months, but we are going ahead, and do our best to fetch up somewhere" (*DRT,* 128). John Tuckey calls these "courageous words of the captain . . . a difficult act to follow." "In projecting a tragedy-trap," Tuckey continues, "Mark Twain had perhaps failed to reckon with his own capacity for rebound and affirmation. His inability to finish the story as planned was less a failure than a success: one senses the resurgence of latent strengths, just when these had seemed about to capitulate to despair" (*DRT,* xiii). Tuckey argues, "Having intended to lead his readers on and spring a tragic ending upon them, Mark Twain had himself been trapped by his own returning courage" (*DRT,* xiii–xiv). But he certainly may not have been trapped; DeVoto summarizes the eight pages of notes accompanying the manuscript, which show that Twain had the whole story worked out, including the ending (*LFE,* 226–27). Twain's notes for the ending show just how tragic and nightmarish a story he projected, with nearly everyone dead before the narrator wakes up to his real life, which he now sees as a dream. Why Twain did not finish his story, and why he stopped at that point, we will never know. With all of these dream narratives left unfinished, it is almost as if he intentionally left them *as dreams.* His notes show that he could have finished the narrative, but perhaps he had learned what he wanted from the fragment.

Deeper than (but certainly including) the biographical concerns we can identify, Twain was up to something, something that concerned him, but that also concerns us. One clue might be the beginning of book 2, where a very odd thing happens narratively: "I have long ago lost Book I, but it is no matter," the narrator tells us. "It served its purpose—writing it was an entertainment to me. We found out that our little boy set it adrift on the wind, sheet by sheet, to see if it would fly. It did. And so two of us got entertainment out of it" (*DRT,* 118). The absurdity of this is striking to the reader: how could we just have read a book 1 that we are then told has been thrown away? And why is that no matter to the narrator? These absurdities and impossibilities do much to reinforce the dream logic; to the dreaming mind, such logical flaws really are of no consequence. But it is precisely these strange moments that serve as messages to the conscious mind, Lacan says. Just as the family members get amusement out of their dream therapy in the midst of their frightening voyage, the writer gets entertainment out of the very act of writing, even if the pages are "lost" (but they are not lost—we are reading them, as perhaps Twain knew we would). Early on, the mate makes the intriguing comment that "a man in his right mind don't put nightmares in the log" (*DRT*, 88). But that is precisely what Mark Twain was bold enough to do: put nightmares in the log and leave them there for us to see.

As DeVoto and Tuckey point out, these ideas on the dreaming and waking self look forward to *The Mysterious Stranger*. All these explorations of consciousness provide insights into what Twain was up to as an artist in his later years. In Lacanian terms, we could say that he was bravely trying to face his Other. Ragland-Sullivan explains the process this way: "Freedom of choice—'self'-creation—cannot reside in consciousness, unless the conscious subject has gained this freedom by peering into its unconscious netherworld."[42] In his last decade, Mark Twain was insistently and heroically trying to explore something he glimpsed about himself, something most people run from. By naming himself with two names, he dramatized the Lacanian split, and then with his dream narratives, he lit out for the territory of the unconscious—and as usual, ahead of the rest.

V. Freeing the Dream: The Mysterious Stranger Manuscripts

"Yes, Austria was far from the world, and asleep," the narrator of *The Chronicle of Young Satan* begins. He continues: "and our village was in the middle of that sleep, being in the middle of Austria. It drowsed in peace in the deep privacy of a hilly and woodsy solitude where news from the world hardly ever came to disturb its dreams, and was infinitely content" (*MTMSM*, 35). The third and most complete of the three manuscript fragments begins with almost the same words, and of course ends with No. 44's famous pronouncement that all of existence is only a dream. Further, the mysterious stranger of the first fragment is named "Philip Traum"—"traum" the German word for "dream." Thus, dreams frame Mark Twain's obsession with this story, the last he was to try to tell. Like "Which Was the Dream?" and "The Great Dark," the fragments are dream narratives, with the strange, disjointed logic of the dream state. They have been variously judged by critics, as the signs of his final despair or as artistic recovery after a long struggle.[43] I align myself with those who see them as an artistic triumph, but even more significantly, I see them as part of Mark Twain's heroic battle to come to terms with his own unconscious, to win a philosophic battle he had been fighting for much of his career. "Dream other dreams, and better," No. 44 tells August near the end; I am arguing that Mark Twain was doing just that, and that he succeeded admirably.

The last fragment, *No. 44, The Mysterious Stranger,* shows his intentions most clearly, is the most nearly finished of the three, and deals most fully with dreams and dream psychology. The episode with the Duplicates and with the ideas of the Dream-Self and Waking-Self show Twain delving into the implications of dreams for our inner workings, revealing the power of metaphorically structured dreams to free us from the nightmare of existence.

When the Duplicates are first introduced, they are more comic than anything else, conjured up by 44 as replacements for the striking print-shop workers. Katzenyammer and his Duplicate fight, and then all the Duplicates emerge and fight their counterparts, but they are so evenly matched that the battle is a draw. In vintage Twain humor, reminiscent of *Those Extraordinary Twins,* each man finds that even though he drinks, he can get only half drunk, because his Duplicate "has gotten the other half of the dividend, and was just as drunk, and as insufficiently drunk, as *he* was" (*MTMSM,* 307). August Feldner, the narrator, is just as affected as everyone else, and responds with an interesting simile: "Every time I met myself unexpectedly I got a shock and caught my breath, and was as irritated for being startled as a person is when he runs up against himself in a mirror which he doesn't know was there" (*MTMSM,* 311).[44] The metaphor of doublings and splits runs throughout Twain's career, of course, but with this narrative, he uses these concepts to make his deepest psychological point.

When 44 now reappears to August, he changes abruptly from telling him about America, which is to be discovered "next fall," to asking about the Duplicates. The shift prompts this comment from August, who explicitly compares 44 to a boy and to a bee, but implicitly describes him in terms of dream psychology: "It was his common way, the way of a boy, and most provoking: careless, capricious, unstable, never sticking to a subject, forever flitting and sampling here and there and yonder, like a bee; always, just as he was on the point of becoming interesting, he changed the subject" (*MTMSM,* 313). But 44 does at last explain who and what the Duplicates are:

> "You know, of course, that you are not one person, but two. One is your Workaday-Self, and 'tends to business, the other is your Dream-Self, and has no responsibilities, and cares only for romance and excursions and adventure. It sleeps when your other self is awake; when your other self sleeps, your Dream-Self has full control, and does as it pleases. It has far

more imagination than the Workaday-Self, therefore its pains and pleas-
ures are far more real and intense than are those of the other self, and its
adventures correspondingly picturesque and extraordinary. As a rule,
when a party of Dream-Selves—whether comrades or strangers—get
together and flit abroad in the globe, they have a tremendous time. But
you understand, they have no substance, they are only spirits. The
Workaday-Self has a harder lot and a duller time; it can't get away from
the flesh, and is clogged and hindered by it; and also by the low grade
of its own imagination." (*MTMSM*, 315)

The Workaday-Selves appear to be "solid," but are "only fictitious flesh
and bone, put upon them by the magician and me. We pulled them out
of the Originals and gave them this independent life" (*MTMSM*, 315).
Apparently, 44 is satisfied with his work, and his comments prefigure much
that will be revealed:

"I've never seen better flesh put together by enchantment; but no matter, it is a pretty airy fabric, and if we should remove the spell they would
vanish like blowing out a candle. Ah, they are a capable lot, with their
measureless imaginations! If they imagine there is a mystic clog upon
them and it takes them a couple of hours to set a couple of lines, that is
what happens; but on the contrary, if they imagine it takes them but half
a second to set a whole galleyful of matter, *that* is what happens! A dandy
lot is that handful of Duplicates, and the easy match of a thousand real
printers! Handled judiciously, they'll make plenty of trouble." (*MTMSM*,
316)[45]

The trouble begins for August when he finds himself in love with Marget,
the master's daughter. In the long episode that follows, Twain fleshes out
his ideas on the Waking-Self and Dream-Self, with fictional situations that
point toward some of the ideas that Freud was pursuing at the time, and
that Lacan was to continue working on later. Marget approaches the invisible August: "She was coming toward me, walking slowly, musing, dreaming, heeding nothing, absorbed, unconscious" (*MTMSM*, 336). In a scene
rife with figurative language and sexual overtones, the two bodies meet:

As she drew near I stepped directly in her way; and as she passed through
me the contact invaded my blood as with a delicious fire! She stopped,
with a startled look, the rich blood rose in her face, her breath came quick
and short through her parted lips, and she gazed wonderingly about her,
saying twice, in a voice hardly above a whisper—
    "What could it have been?" (*MTMSM*, 336)

Mistakenly, August thinks she loves him, just as he does her, but he is soon to find out how complicated the situation is. When he materializes and calls out to her, her response leaves no doubt about her feelings: "She turned upon me a look of gentle but most chilly and dignified rebuke, allowed it a proper time to freeze where it struck, then moved on, without a word, and left me there. I did not feel inspired to follow" (*MTMSM*, 336).

But when August cannot sleep, he wanders the hallways, until he sees "a figure standing motionless in that memorable spot" (*MTMSM*, 337). He does not mean "figure" as a figure of speech, but his language is full of metaphor here, concentrating on this figure that draws him "like a magnet" (*MTMSM*, 337). Their second encounter furthers the sexual tension:

> With a quick movement she lifted her head and poised it in the attitude of one who listens—listens with a tense and wistful and breathless interest; it was a happy and longing face that I saw in the dim light; and out of it, as through a veil, looked darkling and humid the eyes I loved so well. I caught a whisper: "I cannot hear anything—no, there is no sound—but it is near, I know it is near, and the dream is come again!" My passion rose and overpowered me and I floated to her like a breath and put my arms about her and drew her to my breast and put my lips to hers, unrebuked, and drew intoxication from them! She closed her eyes, and with a sigh which seemed born of measureless content, she said dreamily, "I love you so—and have so longed for you!" (*MTMSM*, 338)

Mark Twain had never written such open and convincing scenes of adult intimacy and sexuality as these in *No. 44, The Mysterious Stranger.* In part, he may have realized he was not writing for publication, and so opened himself up and turned off the censors. But a large part of the reason is the subject matter of dreams and the larger point he was making about the freedom of the unconscious, as further events in the text make clear.

When the girl he is kissing will not respond to the name "Marget," August learns (through a kissing game) that she calls herself "Elisabeth von Armin," and that, to her, he is "Martin von Giesbach." August eventually, as he says, "untangled the matter":

> ... the presence of my flesh-and-blood personality was not a circumstance of any interest to Marget Regen, but my presence as a spirit acted upon her hypnotically—as 44 termed it—and plunged her into deep somnambulic sleep. This removed her Day-Self from command and from consciousness, and gave the command to her Dream-Self for the time being. Her Dream-Self was a quite definite and independent personality, and

for reasons of its own it had chosen to name itself Elisabeth von Armin. It was entirely unacquainted with Marget Regen, did not even know she existed, and had no knowledge of her affairs, her feelings, her opinions, her religion, her history, nor any of the other matter concerning her. On the other hand, Marget was entirely unacquainted with Elisabeth and wholly ignorant of her existence and of all other matters concerning her, including her name. (*MTMSM*, 342)

The confusion adds to the romantic comedy: "Marget knew me as August Feldner, her Dream-Self knew me as Martin von Giesbach—*why*, was a matter beyond guessing. Awake, the girl cared nothing for me; steeped in the hypnotic sleep, I was the idol of her heart" (*MTMSM*, 342).

And then August adds yet one more element to the split identities, a third entity of the self that resonates with Freud's formulation of the self, and looks ahead, in a less obvious way, to Lacan:

There was another thing which I had learned from 44, and that was this: each human being contains not merely two independent entities, but three—the Waking-Self, the Dream-Self, and the Soul. This last is immortal, the others are functioned by the brain and the nerves, and are physical and mortal; they are not functionable when the brain and nerves are paralysed by a temporary hurt or stupefied by narcotics; and when the man dies *they* die, since their life, their energy and their existence depend solely upon physical sustenance, and they cannot get that from dead nerves and a dead brain. When I was invisible the whole of my physical make-up was gone, nothing connected with it or depending upon it was left. My soul—my immortal spirit—alone remained. Freed from the encumbering flesh, it was able to exhibit forces, passions and emotions of a quite tremendously effective character. (*MTMSM*, 342–43)

We can see here something like Freud's division of the self—although Twain's three do not clearly align with id, ego, and superego. Also suggestive is a representation of the Lacanian divided self, although there may actually be a clearer parallel to Ralph Waldo Emerson's "transparent eyeball" experience in *Nature*, a philosophical idea with which Twain was familiar.

But we are dealing with Mark Twain, and no matter how serious or philosophical he becomes (and no matter how seriously we take him), he almost always looks for humor in a situation. In this case, he carries the situation to its absurd lengths. August says, "And now a sorrowful thought came to me: all three of my Selves were in love with the one girl, and how could we all be happy?" (*MTMSM*, 343). He mines this confusion for humor, in a series of mistaken-identity scenes between August, his Duplicate (who is named "Emil Schwarz"), Marget, and Elisabeth, none of the four being able to understand quite what is going on as they meet and are either in love or repulsed by the others' presence. But the situation is also serious, and Twain intends to take us to a serious place with all this confusion over split identities. One key moment is when August recognizes his Duplicate's superiority, in another passage rich in metaphor:

> I was always courteous to my Duplicate, but I avoided him. This was natural, perhaps, for he was my superior. My imagination, compared with his splendid dream-equipment, was as a lightning bug to the lightning; in matters of our trade he could do more with his hands in five minutes than I could do in a day; he did all my work in the shop, and found it but a trifle; in the arts and graces of beguilement and persuasion I was a pauper and he a Croesus; in passion, feeling, emotion, sensation— whether of pain or pleasure—I was phosphorus, he was fire. In a word he had all the intensities one suffers or enjoys in a dream! (*MTMSM*, 344)

In Lacanian terms, as Ben Stoltzfus explains in *Lacan and Literature: Purloined Pretexts*, "The discourse of the Other surfaces whenever there is metaphoric or metonymic interplay."[46] The outburst of metaphor in this passage, so unlike the passages that surround it, serves as an important signal. August sees in Emil Schwartz his Other, his unconscious, sees its superiority to him, and the superiority of his Soul to his Duplicate. A bit later, August realizes, because 44 gives him a tape recorder and a camera, that his voice does not sound the same to others as it does to him, and that he does not look to others as he does to himself. His particular words are revealing: " . . . I had been used to supposing that the person I saw in the mirror was the person others saw when they looked at me—whereas that was not the case" (*MTMSM*, 364). A crude Lacanian interpretation would link this moment with the "mirror stage"—and although August is not an infant encountering his mirror image for the first time, his recognition dramatically reenacts that pivotal psychological moment, with the Lacanian effects of both joy and alienation. The description of looking at his Duplicate revolves around metaphor, even down to, again, seeing him as a "figure":

> And here it was again. In the figure standing by the door I was now seeing myself as others saw me, but the resemblance to the self which I was familiar with in the glass was *merely* a resemblance, nothing more; not approaching the common resemblance of brother to brother, but reach-

ing only as far as the resemblance which a person usually bears to his brother-in-law. Often one does not notice that, at all, until it is pointed out; and sometimes, even then, the resemblance owes as much to imagination as to fact. It's like a cloud which resembles a horse after some one has pointed out the resemblance. You perceive it, then, though I have often seen a cloud that didn't. Clouds often have nothing more than a brother-in-law resemblance. I wouldn't say this to everybody, but I believe it to be true, nevertheless. For I myself have seen clouds which looked like a brother-in-law, whereas I knew very well they didn't. Nearly all such are hallucination, in my opinion. (*MTMSM*, 364–65)

Despite descending into absurd humor at the end, the passage touches on an important aspect of the unconscious, this hazy, indistinct sense of self-recognition we experience as we glimpse the hidden parts of our selves. The point becomes even deeper when August finally examines his Duplicate's mentality, and what he finds saddens him: "[H]e was of a loftier world than I, he moved in regions where I could not tread, with my earth-shod feet" (*MTMSM*, 366). The loftier status of the unconscious, however, contains a suggestive and intriguing freedom, a freedom that we see most clearly in the anguish the Duplicate suffers over being bound to a fleshly body. His long speech is full of clusters of metaphor, and is another key glimpse into the voice of the Other: "'Oh, not *that*! I care nothing for that— it is these bonds'—stretching his arms aloft—'oh, free me from *them*; these bonds of flesh—this decaying vile matter, this foul weight, and clog, and burden, this loathsome sack of corruption in which my spirit is imprisoned, her white wings bruised and soiled—oh, be merciful and set her free!'" (*MTMSM*, 369). The nausea of existence comes through as clearly as in any passage in Sartre as he continues: "Oh, this human life, this earthy life, this weary life! It is so groveling, and so mean; its ambitions are so paltry, its prides so trivial, its vanities so childish; and the glories that it values and applauds—lord, how empty! Oh, here I am a servant!—I who have never served before, here I am a slave—slave among little mean kings and emperors made of clothes, the kings and emperors slaves themselves, to mud-built carrion that are *their* slaves!" (*MTMSM*, 369). If the speech stopped here, it would be merely another in a long line of denunciations of "the damned human race," but in his conclusion, as despairing as is his plea, the Duplicate (and behind him, Mark Twain) presents us with a kind of solution and consolation, but not before a shocking outburst:

"To think you should think I came here concerned about those other things—those inconsequentials! Why should they concern me, a spirit of the air, habitant of the August Empire of Dreams? *We* have no morals; the angels have none; morals are for the impure; we have no principles, those chains are for men. We love the lovely whom we meet in dreams, we forget them the next day, and meet and love their like. They are dream-creatures—no others are real. Disgrace? We care nothing for disgrace, we do not know what it is. Crime? We commit it every night, while you sleep; it is nothing to us. We have no character, no *one* character, we have *all* characters; we are honest in one dream, dishonest in the next; we fight in one battle and flee from the next. We wear no chains; we cannot abide them; we have no home, no prison, the universe is our province; we do not know time, we do not know space—we live, and love, and labor, fifty years in an hour, while you are sleeping, snoring, repairing your crazy tissues; we circumnavigate your globe while you wink; we are not tied with horizons, like a dog with cattle to mind, an emperor with human sheep to watch—we visit hell, we roam in heaven, our playgrounds are the constellations and the Milky Way." (*MTMSM*, 370)

Readers who accept Twain's dream psychology have this experience: the Duplicate describes for us our own Dream-Self, our unconscious, which can do all the things he says, and more. We repress that Other, and remember only part of our life in that boundless world, and some of it causes our Waking-Self to feel ashamed and embarrassed. But deep down we know that we are that Other, the self we long to be, the life we long to live. Mark Twain has given us this vision of ourselves, and like the Duplicate, we want to cry out, "[R]elease me from this odious flesh!"

And 44 does free Emil, in a memorable and imaginative scene:

So he told Schwarz to stand up and melt. Schwarz did it, and it was very pretty. First, his clothes thinned out so you could see him through them, then they floated off like shreds of vapor, leaving him naked, then the cat looked in, but scrambled out again; next the flesh fell to thinning, and you could see the skeleton through it, very neat and trim, a good skeleton; next the bones disappeared and nothing was left but the empty form—just a statue, perfect and beautiful, made out of the delicatest soap-bubble stuff, with rainbow-hues dreaming around over it and the furniture showing through it the same as it would through a bubble; then—poof! and it was gone! (*MTMSM*, 381)

This disappearance prefigures in some ways the ending. Metaphorically, it is a picture of the freeing of the dream and of the imagination.

Mark Twain's dream philosophy is intriguing, and again anticipates ideas of Freud and Lacan. In some ways, it is a bit contradictory, even to itself, and in other ways, it does not fully match up with Freud's ideas. Are the Waking-Self and Dream-Self perfect strangers to each other, as he seems to say, or is there some interaction? Even while claiming a complete split between the two, the narrator recognizes at least some interaction, as in this description:

> Always before, I had been tranquilly unconcerned about my Duplicate. To me he was merely a stranger, no more no less; to him I was a stranger; in all our lives we had never chanced to meet until 44 had put flesh upon him; we could not have met if we had wanted to, because whenever one of us was awake and in command of our common brain and nerves the other was of necessity asleep and unconscious. All our lives we had been what 44 called Box and Cox lodgers in one chamber: aware of each other's existence but not interested in each other's affairs, and never encountering each other save for a dim and hazy and sleepy half-moment on the threshold, when one was coming in and the other going out, and never in any case halting to make a bow or pass a greeting. (*MTMSM*, 343)

His metaphor of "Box and Cox lodgers" is largely lost on the modern reader; William Gibson notes that "[t]he comparison is especially apt since Box was a journeyman printer in John Madison Morton's farce of 1847, *Box and Cox*" (*MTMSM*, 481n). Even with the obscure reference, we can understand the point, and that "half-moment on the threshold" certainly rings true in our experience with dreams, the liminal moments of falling asleep and waking up, the mysterious hypnagogic state that we experience each night and each morning, all our lives.

In fact, Twain seems actually to have believed in these ideas about the Waking-Self and the Dream-Self. In a letter to Joseph Twichell written on July 28, 1904, he lays out these ideas as his own, and seems to have believed in them fully. According to Gibson, Twain's friend and pastor had asked "how life and the world had been looking to Clemens" (*MTMSM*, 30). The letter, which Gibson reprints in *Mark Twain's "Mysterious Stranger" Manuscripts,* could have come almost verbatim from the pages of *No. 44:*

> (A *part* of each day—or night) as they have been looking to me the past 7 years: as being NON-EXISTENT. That is, that there is *nothing*. That there is no God and no universe; that there is only empty space, and in it a lost and homeless and wandering and companionless and indestructible *Thought*. And that I am that thought. And God, and the Universe, and Time, and Life, and Death, and Joy and Sorrow and Pain only a grotesque and brutal *dream*, evolved from the frantic imagination of that insane Thought.

By this light, the absurdities that govern life and the universe lose their absurdity and become natural, and a thing to be expected. It reconciles everything, makes everything lucid and understandable: a God who has no morals, yet blandly sets Himself up as Head Sunday-school Superintendent of the Universe; Who has no idea of mercy, or justice, or honesty, yet obtusely imagines Himself the inventor of those things; a human race that takes Him at His own valuation, without examining the statistics; thinks itself intelligent, yet hasn't any more evidence of it than had Jonathan Edwards in his wildest moments; a race which did not make itself nor its vicious nature, yet quaintly holds itself responsible for its acts.

But—taken as unrealities; taken as the drunken dream of an idiot Thought, drifting solitary and forlorn through the horizonless eternities of empty Space, these monstrous sillinesses become proper and acceptable, and lose their offensiveness. (*MTMSM*, 30)

We must be careful in reading Mark Twain's letters, on guard always for tone; many critics have been "sold" by Twain in a letter that contains a wink and a nudge the too-serious might miss. Gibson explains, "It would be a mistake, however, to consider this letter unmixed autobiography. It is a moving document, written by Samuel Clemens, who suffers; it is equally a letter by Mark Twain, the long-committed artist who creates" (*MTMSM*, 31). The point is well taken, but the neat split Gibson makes between Clemens the man and Mark Twain the artist is a bit too pat. The fact that Twain wrote this letter to his minister, as Gibson says, "not long before Twain either wrote or had firmly in mind his last chapter" (*MTMSM*, 29), seems to be evidence that these were not just creative ideas, but a part of his actual beliefs. In fact, by taking a look back at some earlier works, we can see them as the culmination of a long line of thought he had been working on for much of his career.

What we are here calling the unconscious, Mark Twain was in the 1870s and 1880s labeling "Conscience," a part of himself he seemed to be at war with in works such as *Adventures of Huckleberry Finn* and "The Facts Concerning the Recent Carnival of Crime in Connecticut." Huck's pronouncement on Conscience is a kind of solution for him: "If I had a yaller dog that didn't know more than a person's conscience does, I would pison him" (*HF*, 290). In a fuller sense, Twain explores the idea in "Carnival of Crime," one of his most inventive, imaginative, humorous, and at the same time, serious works, which Gibson calls "a brilliant narration of the conflict between 'Twain' and his conscience or superego." The climactic moment prefigures a main idea Twain would develop decades later in *No. 44*: "With an exultant shout I sprang past my aunt, and in an instant I had my life-long foe by the throat. After so many years of waiting and longing, he was mine at last. I tore him to shreds and fragments. I rent the fragments to bits. I cast the bleeding rubbish into the fire, and drew into my nostrils the grateful incense of my burnt-offering. At last and forever, my Conscience was dead!" The narrator's next line makes the irony complete: "I was a free man!" (*CTSS1*, 149). Even in his humor, he makes, in 1876, a profound statement about our psychological make-up. "Since that day my life is all bliss," the narrator tells us. "Bliss, unalloyed bliss. Nothing in all the world could persuade me to have a conscience again" (*CTSS1*, 149).

We see the liberating effect later on in works like "The Mad Passenger," which is a long digression from "The Great Dark," a fragment embedded in and then detached from a fragment: "In his [the Mad Passenger's] tongue there were no exact equivalents for our words *modesty, immodesty, decency, indecency, right, wrong, sin*" (*DRT*, 135). We see the oppressive effect of the conscience on Mark Twain (and on the reader) in works such as *Letters from the Earth*, where the aging writer's anger can not get past the hypocrisy and crippling psychology of what he calls "the damned human race." In dreams we are free, but in the reality of the world that we are tied to, we are damned. Since 1960 or so, the critical pendulum has swung far to the side of the bitter Twain who pronounces us (and himself) damned, but increasingly in recent years, critics are recognizing the creative, liberating side of the equation. An idea from "The Mad Passenger" rids us of the central problem of Twain's apparent inconsistency, an idea that finds its full fruition in *No. 44*. The passage is worth examining in full:

> He said that in most details the civilization of his country was the counterpart of that which prevailed among the highest civilizations of dreamlands like the World, and that a citizen of that unreal planet would be quite at home in his Empire, and would find it quite up to date in matters of art, erudition, invention, architecture, etc.
>
> That seemed strange, but he said there was properly nothing strange about it, since dreamlands were nothing but imitations of real countries created out of the dreamer's own imagination and experience, with some help, perhaps, from the Superintendent of Dreams. At least that was his belief, he said, and he thought it reasonable and plausible. He had noticed that in Jupiter, Uranus, and in fact in all the other dream-countries he found things about as they were at home, and apparently quite real and natural as long as the dream lasted. (*DRT*, 135)

Thus, the dream and the dreamer are the creators. Mark Twain puzzled over the dream as a way to understand, a way to create.

The problem lies in the difference between us and a creature like No. 44. This difference is illuminated in a burst of metaphor when 44 fills August with the language of his own country to let August see what thought is like on 44's plane. His explanation makes everything clear: "Now then, things which have puzzled you heretofore are not a mystery to you any more, for you are now aware that there is nothing I cannot do—and lay it on the magician and increase his reputation; and you are also now aware that the difference between a human being and me is as the difference between a drop of water and the sea, a rushlight and the sun, the difference between the infinitely trivial and the sublime!" (*MTMSM*, 319). Later, he distinguishes his kind of thought from a human's:

> "A man *originates* nothing in his head, he merely observes exterior things, and *combines* them in his head—puts several observed things together and draws a conclusion. His mind is merely a machine, that is all—an *automatic* one, and he has no control over it; it cannot conceive of a *new* thing, an original thing, it can only gather material from the outside and combine it into new *forms* and patterns. But it always has to have the *materials* from the *outside*, for it can't make them itself. That is to say, a man's mind cannot *create*—a god's can, and my race can. That is the difference. *We* need no contributed materials, we *create* them—out of thought. All things that exist were made out of thought—and out of nothing else." (*MTMSM*, 332–33)

His description of observing and combining could be a definition of metaphor and the metaphor-making principle, and the description of the mind as an automatic machine is itself a metaphor. But what would happen if our minds were not what we think of as "human," but like the mind of No. 44? I am proposing that Mark Twain was actually seriously arguing just that: we *can* be like No. 44, and indeed we already are. Not only can we have the freedom of the Dream-Self, we can have the ultimate freedom of the self that dreams the dream. In essence, just as No. 44 frees August at the end, Mark Twain is imaginatively freeing himself, and I am arguing the reader can also, if he or she is willing. Not that each of us is the only being in existence and has created the whole world by dreaming it, but that each of us is capable of the complete creation of a complete world. The writer, the good writer, does that, and for thousands of years, readers have been willing to believe in the reality of those "created" worlds. The study of literature shows how seriously we take "fiction." Would not most avid readers agree that they know some "fictional" characters better than they know many of their "actual" friends? (Or to tell the honest truth, *like* some of them better?) From the age of five or six, many people spend a good portion of their lives in one book after another, often with the sense that the book has *become* reality. Who is to say that it is not? That experience certainly seems "real" to the absorbed reader. And then there are dreams, where we spend approximately one-third of our lives—and even though we remember only a very small portion of our lives there, when we are in it, the dream world certainly seems real: sometimes frighteningly so, sometimes pleasurably. Sometimes, the dream sets us free.

The artist dreams a world, then shares it with us. Artists tell us that the worlds they dream are real worlds to them, at least during the act of creation. If we turn off our rational minds, we know deep within us that these "imaginary" worlds are real. And even more incredibly, *we* are artists every night in our dreams. When we are in the dream, we know the dream world is the real world. It is only when we wake back into the "real" world that the dream world seems absurd and begins to fade away. It is only because we are slaves to our rational minds that we do not continue to see the dream as real too. How can we trust "rationality" if it is the only way we have to judge reality, yet it denies the reality of an experience that a part of us knows is real, a part repressed by our rational selves? Mark Twain recognized something about the reality of his other self and was trying to tell us that we are the same—if we will wake up to that other reality.

At the end of the fragment, No. 44 is addressing August, but what if we choose to take that second-person pronoun personally and listen to him talking to each of us? The ending is the ultimate metaphor, and the metaphor has the power to set us free. *"Life itself is only a vision, a dream,"* 44 tells August and the reader. There is that metaphor again, the metaphor of metaphors, the one that was so disturbing in "The Great Dark," but so liberating in this last dream text. August reacts with wonder: "It was electrical. By God I had had that very thought a thousand times in my musings!" The words are so familiar, but consider them not as mere metaphor, not as mere fantasy, but perhaps as an actual truth that Mark Twain had discovered in his passage into the other side, a truth that others have told us, before and since:

> *"Nothing* exists; all is a dream. God—man—the world,—the sun, the moon, the wilderness of stars: a dream, all a dream, they have no existence. *Nothing exists save empty space—and you!"*
>
> "I!"
>
> "And you are not you—you have no body, no blood, no bones, you are but a *thought.* I myself have no existence, I am but a dream—your dream,

creature of your imagination. In a moment you will have realized this, then you will banish me from your visions and I shall dissolve into the nothingness out of which you made me. . . ." (*MTMSM*, 404)

This is not 44 talking to August, but Mark Twain talking to us. We dreamed him, and he is dissolving. But he has more to say before he goes: "I am perishing already—I am failing, I am passing away. In a little while you will be alone in shoreless space, to wander its limitless solitudes without friend or comrade forever—for you will remain a *Thought*, the only existent Thought, and by your nature inextinguishable, indestructible. But I your poor servant have revealed you to yourself and set you free. Dream other dreams, and better!" (*MTMSM*, 404).

I risk a personal comment here: I know this to be true. I know that I have the power in me to dream other dreams, and better. I know that the miracles of this world have come when a few brave souls have let themselves go, let their rational selves go, and let their real selves dream—and then have told us about it. We call them crazy, we shun them, we banish them, and often we kill them. Or we consign them to the rank of "mere humorist," God's fool.

Mark Twain had a clue about the dream, he had it all along, and he made the courageous decision to follow it to the end, to follow the metaphor to its conclusion, no matter where it took him. Along the way, he often had to joke, or pretend to joke, in order to figure it out and tell us, but a joke is as good as a dream when it comes to that kind of exploration. It was a long journey, from a dream about a frog to a dream that tells us that life is only a dream.

When that frog jumped, he landed "solid as a gob of mud." What can be more real than that, or more perfect? Aristotle said, "But the greatest thing by far is to be a master of metaphor." He was not, of course, talking merely about figures, or even merely about being a poet. He was, fundamentally, talking about seeing through the lie of apparently solid reality to the metaphorical nature of all our perception, about recognizing the metaphor as a metaphor, of not being fooled, of mastering metaphor—which is to say, mastering our own created, metaphorical selves. He was talking about, among other people, Mark Twain. "Mark Twain" is the master metaphor created by a master of metaphor. What we thought was just a matter of style is, in actuality, a matter of the deepest essence.

Coda

Mark Twain Studies and the Myth of Metaphor

We are now at the final level of analysis where, having become to some degree aware of the metaphors involved, we proceed to re-use them instead of being used by them. But need we use the same ones? If we are aware, we can stop and think. We can choose our metaphors. We are no longer duped citizens of the city-state of Oz, but the Wizard of Oz himself.

—Colin Turbayne, *The Myth of Metaphor*

Metaphor reveals much about Mark Twain's works, but it can also reveal something important about Mark Twain's critics. As we have seen, metaphor, so fundamental to language, has power to reveal what might otherwise remain hidden, and it can do the same for critical ideas, and even the direction of Mark Twain studies in general. An examination of roughly a decade's worth of book-length studies of Mark Twain will not only give a sense of the direction of Mark Twain scholarship, but also point out some of its distortions, past and present. By recognizing distortions, we do not necessarily get any closer to the truth, but we at least become aware that we are in the midst of distortion, and thus do not mistake the distortion for the truth.

As a brief reminder, Colin Turbayne's 1962 study, *The Myth of Metaphor*, traces the way metaphor passes through several stages. Turbayne makes a distinction between "using a metaphor and being used by it"; if we, as he describes it, "mistake[e] the model for the thing being modeled," we become what he calls "a victim of metaphor."[1] I used his argument in discussing *Huckleberry Finn* in Chapter 2, but his ideas can also apply to those of us who read and study Mark Twain.

What, then, are the metaphors that have governed Mark Twain studies? There are many, but clearly the most dominant and persistent have been the metaphors of doubling, of twinness, of the split. This metaphor is so firmly ingrained in our critical vocabulary that some of us may be unable to see it as a metaphor; after all, we are talking about Mr. Clemens and Mark Twain, the river vs. the shore, a sound heart and a deformed conscience, reality and dream, white and black, male and female. No doubt these paired phrases bring specific articles and books to mind. But do we see these splits and oppositions and divisions because they are there, in both the writer and his texts, or because that is the metaphor we have embraced so fully that we do not even recognize it as a metaphor anymore, and thus, victims of the metaphor, the split is all we can see?

To illustrate the point, let us imagine for an example that the metaphorical way we perceived Mark Twain and his works were in triangles, instead of splits. We would then see what we formerly saw as oppositions, but with a third, mediating element: Samuel Clemens/constructed persona/Mark Twain, the river/the raft/the shore, sound heart/language conflict/deformed conscience, reality/perception/dream, white/mulatto/black. Given such a formulation, Mark Twain studies would have a very different history and content.[2]

One immediate response to my questioning of these splits and oppositions in Mark Twain studies would undoubtedly be that the splits and oppositions came originally from Mark Twain (or Samuel Clemens) himself. Turbayne has an answer for this objection: "A great metaphor made by a genius, and treated as metaphor, always tends to pass into a later stage in its life. The more effective it is in the realm of make-believe the more seriously it comes to be believed in until it is taken literally, by posterity, or by the great man's contemporaries, or even by himself. It awaits an iconoclast from a later age who will explode it as myth."[3] The metaphor, then, becomes a myth. Mark Twain's metaphor has been taken literally by all three groups Turbayne mentions—posterity, his contemporaries, and to some extent, himself—and a number of iconoclasts have attempted to explode the myth. It is to these iconoclasts that I now turn my attention.

Rather than begin with recent critics, I must go back to the two original iconoclasts in our debates, Van Wyck Brooks and Bernard DeVoto, because several recent critics also begin with them and are very consciously engaged in the ongoing debate these two set up so long ago. To quote Brooks is to recognize how early (in 1920, ten years after Mark Twain's death) an iconoclast stepped forth to try to explode the myth of the "Mark Twain" duality metaphor:

He seems to exhibit himself, on the one hand, as a child of nature conscious of extraordinary powers that make all the world and even the
Almighty solicitous about him, and, on the other, as a humble, a humil-
iated man, confessedly second-rate, who has lost nine of the ten talents
committed to him and almost begs permission to keep the one that
remains. A great genius, in short, that has never attained the inner control which makes genius great, a mind that has not found itself, a mind
that does not know itself, a mind that cloaks to the end in the fantasy of
its temporal power the reality of some spiritual miscarriage!

The metaphor of division is clear here, but even more so in another quotation. Note the string of metaphors as Brooks attempts to describe and
define Mark Twain: "From his philosophy alone, therefore, we can see that
Mark Twain was a frustrated spirit, a victim of arrested development, and
beyond this fact, as we know from innumerable instances the psycholo-
gists have placed before us, we need not look for an explanation of much
of the chagrin of his old age. He had been balked, he had been divided, he
had even been turned, as we shall see, against himself; the poet, the artist
in him, consequently, had withered into the cynic and the whole man had
become a spiritual valetudinarian."[4] Brooks's title itself, *The Ordeal of Mark
Twain*, announces its metaphorical emphasis, as titles often do, whether
their authors recognize it or not; figuring Mark Twain's life and career as
an "ordeal," his book set the tenor for the debate that has continued to this
day. In Turbayne's terms, Brooks is both the iconoclast who tries to explode
a myth and the creator of a new metaphor that itself becomes a myth.

That metaphor, of course, was answered in 1932 by Bernard DeVoto in
his book *Mark Twain's America*. Rather than a metaphorical emphasis,
DeVoto's title seems to emphasize a metonymic connection, as the following quotation shows:

Somewhere in the person of Mark Twain . . . must have been an artist—
as American.
    The artist's career is worth a summary. More widely and deeply than
any one else who ever wrote books, he shared the life of America. Printer,
pilot, soldier, silver miner, gold-washer, the child of two emigrations, a
pilgrim in another, a sharer in the flush times, a shaper of the gilded age—
he, more completely than any other writer, took part in the American
experience.

DeVoto's metonymic focus finally amounts to a metaphor, a metaphor that
directly challenges Brooks's: the artist as American, and finally, the artist

as America. Consider this string of metaphors in his description of Mark Twain's move to the East: "He was the frontier itself"; "He was, that is, a savage"; "He was anarchy."[5]

I am treading on very well-worn ground in reviewing the Brooks-DeVoto debate, but my emphasis on the metaphorical nature of the debate makes the review worthwhile. I refer again to the influential theorist Roman Jakobson, whose 1956 article "Two Aspects of Language and Two Types of Aphasic Disturbances" has been very important in a number of fields, including both structuralist and post-structuralist literary theory. What Jakobson's editors called a "fundamental polarity of language" can apply even to critical approaches.[6] Thus, we can make the quick distinction that because of Brooks and DeVoto, Mark Twain studies have been founded on a conflict between metaphor and metonymy, and we are then able to chart subsequent studies as being either predominantly one or the other.

I see several trends in recent criticism, especially in regard to metaphoric underpinning. These break down not only by metaphor/metonymy, but also by an attempt to deal with Mark Twain's doubleness and identity, as well as by an attempt to define him and his work in new ways. A number of studies are very clearly metonymic in nature, examining Mark Twain and his works in connection with a specific topic or idea. The titles of these works make their metonymic focus clear: *Mark Twain and the Art of the Tall Tale,* by Henry B. Wonham; *Mark Twain and Shakespeare,* by Anthony J. Berret; *Mark Twain's Languages,* by David R. Sewell; *Mark Twain and Science,* by Sherwood Cummings; *Mark Twain and the Feminine Aesthetic,* by Peter Stoneley; *Mark Twain, Culture and Gender,* by J. D. Stahl; *Mark Twain in the Company of Women,* by Laura E. Skandera Trombley; *The Courtship of Olivia Langdon and Mark Twain,* by Susan K. Harris; *Twain's Heroes, Twain's Worlds,* by Andrew Hoffman; and *Mark Twain and William James,* by Jason Gary Horn. Each of these works makes a metonymic connection between Mark Twain and the particular topic in question, and the connection forces a metonymic shift in our understanding of Twain. For example, Stoneley gives this explanation of why he uses a man to study a feminist issue, with language that highlights the metonymic shift: "Mark Twain is a representative example of a man who tried, with a variety of techniques, to both enforce and moderate the cult of femininity. He can be used to suggest the extended integration of masculine and feminine values, the uses that the feminine aesthetic had for men, and to illustrate the threat that 'excessive' femininity contained. For although Twain is usually associated with a boyish, picaresque world, he returned throughout his career to the questions raised by the role and nature of the feminine aesthetic." Similarly, Harris recounts the usual metaphoric representation of Twain to argue for a reappraisal of Olivia Langdon's importance, a reappraisal that forces a metonymic shift in our perception of Twain: "Mark Twain may have been as saintly or as devilish, as sane or as neurotic, as passive or as manipulative, as he has been painted by the various biographical camps that have tackled him, but he cannot be assessed without genuine attention to the people with whom he daily interacted—and the emphasis here must be on interaction. Perhaps because it was composed of women, the family that most of Twain's early biographers portray is flat, a collective background for Mark Twain's angst and antics."[7] If such a metonymic approach is successful in convincing the reader of its validity, the approach finally becomes metaphoric, as the writer makes us see Mark Twain anew. Clearly, given the work of Stoneley, Stahl, Skandera Trombley, Harris, and others, we are in the midst of a major metonymic shift as regards Mark Twain and women, one that will undoubtedly create a new picture of him. Similar metonymic shifts are always occurring with any writer, and we can see from the list above the other kinds of shifts occurring in Mark Twain studies as critics turn their attention to various matters.

A number of other works are more metaphoric in approach (but note that their subtitles often reveal a metonymic connection): *Was Huck Black?: Mark Twain and African-American Voices*, by Shelley Fisher Fishkin; *Writing "Huck Finn": Mark Twain's Creative Process*, by Victor Doyno; *Sentimental Twain: Samuel Clemens in the Maze of Moral Philosophy*, by Gregg Camfield; *Acting Naturally: Mark Twain in the Culture of Performance*, by Randall Knoper; and *Mark Twain on the Loose: A Comic Writer and the American Self*, by Bruce Michelson. Still others are fully metaphoric: Tom Quirk, *Coming to Grips with "Huckleberry Finn"*; Jeffrey Steinbrink, *Getting to Be Mark Twain*; Andrew Hoffman, *Inventing Mark Twain*. Looking at two studies of the late 1980s by Forrest G. Robinson and Susan Gillman, we can see from their titles, *In Bad Faith* and *Dark Twins*, respectively, their predominantly metaphoric nature. Significantly, however, in each of their subtitles is embedded a metonymic reference to *DeVoto's* title: Robinson's *The Dynamics of Deception in Mark Twain's America* and Gillman's *Imposture and Identity in Mark Twain's America*. Robinson makes metaphoric connections between America's bad faith over what he calls "race-slavery" and two texts: *Tom Sawyer* and *Huckleberry Finn*; thus, *Huckleberry Finn* becomes, metaphorically, "a direct, anguished meditation on the affliction itself, the environment through which it spreads, and the tortuous pattern of its operation in the minds of its agents and victims and witnesses." As Turbayne says, "A new theory, even one not metaphysical, like a new pair of spectacles, changes the facts. . . . New theories not only save the appearances; they change them, and even create new ones."[8] What any critic tries to do is to change our metaphoric relation to the text or author, to make us read, in Robinson's case, a text we have formerly read as a comic masterpiece or as a coming-of-age adventure story or as a satire on society's shams now as "a direct, anguished meditation." Part of the resistance many readers may have to such an interpretation comes from the distance between such a new reading and our previous metaphoric stance toward the novel. When a critic tries to change our metaphoric stance so radically, he or she takes on even more of a burden of proof than that usually shouldered by critics.

Gillman's study demands a smaller metaphoric shift in the reader, examining as it does what she calls the "critical language of twinning, doubling, and impersonation [that] has . . . developed around" Mark Twain. I would argue, of course, that it is not merely a critical *language* of twinning, but a *metaphor* that shapes the way we form our critical language about the writer. Gillman posits that "Mark Twain presses his investigations of twinness to the point where coherent individual identity collapses," which includes the Clemens/Mark Twain split. A few pages later, she goes even further, and I would propose that she begs the question, referring to "Mark Twain's own unstable personal identity." This point leads to her thesis: "My approach to the subject that might be called by its nineteenth-century name of 'duality' is to (re)create the dialogue between Twain's language of identity and the cultural vocabularies available to him." This sentence is full of metaphorical implications, but I find especially intriguing the central metaphorical term "re-create," which Gillman further complicates by putting "re" in parentheses. As she no doubt intends, she gives the term a double meaning, but when we consider the word(s) as metaphorical, that move becomes somewhat troubling. Which is it: create or re-create? Gillman seems to recognize that she is creating rather than re-creating when she admits that "it will be *my* Mark Twain and *my* nineteenth-century that emerge."[9] Both Gillman and Robinson seem to be appropriating DeVoto's metonymic phrase and stance—"Mark Twain's America"—but with a complete reversal, so that their argument shares more in spirit with Brooks's than DeVoto's. Clearly, we remain engaged in the same debate Brooks and DeVoto were engaged in seventy-five years ago, not just over our metaphorical vision of Mark Twain, but also over our vision of America.

In fact, I am struck by the number of recent studies that begin with a discussion of the Brooks-DeVoto argument, showing not only how central the debate remains, but also how aware Mark Twain critics generally are of our critical history. Guy Cardwell's controversial 1991 book, *The Man Who Was Mark Twain*, not only begins with the debate, but also highlights the debate's metaphorical nature. His opening chapter is basically a reprint of his article "Mark Twain: The Metaphoric Hero as Battleground" (1977), in which he uses the terms "metaphor" and "synecdoche" (often considered interchangeable with "metonymy"), yet curiously never mentions Jakobson directly. In fact, even though he seems aware of the metaphoric nature of his approach, he seems not to be aware of some of its implications. For example, early on he states that "[a]n obvious step toward ordering the chaos is to attempt to disentangle Samuel Clemens from his metaphoric roles." Using and recognizing metaphor is good, but we cannot "disentangle Samuel Clemens from his metaphoric roles"; as Turbayne argues, all we will do is get enmeshed in *another* metaphoric role. Cardwell's stated intention is "to undermine superstitiously devised memorial statues that have been cherished as acceptable likenesses," but every act of undermining is actually the erection of another statue, even if the undermining critic does not recognize that.[10] The negative reaction to Cardwell's book came in part because his metaphorical presentation of Mark Twain as a masturbating, impotent pedophile with a gambling problem is so far from our shared metaphorical image.

One of the reasons we need to be metaphorically aware is so that we can avoid works such as Cardwell's (or, to go back, such as Brooks's, or even DeVoto's). It is a temptation for a critic or biographer to attempt to strip away the metaphorical myth and arrive at the "truth." But what he or she is really doing is substituting one metaphor for another. Turbayne makes this point emphatically: "The attempt to re-allocate the facts by restoring them to where they 'actually belong' is vain. It is like trying to observe the rule 'Let us get rid of the metaphors and replace them by the literal truth.' But can this be done? We might just as well seek to provide what the poet 'actually says.'" As critics and biographers, we do seem so often to be trying to do just this; we all seem to be engaged in "an essay in the correction of ideas," as DeVoto calls his book on his dedication page. That impulse combined with our own metaphors can lead us into some interesting places. Consider this example from Laura Skandera Trombley's introduction to *Mark Twain in the Company of Women*:

> Past criticism by both men and women has wrongly dismissed Twain as being anti-female and has come to portray Twain almost as a caricature of the "man's man," far removed from the realm of women. I find this view fallacious.

Some feminist critics have responded to this conception of Twain by repeatedly attacking and finally dismissing him, yet it is questionable whether critics have been responding to the man or to an invention of past biographies. Thus, central to my work is the challenge of distinguishing the person from the plethora of published opinion. My intention is to dynamite this hollow creation and reveal Twain as he really was, an author so dependent upon female interaction and influence that without it the sublimity of his novels would have been lost.[11]

Skandera Trombley has reacted to a metaphorical definition of Mark Twain as a "man's man" with the metaphorical act of dynamiting, but what has she replaced that hollow image with? If we accept Turbayne, not with "Twain as he really was." Does this mean, then, that we can't make any point, that we can't write anything? Turbayne offers this answer:

> I have said that one condition of the use of metaphors is awareness. More accurately speaking, this means *more* awareness, for we can never become wholly aware. We cannot say what reality is, only what it seems like *to* us, imprisoned in Plato's cave, because we cannot get outside to look. The consequence is that we never know exactly what the facts are. We are always victims of adding some interpretation. We cannot help but allocate, sort, or bundle the facts in some way or another. Thus the second level of analysis which purported to reveal process and procedure purged of metaphysics was at best an approximation.[12]

What Skandera Trombley has done, rather than show "Twain as he really was," is to make a very convincing new metaphor of Mark Twain as a "woman's man," a metaphor arising from her metonymic examination of Mark Twain in the company of women. She, Stoneley, Stahl, and others are engaged in a new metaphoric creation of Mark Twain as regards his relations with women, a new metaphoric creation that is already changing our image of Mark Twain. All I am arguing is that it is better that we be aware of the metaphoric nature of that image rather than to fall into the trap of thinking that we are finally getting at "the real Twain."

In fact, what my examination of recent Mark Twain studies reveals is the extent and the number of ways that metaphoric image is being changed. By metaphorically seeing, or rather *hearing*, Huck as black, Shelley Fisher Fishkin is, like others, changing our view of Mark Twain and his works in their metonymic relation to African-American issues. Still, such a radical metaphoric shift makes her claim hard for many readers to accept. At least part of the reluctance of some to accept her theory that "Sociable Jimmy" provided Mark Twain the voice for Huck Finn lies embedded in the metaphorical language of her claim: "[A]s an engaging black child he encountered in the early 1870s helped him reconnect Twain to the cadences and rhythms of black speakers from Twain's own childhood, he inspired him to liberate a language that lay buried within Twain's own linguistic repertoire and to apprehend its stunning creative potential."[13] The metaphors "reconnect," "liberate," and "buried" seem to lie at the heart of some readers' objections to Fishkin's assertion, suggesting as they do that this particular encounter somehow reconnected Mark Twain to a language that many would argue he had never lost touch with in the first place. But even if the "Sociable Jimmy" theory fails to win over everyone, her other, broader claims about African-American influence will no doubt prove enduring and image-altering, especially coupled with her continuing work on race, as well as the work of other scholars and critics. As on the question of women, we are in the midst of a dramatic metaphoric shift in the question of Mark Twain and race. The Mark Twain of the twenty-first century will likely be very different from the Mark Twain of the nineteenth, or even the twentieth.

An exciting area of recent inquiry goes back to that question of doubles and identity, the metaphor that has proved the most persistent and shaping throughout the history of Mark Twain studies. In *Mark Twain on the Loose,* Bruce Michelson uses the controlling metaphor of wildness to recover Twain from the domestication Michelson sees him as undergoing at the hands of critics and biographers. But rather than using wildness as a defining term, Michelson warns against any attempts at definition: "To try to define or *con*fine Mark Twain ideologically is therefore a risky business, for the range and reflexivity of his own work can easily outrun—or overthrow—discourse about economic and political configurations of the self." His metaphor for Mark Twain's humor is its "absolute fluidity," the same metaphor Don Florence uses throughout *Persona and Humor in Mark Twain's Early Writings.* Rather than an evasion, I see this metaphor as one that will allow us to take a new look at Mark Twain, a look not defined by or confined by oppositions and dualities. Michelson poses this question: "Is it possible that this 'self' that Mark Twain seems to exemplify in American culture, this literary-mythological identity with such stubborn appeal, defines itself by how it refuses and evades, rather than by how and what it affirms?"[14] In a similar vein, we have J. D. Stahl's announcement that he is "not attempting to 'invent' a new text or a new author. I am simply trying to see, without some of the preconceptions which it is easy to bring to familiar—and unfamiliar—texts, what is there in the texts that is not necessarily easy to see."

Or we have Gregg Camfield's questioning the oppositions that Henry Nash Smith and others have set up, asserting that such "polar oppositions [as "democracy versus elitism, freedom versus constraint, pragmatic realism versus sentimental idealism"] . . . begin to collapse if put under pressure."[15] Andrew Hoffman explains why over a decade ago he refused to use the biographical approach (he has used a biographical approach in his recent full-length biography, of course), saying that the idea of a "divided Twain" has "stalled" Twain criticism: "Twain's bifurcated self has been made to account for so much in Twain's fiction that the fiction itself risks being lost in this simplistic code. The skeleton key of 'divided Twain' threatens to turn the wonder of entering the maze of Twain's work into a walk down a well-lit corridor."[16]

Such moves are, of course, themselves metaphorical. But clearly there is a metaphoric battle being waged over Mark Twain, a battle in many ways like the battle between Brooks and DeVoto earlier in the century. Critics such as Robinson and Gillman present us with a Mark Twain who is metaphorically bound by his culture, his race, his gender, while critics such as Michelson counter with a metaphorically more loose writer and person, allied with critics such as Skandera Trombley and Fishkin, who are altering the metonymic representation of Mark Twain. The stakes in this battle are high: the result will be our new Mark Twain, or at least the new way we perceive him. My central point is that we must always remain aware of the *metaphorical* nature of the battle.

A number of recent critics explicitly acknowledge the metaphorical nature of their approaches. For example, Richard S. Lowry, in *"Littery Man": Mark Twain and Modern Authorship*, discusses Europe as a metonymic series and examines the metaphors of *Life on the Mississippi*; Maria Ornella Marotti in *The Duplicating Imagination* traces the space/time and writing/printing metaphors in the *Mysterious Stranger* manuscripts, as well as calling "duplication" the central metaphor of Twain's late work; and Susan K. Harris, in *The Courtship of Olivia Langdon and Mark Twain*, figures the courtship as a series of tropes, rightly reading Mark Twain's letters as centered around various metaphors—the language of material possession as one example.[17] But at this moment of re-vision, it becomes vitally important that we all constantly stay metaphorically aware; otherwise, we will remain, in Turbayne's terms, "victims of metaphor." Turbayne sums up his argument this way:

We are now at the final level of analysis where, having become to some degree aware of the metaphors involved, we proceed to re-use them instead of being used by them. But need we use the same ones? If we are aware, we can stop and think. We can choose our metaphors. We are no longer the duped citizens of the city-state of Oz but the wizard of Oz himself.

Perhaps the best way to avoid being victimized by a metaphor worn out by over-use is to show that it is expendable. The best way to do this is to choose a new one. If the operation, just described, of presenting the literal truth is naïve, this one is sophisticated.

Clearly, we are engaged in choosing a new metaphor for Mark Twain. Turbayne says that "a new metaphor changes our attitude to the facts." That is what happens with a new critical metaphor, especially one we accept. The metaphor does not change the text, or change Mark Twain. All it does is change our attitude—and note that "attitude" is itself a metaphor. Attitude is important, not only for us as scholars and critics and teachers, but for the culture at large. I quote Tom Quirk on this point: "Somehow our attitude toward Twain and *Huckleberry Finn* matters—matters as a response to a cultural property, to be sure, but it matters as well because the novel challenges our tepid commitments and false assurances and promotes values we do not as yet own."[18]

I am not proposing myself as either the genius or the iconoclast who makes the new metaphor, to use Turbayne's labels. Instead, I propose as our iconoclastic genius Louis J. Budd, with these words from *Our Mark Twain:*

My insisting on his success [in creating a persona] does not mean to concede Twain's dishonesty with or about himself. His moods of self-accusation often plunged to the edge of irrationality, and he regularly warned the public that his character was flawed. He also warned it that he was posturing.

At the risk of sounding like Twain's official biographer, Albert Bigelow Paine, I proceed in the tone of gratitude that his posturing worked and gave us both his writings and his public personality. We would not have these writings as they now stand if he had shaped a substantially different life; biographers once understood that principle better than does the guild today. Within and beyond his books Twain reinforced qualities crucial to the happiness and perhaps survival of humankind: delight in experience, emotional spontaneity, and irreverence toward pomposity, petrified ideas, injustice, and self-pride. The function of a humorist centers in a liberating aggression that can spin toward tedious venom or anarchy. But effective naysaying carries over into affirmation. Twain reinforced some old and some modern values: courage in the face of dishonest or carping criticism, candid self-judgment that humbles the delusion of being able to gauge interpersonal reality without error, flexibility of mind and response (when his career is perceived as it happened rather than simplified to suit some theory), respect for the integrity of others, concern for the common welfare, and rapt awareness sweeping from the submicroscopic to the cosmic. While holding no monopoly on those values, Twain embodied them uniquely. My analysis tries to catch that rounded uniqueness, which serves us better than the flattened models that the mass or elitist media keep manufacturing.[19]

There: "rounded uniqueness." There is a new metaphor, one we can build on in interesting and fruitful ways.

Notes

Introduction

1. "Metaphor," 136; Paul Ricoeur, *The Rule of Metaphor: Multidisciplinary Studies of the Creation of Meaning in Language*, 18.

2. Wayne C. Booth, "Metaphor as Rhetoric: The Problem of Evaluation," 48–49.

3. Colin Murray Turbayne, *The Myth of Metaphor*, 91.

4. Phillip Stambovsky, *The Depictive Image: Metaphor and Literary Experience*, 103–4.

5. Ibid., 113.

6. I. A. Richards, *The Philosophy of Rhetoric*, 90, 92.

7. Ibid., 116, 125.

8. Ibid., 135.

9. William M. Gibson, *The Art of Mark Twain*, 27.

1. Figuring "Mark Twain"

1. The story has had numerous titles; for simplicity, I will refer to it generically as "The Jumping Frog."

2. I use "Mark Twain" to distinguish the character of the narrator from the writer Mark Twain—here, as so often, there is a clear difference, and a distance between the persona of the narrator and the writer himself.

3. There are at least five published versions of this story from 1865 to 1875. Twain spent a great deal of time revising and polishing "The Jumping Frog," unlike other pieces in his career, and the 1875 version seems to represent his final intentions. Simon Wheeler's figurative language is virtually unchanged throughout the many versions, except for dialect markings, which Twain obviously cared about very deeply. Henry B. Wonham makes a similar point, commenting on the changes in the three early versions: "His revision added nothing either to the substance of Wheeler's tale or to the yarn spinner's easygoing narrative style." *Mark Twain and the Art of the Tall Tale*, 68. Even so, since Twain cared so much about even the slightest change in this story, it seems proper to quote from the version as he finally left it.

4. Richard Wilbur, *New and Collected Poems*, 10. I am indebted to Bruce Michelson for the connection to Wilbur's poem.

5. George Lakoff and Mark Johnson, *Metaphors We Live By*, 4–5, 17, 15–16.

6. See especially Paul Baender, "'The Jumping Frog' as a Comedian's First Virtue"; Edgar M. Branch, "'My voice is still for Setchell': A Background Study of 'Jim Smiley and His Jumping Frog'"; Sydney J. Krause, "The Art and Satire of Twain's 'Jumping Frog' Story"; and Paul C. Rodgers Jr., "Artemus Ward and Mark Twain's 'Jumping Frog.'" In a classic study of Twain's manipulation of his persona and point of view, John C. Gerber discusses "The Jumping Frog" in "Mark Twain's Use of the Comic Pose." For an excellent overview, both of the story's publication and of its critical history, see James D. Wilson, *A Reader's Guide to the Short Stories of Mark Twain*, 163–76. Tom Quirk devotes several pithy pages to the story in *Mark Twain: A Study of the Short Fiction*, esp. 23–29. Quirk notes the effect of some of the metaphorical language: "These fantastic similes have the feel of unmediated originality because the author has so managed the dramatic presentation that Simon Wheeler seems earnestly to spin out his yarn with spontaneous association and halting confusion" (27). Gibson asserts that "Mark Twain's metaphors help make these creatures characters in a fable." *Art of Mark Twain*, 74. See also James M. Cox, *Mark Twain: The Fate of Humor*, 24–33; and Bruce Michelson, *Mark Twain on the Loose: A Comic Writer and the American Self*, 25–33. For a recent critical examination, see Peter Messent, "Caught on the Hop: Interpretive Dislocation in 'The Notorious Jumping Frog of Calaveras County.'" Messent ably crawls through the accumulated critical thickets and argues, convincingly, that the story turns on "the relativity of voices and the indeterminacy of values" (37). We are in essential agreement about the effects of the various levels in the story: "Our interpretive bearings are being constantly disconcerted, redirected, even frustrated, as the various strands of the story both reflexively inform each other and yet resist any totalizing critical impulse. Disorientation, indeed, operates to both central stylistic and thematic effect in the story. The upsetting of expectations, which its various narratives repetitively trace, is formally reproduced in its problematization of interpretive stability and certainty." Messent, "Caught on the Hop," 39. For an updated version of his argument, see Peter Messent, *The Short Works of Mark Twain*, 24–39.

7. Lakoff and Johnson, *Metaphors We Live By*, 51.

8. Richards introduces the terms "vehicle" and "tenor" to name the parts of a metaphor, and wonders that no such terms had been used before. *Philosophy of Rhetoric*, 96.

9. In the 1865 version, the camp's name is given as "Boomerang," which is also metaphorically interesting (as well as ironic). Twain uses both "Boomerang" and "Angel's Camp" in the three versions reprinted in *ET&S2*, 273–88.

10. Kenneth S. Lynn discusses the use of lawyers as narrators for much of southwestern humor in *Mark Twain and Southwestern Humor*. Another early Twain sketch (1863) that depends for its humor on the language of the law is "Ye Sentimental Law Student" (*ET&S1*, 215–19).

11. A number of critics discuss the framework structure, including Lynn, *Mark Twain and Southwestern Humor*, 145–47; and Walter Blair and Hamlin Hill, *America's Humor from Poor Richard to Doonesbury*. For a detailed discussion of structure, see Krause, "Art and Satire," 562–76.

12. For a discussion of the "double deadpan" or "double poker face," see Baender, "'The Jumping Frog'"; and Pascal Covici Jr., *Mark Twain's Humor: The Image of a World*, 51–52. Messent analyzes the "double deadpan" (or its absence) in "Caught on the Hop," 36–39. For historical background on the use of deadpan humor, see Randall Knoper, *Acting Naturally: Mark Twain in the Culture of Performance*, 55–61.

13. Cox, *Mark Twain*, 32, 33.

14. Guy Cardwell pictures Mark Twain as "a compulsive gambler" in *The Man Who Was Mark Twain: Images and Ideologies*, 87, and he uses several quite unflattering por-

traits and psychological analyses of gambling to paint Twain in a more unflattering light than any other critic or biographer has done. While Twain probably did not have as severe a problem as Cardwell claims, clearly there is abundant evidence in his life and his works of plenty of experience with the world of chance.

15. For a reliable and balanced account of Twain's literary biography, see Everett Emerson, *Mark Twain: A Literary Life*. See also Emerson, *The Authentic Mark Twain: A Literary Biography of Samuel L. Clemens*. Of the narrator of *Roughing It*, Emerson points out, "He reminds the reader repeatedly in the early chapters that he has traveled to Europe and the Holy Land; he suggests that these experiences, as well as the ones he is telling about, made him what he is now. As a result, the reader is encouraged to feel that he is hearing the voice of the authentic Mark Twain, who is providing his autobiography. Here the writer provides answers to some implied questions. How did there come to be this humorist, this skeptical, sometimes cynical character? Who is this frank, confidential, justice-seeking comic writer, whose graceful but firm prose seems to fit him like a glove? The writer's Western experience provides explanations." *Mark Twain: A Literary Life*, 74. For a biographical account focused on the creation of the persona, specifically on the crucial years 1868 to 1871, see Jeffrey Steinbrink, *Getting to Be Mark Twain*. Steinbrink maintains: "In many respects the invention of that identity was the work of a lifetime, an ongoing effort at self-discovery, self-fashioning, and self-promotion that Clemens managed with inexhaustible dexterity. But the animal assumed its essential shape—grew to its adult, if not mature, proportions—between 1868 and 1871 . . ." (xiii).

16. Henry Nash Smith, *Mark Twain: The Development of a Writer*, 53, 55. Among earlier studies, readers should not overlook the chapter on *Roughing It* in Franklin R. Rogers, *Mark Twain's Burlesque Patterns*, 61–81. Lynn relates the narrative to the topic of his groundbreaking book, *Mark Twain and Southwestern Humor*. See also Robert Regan, *Unpromising Heroes: Mark Twain and His Characters*. Among more recent books on Twain's writing, the following devote considerable attention to *Roughing It*: Wonham, *Art of the Tall Tale*, 89–111; Michelson, *Mark Twain on the Loose*, 63–74; Don Florence, *Persona and Humor in Mark Twain's Early Writings*, 93–139; and Richard S. Lowry, *"Littery Man": Mark Twain and Modern Authorship*, 65–75.

17. As I will discuss, Florence has examined this passage in light of its metaphorical nature in *Persona and Humor in Mark Twain's Early Writings*. I had made my initial analysis before I read Florence's book, and while many of our ideas about the way metaphor works in the passage are very similar, we reach quite different conclusions. I am indebted to him for sharpening my ideas about the passage and about *Roughing It*.

18. Rather than the linguistic humor of the passage, Lawrence I. Berkove focuses on its darker undertones in "The Trickster God in *Roughing It*." He emphasizes Buck Fanshaw rather than Scotty Briggs in his analysis.

19. Richard Bridgman, *Traveling in Mark Twain*, 35; Lynn, *Mark Twain and Southwestern Humor*, 168; Smith, *Mark Twain*, 61, 63.

20. Covici, *Mark Twain's Humor*, 102–3; David R. Sewell, *Mark Twain's Languages: Discourse, Dialogue, and Linguistic Variety*, 132. While he does not focus specifically on metaphor, Philip Burns makes an argument similar to mine in its topic and conclusions in his article "Fabrication and Faultline: Language as Experience in *Roughing It*." Burns charts the narrator's linguistic experience, pointing out the prevalence of "language without shared meaning" in the Scotty Briggs episode and throughout. His conclusion is one with which I heartily agree, that the gap between the narrator's expectation and his experience comes about through a "collapse of language" (254, 263). Lowry sees in *Roughing It* "the central trope of Twain's autobiography of authorship." *"Littery Man,"* 70. Lowry's conclusion on *Roughing It* is similarly metaphorically aware: "The tropes of a commodified world of fictional spectacle that he employed in his early books—

tourism and prospecting—would reappear only sporadically throughout the rest of his writing. But his understanding of how the promiscuous mix of culture and economics set social values would never cease to shape his best work" (75). Florence, as I have noted, is even more focused on metaphor. Besides his extended examination of the Scotty Briggs episode, he makes a number of comments about the ways various elements in *Roughing It* serve as metaphors; for example, "The Washoe Zephyr might be a metaphor for the mind itself, with its different grades or layers of consciousness, distortion, and exaggeration," and later, "Twain gives us another metaphor for life's incomprehensibility and the mind's restlessness." *Persona and Humor,* 124, 133.

21. Florence, *Persona and Humor,* 109.

22. J. R. Searle, *Expression and Meaning,* 85; Lakoff and Johnson, *Metaphors We Live By,* 3.

23. Philip D. Beidler, "Realistic Style and the Problem of Context in *The Innocents Abroad* and *Roughing It,*" 46. Florence disagrees with Beidler's point: "Actually, Twain implies that both linguistic worlds are founded upon fantasy and that 'truth' lies not in something clearly perceived and objectively rendered but in imaginative expressions. Far from reaching an impasse, Twain indicates that both languages are cut from figurative cloth." *Persona and Humor,* 109. While I agree with Beidler that the two are at an impasse, my further argument will show some agreement with Florence about ultimate transcendence, although with a difference in emphasis on when and how that transcendence is attained. See also Messent's position: "There is no favoring of western language and value here. A rejection of genteel forms of language is implied in the failure of its rhetorical forms and elaborate but well-worn turns of phrase adequately to connect with the facts of western life. But vernacular forms of language are not thereby rendered fully admirable." *Mark Twain,* 52.

24. Sewell, *Mark Twain's Languages,* 132–33; Covici, *Mark Twain's Humor,* 103.

25. Smith, *Mark Twain,* 63.

26. Florence, *Persona and Humor,* 110–11.

27. Pascal Covici Jr., "Buck Fanshaw's Funeral," 103. Gibson calls the episode "a bravura performance" and "a kind of 'language experiment,' as Whitman sometimes spoke of his *Leaves of Grass.*" *Art of Mark Twain,* 10, 9.

28. Florence concludes his examination of the episode with this point: "Despite linguistic discords, the Scotty Briggs anecdote is a joyous harmony. We are not to *choose* between these two languages, or any other languages; instead, we are to become imaginatively inclusive, coming to understand differing systems of metaphor, as Scotty and the minister come to understand each other." *Persona and Humor,* 111. While I agree with Florence about the passage's complexity and with his overall argument against the dichotomies and conflicts that have often dominated Twain criticism, I disagree with his description of the episode as "joyous harmony" and the fact that we are not to choose. If the minister and Scotty finally do come to an understanding, it takes, as the passage shows, a number of years. My emphasis is on the conflict; Florence's seems to be on the ultimate conclusion. As I argue in the remainder of this section, the conflict between metaphorical levels that drives this particular episode is central to the whole book and, even more importantly, to Twain's establishment of his skill with metaphor.

29. Carl F. Wieck examines this phrase and the preface to *Roughing It,* as well as the prefaces to a number of Twain's other works, in *Refiguring "Huckleberry Finn,"* 128–29.

30. Smith, *Mark Twain,* 54–56.

31. Although Smith asserts that the vernacular and the genteel are in clear conflict, he recognizes complexity and ambiguity in the situation: "The attitudes from back home are shown to be ridiculous in comparison with the coyote's secret—a secret that seems actually to release him from the laws of nature. It is true that the exact content of the vernacular values is not made clear; they are somewhat hypothetical, they are suggested

rather than specified. Yet the coyote with his ambiguous smile is perhaps the more impressive because of the air of mystery that surrounds him." *Mark Twain,* 55–56. Tom Towers disagrees with Smith's emphasis on initiation. Towers argues that reading *Roughing It* as an initiation is distortive and obscures the true unity, which he says is a pattern of increasing disillusionment. Towers, "'Hateful Reality': The Failure of the Territory in *Roughing It,*" 4. While Towers makes a strong case, one might argue that disillusionment is often a key experience in initiation. Florence argues against such dualities, and instead offers "a pattern of humorous transcendence, expressed through the interplay of anecdotes and perspectives in the narrative." *Persona and Humor,* 95. As I note elsewhere, Florence makes metaphorical language central to his argument.

32. Cox, *Mark Twain,* 104, 90–91; Gérard Genette, *Figures of Literary Discourse,* 204.

33. Susan Gillman, *Dark Twins: Imposture and Identity in Mark Twain's America,* 1.

34. Gerber, *Mark Twain,* 13.

35. Kenneth Burke, *A Grammar of Motives,* 503.

36. Burke, *A Grammar of Motives,* 503. Michael Shapiro and Marianne Shapiro discuss the tendency of metonymy to slide into metaphor: "While taking account of the high incidence of semantic fading among tropes in nonpoetic discourse, we must also acknowledge the fact that a metonymy, even at its original creation in literary texts, is already on the way to becoming a metaphor. . . . Every metonymy thus contains the potential for sliding into metaphor." *Figuration in Verbal Art,* 34.

37. In common practice, scholars and critics use "Samuel Clemens" when referring to the man and his life, and "Mark Twain" when referring to the writer and his works. The split is not that neat, of course, which can cause problems for Clemens/Twain scholars. Some writers insist that the name "Mark Twain" must not be split, that it is an error to refer to "Twain." Bernard DeVoto called him "Mark."

38. Most metaphor critics consider synecdoche a subset of metonymy, or treat the two as interchangeable, just as most routinely consider simile a subset of metaphor. Arguments have been made against both critical moves, but metaphor and metonymy are firmly entrenched as the dominant figures, mainly because of Roman Jakobson's formulation.

39. He refers to himself thusly in *Those Extraordinary Twins,* 119. Robert A. Wiggins uses that phrase to provide the title of his book *Mark Twain: Jackleg Novelist.*

40. See, for example, the discussion of the pen name in R. Kent Rasmussen, *Mark Twain A to Z,* 303.

41. Emerson, *Mark Twain,* 11–12. For the fullest discussion of the origin of the name, see Horst H. Kruse, "Mark Twain's *Nom de Plume:* Some Mysteries Resolved."

42. Walter J. Ong, "Metaphor and the Twinned Vision," 42.

43. Ibid., 43.

44. Ibid., 45, 46.

45. Ibid., 48.

2. Figuring the River

1. Genette, *Figures of Literary Discourse,* 204.

2. Philip Wheelwright, *Metaphor and Reality,* 71–72.

3. For insightful and foundational readings of the opening scene, see Walter Blair, *Mark Twain and Huck Finn,* 43–47; and Smith, *Mark Twain,* 72–75. For discussions of "Old Times on the Mississippi," see the following: Smith, *Mark Twain,* 71–81; Cox, *Mark Twain,* 105–26; Gibson, *Art of Mark Twain,* 53–65; Wonham, *Art of the Tall Tale,* 112–23; and Lawrence Howe, *Mark Twain and the Novel: The Double-Cross of Authority,* 14–72. Howe's reading of "Old Times on the Mississippi" deftly traces metaphorical and

metonymical patterns, although his argument centers less on language and style and more on Twain's development as a writer.

4. David Lodge, *The Modes of Modern Writing: Metaphor, Metonymy, and the Typology of Modern Literature*, 73; Roman Jakobson, "Two Aspects of Language and Two Types of Aphasic Disturbances," 74, 90.

5. A number of critics and theorists have raised objections to Jakobson's opposition of metaphor and metonymy, most centering on what they perceive as a simplistic duality, endemic, they say, to structuralist criticism. I quote Maria Ruegg at length to give a full sense of typical objections: "The use of the terms 'metaphor' and 'metonymy' by both Jakobson and Lacan is of particular interest: first of all, because it illustrates a number of characteristic structuralist tendencies—the tendency to reduce complex givens to the terms of a simple binary opposition; the tendency to make universal generalizations on the basis of purely hypothetical and unverifiable 'structures'; the tendency to ignore logical inconsistencies within the binary oppositions themselves. And secondly, the use of 'metaphor' and 'metonymy' is of interest because it reveals the extent to which structuralism, despite the pretense of radical novelty, remained firmly entrenched in the most traditional of metaphysical idealisms; for it was the use of such terms—terms which have always depended on classical theories of language, the very theories structuralism so categorically rejected—that permitted structuralism to dismiss the Western metaphysical tradition, while at the same time reaffirming it. . . . It is only on the most superficial level, however, that such a distinction can function, and even then, the grossly oversimplified caricatures to which it gives rise are so general as to be virtually meaningless." Ruegg goes on to argue that the distinction between the two figures is not clear, that distinguishing a difference is "at best unfruitful, and at worst, a misleading oversimplification of what language does." Her argument concludes with this point: "If Jakobson's attempt to analyze language in terms of a simple binary rhetoric leads to logical inconsistencies, it is, first of all, because he treats what are in fact the very subtle, and often undecidable *differences* between metaphor and metonymy in terms of an absolute *opposition* which imposes an either/or choice at all levels of the analysis. And secondly, it is because he attempts to maintain a strict dualism between the two poles, even though he is forced to admit that the language of analysis (the 'metalanguage') is itself essentially a 'metaphoric' process, which naturally tends to *privilege* metaphor over metonymy." "Metaphor and Metonymy: The Logic of Structuralist Rhetoric," 142, 143–44, 145, 147. Hugh Bredin sees an even starker dead end in Jakobson's theoretical position: "What can now be seen, I believe, is what a straitjacket this has made of language. We do not live in a binary world. And there are more ways of organizing our ideas and our knowledge than two. Indeed, there are more types of discourse (and many more types of rhetorical figure) than two. The endless variety of discourse expresses the inexhaustible complexity of things, and the organizing principles of language are instruments, not determinants, of that expression." "Roman Jakobson on Metaphor and Metonymy," 102. For a good summary of the major theoretical objections to Jakobson's theory, see Christina Brooke-Rose, *A Structural Analysis of Pound's "Usura Canto": Jakobson's Method Extended and Applied to Free Verse*, 1–10. In defense of Jakobson, Krystyna Pomorska and Stephen Rudy make this counterargument: "Jakobson's critics—especially those insufficiently acquainted with modern linguistics—have singled out this idea [the opposition of metaphor and metonymy] for attack. But their misunderstanding stems from two sources: on the one hand, they usually mistake metaphor and metonymy for mere figures of speech, as opposed to pervasive forces organizing language in operation; on the other hand, they fail to appreciate that the metaphor/metonymy opposition is not an absolute one, but rather a tendency." *Verbal Art, Verbal Sign, Verbal Time*, 171. In spite of the serious objections to Jakobson, his work continues to be important and influential. In my use of Jakobson, I have tried

to keep these objections in mind and read with an eye toward tendencies and inter-connections rather than absolute binary opposites. In any discourse, both metaphor and metonymy are present, shifting constantly, penetrating one another, but with one pre-dominant over the other. I have certainly found Jakobson's ideas about metaphor and metonymy to be a powerful tool for reading Mark Twain.

6. Jakobson, "Two Aspects of Language," 91–96; Linda R. Waugh and Monique Monville-Burston, eds., in Roman Jakobson, *On Language*, 17.

7. Lodge, *Modes of Modern Writing*, 80–81.

8. Jakobson, "Two Aspects of Language," 95–96; Lodge, *Modes of Modern Writing*, 100–101.

9. Genette, *Figures of Literary Discourse*, 204.

10. For a compelling argument tracing the progression from metaphor to symbol, see Wheelwright, *Metaphor and Reality*, 92–152.

11. Leo Marx, *The Machine in the Garden: Technology and the Pastoral Ideal in America*, 321–24.

12. While critics who are judging "Old Times on the Mississippi" from a standpoint of narrative development find the ending somewhat flat, Gregg Camfield highlights the importance of Twain's comments on labor relations in this section: "Twain pub-lished this detailed portrait of labor conditions in antebellum America at precisely the moment when these conditions were moving to the center of American conscious-ness. . . . Remarkably, Twain's vision is without obvious bias either for or against unions. At the beginning of America's political engagement in 'the labor question,' Twain pres-ents an open mind, one that would take both sides at different times." *The Oxford Companion to Mark Twain*, 409, 410.

13. Genette, *Figures of Literary Discourse*, 204.

14. John Seelye, introduction to *LOM*, xxvii.

15. John C. Gerber, "*Adventures of Tom Sawyer, The*," 14; Gibson, *Art of Mark Twain*, 99; Messent, *Mark Twain*, 67–68.

16. Gibson, *Art of Mark Twain*, 99; Blair, *Mark Twain and Huck Finn*, 57; Smith, *Mark Twain*, 82. See Alan Gribben, "'I did wish Tom Sawyer was there': Boy-Book Elements in *Tom Sawyer* and *Huckleberry Finn*"; and Marcia Jacobson, *Being a Boy Again: Autobiography and the American Boy Book*. Gribben asserts that Aldrich's novel "tutored him [Mark Twain] in creating a sentimental, dignified, patronizing adult persona." "'I did wish,'" 158.

17. Gerber, "*Adventures of Tom Sawyer*," 14. Wonham has already noted a narrative split. In *Mark Twain and the Art of the Tall Tale*, 128–32, he adroitly outlines what he calls a contest for narrative authority between the narrator and Tom Sawyer, with Tom serv-ing as the tall-tale narrator who subverts the main narrator's conventional values. Wonham's point is persuasive and powerful, but I am arguing that the narrative con-test is even more complex.

18. Smith, *Mark Twain*, 83. The narrator I am calling "Author" could also be an exam-ple of what Michelson calls a "Petrified Man." Michelson, *Mark Twain on the Loose*, 14–18.

19. Gerber, "*Adventures of Tom Sawyer*," 14.

20. Smith, *Mark Twain*, 84.

21. Wonham, *Art of the Tall Tale*, 139. Wonham makes a reference to Bakhtin, noting that *Tom Sawyer* could be termed a "heteroglot" novel (194–95). Obviously, the addi-tion of yet another narrative voice, as I am claiming, would only intensify this effect. Wonham makes a related but slightly different argument in another essay. In addition to the contest between the narrator and Tom Sawyer, he notes a split in the narrator himself: "Like the novel's author, the narrator of *Tom Sawyer* seems trapped between two attitudes toward his material, one detached and ironic, the other engaged and

romantic, and he remains peculiarly undecided about which attitude he prefers." "Undoing Romance: The Contest for Narrative Authority in *The Adventures of Tom Sawyer*," 228. I am arguing for a more pronounced and intentional split, seeing two narrators rather than one narrator with divided attitudes. See also the discussion of *Tom Sawyer* in Lowry, "Littery Man," 76–111. Lowry also focuses on "Author," arguing for a kind of doubling in which Twain presents himself partly through his autobiographical correspondences with Tom and partly through his performance as a writer. "Littery Man," 77.

22. Smith, *Mark Twain*, 82–83, 84, 85.

23. Forrest G. Robinson, *In Bad Faith: The Dynamics of Deception in Mark Twain's America*, 2, 45–46, 4, 48.

24. Ibid., 47.

25. Ibid., 48, 53.

26. Blair, *Mark Twain and Huck Finn*, 56, 56–57, 57.

27. David E. E. Sloane, *"Adventures of Huckleberry Finn": American Comic Vision*, 23.

28. Turbayne, *Myth of Metaphor*, 24, 25–26, 27.

29. For another reading of Huck's interactions with these characters in the opening parts of the novel, see Sloane, *"Adventures of Huckleberry Finn,"* 34–49. Part of Twayne's Masterwork Series, Sloane's book is advertised as "a student's companion of the novel," but it will enlighten even those who think they know this novel "by the back" (to quote Jim).

30. For a good discussion of the controversy over and censorship of *Huckleberry Finn*, see Elaine Mensh and Harry Mensh, *Black, White, and "Huckleberry Finn,"* 3–16, 102–15. As Mensh and Mensh conclude, "The intensity and longevity of these clashes are a compelling reminder that the *Huckleberry Finn* controversy is not only over fictional black-white relations, but also—or rather primarily—over real ones" (118). See also Jonathan Arac, *"Huckleberry Finn" as Idol and Target: The Functions of Criticism in Our Time*, 63–89. Gregg Camfield discusses the sentimental nature of Jim's vision: "Although few supporters of the book like to admit it, such a vision of racial harmony stems ultimately from a sentimental view of the world, a view that Twain, though he also disliked to admit it, to a large degree shared." *Sentimental Twain: Samuel Clemens in the Maze of Moral Philosophy*, 5.

31. For a compelling analysis of the scene of Buck's death, see Victor A. Doyno, "Presentations of Violence in *Adventures of Huckleberry Finn*."

32. For readings of chap. 31, see Cox, *Mark Twain*, 180–84; Sloane, *"Adventures of Huckleberry Finn,"* 114–23; and Michelson, *Mark Twain on the Loose*, 135–41. For a somewhat contrarian view, see Michael J. Kiskis, "Critical Humbug: Samuel Clemens' *Adventures of Huckleberry Finn*." For perhaps the ultimate contrarian view, see Arac, *"Huckleberry Finn" as Idol and Target*, 37–62.

33. The controversy over the ending was a dominant critical concern beginning in the 1950s, and in many ways continues today. A bibliography of critical comment would be voluminous in itself; a good introduction and overview is provided in Gerald Graff and James Phelan's edition of *Adventures of Huckleberry Finn*, 277–355.

34. Turbayne, *Myth of Metaphor*, 26, 27.

35. Ibid., 64, 65, 95.

36. The racial issues of the novel have been examined in several recent book-length studies; see James S. Leonard, Thomas A. Tenney, and Thadious M. Davis, eds., *Satire or Evasion?: Black Perspectives on "Huckleberry Finn"*; Shelley Fisher Fishkin, *Was Huck Black?: Mark Twain and African-American Voices*; Jocelyn Chadwick-Joshua, *The Jim Dilemma: Reading Race in "Huckleberry Finn"*; Mensh and Mensh, *Black, White, and "Huckleberry Finn."* Messent devotes a chapter to the subject, "Racial Politics in *Huckleberry Finn*," in his book, *Mark Twain*, 86–109. For a good introduction and

overview of the controversy over race in the novel, see Graff and Phelan, *Adventures of Huckleberry Finn*, 356–470.

37. Ricoeur, *Rule of Metaphor*, 40.

38. See especially Chadwick-Joshua's argument in *The Jim Dilemma*, 53–59.

39. Genette, *Figures of Literary Discourse*, 204.

40. David L. Smith, "Huck, Jim, and American Racial Discourse," 107. In his study of the minstrelsy tradition, Eric Lott examines the way Pap is "blacking up" in his "govment" speech. Lott looks at the way race, class, and gender work in and complicate blackface minstrelsy; he argues that the mulatto "threatens the status of Pap's own working-class whiteness." He continues: "Conversely, Twain's sly construction of this scene so that Pap, covered with mud after a drunken night in the gutter, is actually blacker than the hated 'mulatter' free man suggests the underlying 'racial' equations between black and working-class white men that occasionally called forth in the minstrel show interracial recognitions and identifications no less than the imperative to disavow them. And the fact that Twain's fantasy of racial harmony, of Jim and the adolescent Huck, could occur only by excluding conventional manhood altogether reminds us here of the gender dynamic through which the intersections of race and class, in the minstrel show as elsewhere, were lived." *Love and Theft: Blackface Minstrelsy and the American Working Class*, 35. Mensh and Mensh argue that Pap's "blacking up" is *not* a metaphor "for the common origins of black and white." *Black, White, and "Huckleberry Finn*," 72. For another perceptive reading of the scene, see James S. Leonard, "Huck, Jim, and the 'Black-and-White' Fallacy," 144–45.

41. Chadwick-Joshua calls this moment "the turning point" in the novel. *The Jim Dilemma*, 56. Victor A. Doyno has shown how Twain's revisions of this passage "give Jim even more dignity, a sharper memory, and more self-control." He also specifically looks at the changes involving the word "trash": "The explicit linkage of Huck with his father's low status and with his father's despicable habit of drawing shame upon himself and upon those associated with him leads Huck to a self-liberating moment. Huck recognizes the truth of Jim's statement, decides to reject his paternal 'trash' style, and acts with personal integrity and independence to apologize to a slave for his own thoughtlessness and for the indignity and emotional harm he had inflicted. This self-transformation is precisely what Tom Sawyer, later in the novel, is not able to achieve." *Writing "Huck Finn": Mark Twain's Creative Process*, 377. Mensh and Mensh note the metaphorical underpinnings of this key scene: "In this passage, Jim uses ambiguity, dual meaning, and metaphor to such effect that one wonders why he is so easy to fool, so gullible that he suspects nothing until the prankster taunts him with the truth." *Black, White, and "Huckleberry Finn*," 54.

42. Smith, "Huck, Jim, and American Racial Discourse," 104; Genette, *Figures of Literary Discourse*, 204; Toni Morrison, *Playing in the Dark: Whiteness and the Literary Imagination*, 63.

3. Figuring Metaphor

1. Emerson, *Mark Twain*, 167. For critical analysis of "The Private History of a Campaign That Failed," see Cox, *Mark Twain*, 190–97; Tom Quirk, *Mark Twain: A Study of the Short Fiction*, 83–85; and Messent, *Short Works of Mark Twain*, 133–51. Messent does an especially good job of setting the piece in the context of its publication in the *Century* (140–44). My argument about the confusion of allegiance is very similar to his. Note Messent's focus on the figurative: "The militaristic values that stand squarely behind the whole *Century* series are, to a considerable degree then, metaphorically shot to tatters here" (146).

2. *Webster's Third New International Dictionary of the English Language Unabridged*, 1993, s.v., "palliate."

3. Michelson, *Mark Twain on the Loose*, 14.

4. For readings of this pivotal scene, see Quirk, *Mark Twain*, 84; and Cox, *Mark Twain*, 192–95. Disagreeing with Bernard DeVoto, who reads the passage as an example of "lonely realism" in *Mark Twain's America*, 114, Cox asks, "But is such power really present in the style? The entire texture of the passage is given over to all the stock responses of the most maudlin melodrama." *Mark Twain*, 194. Cox reads the whole piece as a failure, a failure of Mark Twain to confront the central historical event of his time, an event he evaded. I disagree, as my argument shows, but Cox's argument is, as usual, worth noting and considering.

5. Walter Blair discusses some of the similarities of point of view, technique, and humor between *1601* and *Huckleberry Finn*, as well as suggesting the titles Twain was reading that triggered *1601*: "The FART; Famous for Its Satyrical Humor in the Reign of St. Anne" and "The Second Part of the FART; or the Beef-eaters Appeal to Mr. D'Urfey," two bawdy poems included in Thomas D'Urfey's *Wit and Mirth, or Pills to Purge Melancholy*, published in London in 1719. The plots of the poems resemble that of *1601* closely: a fart of unknown origin, a questioning of those present, accusal of a yeoman, and his proof of who was the culprit. Blair, *Mark Twain and Huck Finn*, 96–97. Howard Baetzhold suggests a similarity to certain tales in Marguerite of Navarre's *Heptameron*, a book patterned after Boccaccio's *Decameron*. Twain purchased *Heptameron* in 1875, one year before the composition of *1601*. Further, in *1601* Raleigh attributes his final anecdote to "ye ingenious Margrette of Navarre." Baetzhold, *Mark Twain and John Bull*, 82.

6. Van Wyck Brooks, *The Ordeal of Mark Twain*, 227. Martha Anne Turner adroitly refutes Brooks: "[T]he satire reveals conspicuously a side Twain fought to preserve. That he succeeded in giving expression to his ribald Anglo-Saxon nature, which both his editor-friend William Dean Howells and the purist influence of his wife tended to suppress, is significant. There was not literary emasculation of Mark Twain. What is of further importance, *1601* uncovered the man himself beneath the trappings of convention—the man who like Lincoln was descended from sturdy pioneer stock. Moreover, as an avowed opponent of sham and hypocrisy with an equal aversion to puritanism and censorship of the press, Twain deals all three a shocking blow in *1601*." "Mark Twain's *1601* through Fifty Editions," 10. More recently, J. D. Stahl deals with *1601* at length, seeing in Elizabeth and the other women proof of "female power." *Mark Twain, Culture and Gender: Envisioning America through Europe*, 55–65. Stahl's insightful analysis is the fullest and best commentary on the piece by a Twain critic, instructive to read alongside Erica Jong's introduction to it in the Oxford Mark Twain.

7. Erica Jong, introduction to *"1601" and "Is Shakespeare Dead?,"* xxxiv–xxxv, xxxvi, xxxvi–xxxvii.

8. I refer to Louis Budd's Library of America edition rather than the Oxford Mark Twain, partly because of its wider availability, but mainly because of its readability. As delightful as the Oxford Mark Twain's reprinting of the facsimile first edition is (and it truly is a work of the typesetter's art), it is quite difficult to read.

9. Stahl makes the excellent point that all of the women's ages are given, while among the men, only Beaumont's is. *Mark Twain, Culture, and Gender*, 55–56.

10. Robert Rogers, *Metaphor: A Psychoanalytic View*, 59, 60, 62.

11. Ibid., 14, 62–63, 59, 64.

12. Ibid., 77, 85, 92, 93, 94.

13. Mikhail Bakhtin, *Rabelais and His World*, 319, 320. Stahl makes a full argument on this point, focusing especially on Elizabeth and her portrayal by Twain in a number of works. Stahl, *Mark Twain, Culture, and Gender*, 55–65. Guy Cardwell sees *1601* as one of

"Clemens's jokes at the expense of women." *The Man Who Was Mark Twain*, 170. I disagree, of course; overall, the joke is certainly much more on the men in this piece. One small but significant point I might make about the language: according to the *OED*, these so-called "dirty words" in the piece—"shit," "piss," "bollocks," and "fart"—were all considered Standard English in 1601, variously being labeled as vulgar later, up to the nineteenth century. *Oxford English Dictionary, Compact Edition*. According to Eric Partridge, "cunt" was Standard English until the end of the fifteenth century; after 1700, it was considered not only vulgar but also obscene, meaning that it constituted a legal offense in print. *A Dictionary of Slang and Unconventional English*, 278. We cannot know whether Twain knew about the words' histories (he may well have), but the contrast between his time (and ours) and Elizabeth's is still striking.

14. Bakhtin, *Rabelais and His World*, 378, 403, 336.

15. Gibson, *Art of Mark Twain*, 77. The manuscript of "A True Story" is in the Clifton Waller Barrett Library of American Literature, Special Collections, University of Virginia Library. For information on and analysis of the story, see James D. Wilson, *A Reader's Guide to the Short Stories of Mark Twain*, 267–74; Messent, *Short Works of Mark Twain*, 60–66; Gibson, *Art of Mark Twain*, 76–80; and Quirk, *Mark Twain*, 57–62.

16. Messent notes the change in *Short Works of Mark Twain*, 62, as does Quirk in *Mark Twain*, 59. In *Was Huck Black?*, Fishkin discusses the change, asking, "was [Twain] . . . improving on Mary Ann Cord's original story, or merely revising his record of it to read more accurately?" (33). My argument suggests that the second possibility is highly unlikely. For a compelling argument from Mary Ann Cord's descendants, who do not recall her ever using such a phrase, see Herbert Wisbey, "The True Story of Auntie Cord," 1–3. In regard to Twain's revisions, Victor A. Doyno, the leading expert on Twain's habits of composition, has told me that he finds such insistent crossing out to be quite uncharacteristic for Mark Twain (personal communication).

17. The manuscript of "The Invalid's Story" is in the Clifton Waller Barrett Library of American Literature, Special Collections, University of Virginia Library. For a good overview and bibliography, see Wilson, *Reader's Guide*, 147–52.

18. For analysis of "Baker's Blue-jay Yarn," see Wilson, *Reader's Guide*, 153–61; Quirk, *Mark Twain*, 76–80; and Gibson, *Art of Mark Twain*, 66–71.

19. DeVoto, *Mark Twain's America*, 251.

20. For critical comment on "The Man That Corrupted Hadleyburg," see Wilson, *Reader's Guide*, 199–216; Quirk, *Mark Twain*, 102–8; Gibson, *Art of Mark Twain*, 89–95; and Michelson, *Mark Twain on the Loose*, 179–87. Quirk notes that in this story "Twain seldom pauses to indulge in the sort of lavish humorous metaphors that characterize his earlier work." *Mark Twain*, 104.

21. Burke, *A Grammar of Motives*, 516–17.

22. Analysis of the *Huckleberry Finn* manuscript has largely come from Victor A. Doyno. He studies the second half of the manuscript in *Writing "Huck Finn": Mark Twain's Creative Process*. The first half of the manuscript was discovered as Doyno's book was being published; his examination of the first half is *Beginning to Write "Huck Finn": Essays in Genetic Criticism*, included in Victor A. Doyno and Robert Berthoff, eds., *"Huck Finn" CD-ROM: The Complete Buffalo and Erie County Public Library Manuscript*.

23. In this discussion, I am quoting from the CD-ROM *Huck Finn* manuscript, so I do not include parenthetical book page numbers.

24. For a definitive account of the composition and typesetting of the novel, see the introduction to textual apparatus in *Adventures of Huckleberry Finn*, ed. Victor Fischer and Lin Salamo with the late Walter Blair, 663–794. The rediscovery of the first half of the manuscript and the insightful work by the editors at the Mark Twain Project clear up many questions and overturn a number of long-held assumptions about the composition of the novel.

25. Leo Marx, "The Pilot and the Passenger," 59.

26. Ibid.

27. Kenneth E. Eble, *Old Clemens and W.D.H.: The Story of a Remarkable Friendship*, 68, 64; René Wellek and Austin Warren, *Theory of Literature*, 197.

28. Genette, *Figures of Literary Discourse*, 204, 50.

29. For a full account of the relationship between Samuel Clemens and his older brother Orion, an account that counters many previous assumptions about the two, see Philip Ashley Fanning, *Mark Twain and Orion Clemens: Brothers, Partners, Strangers*.

30. William Dean Howells, *My Mark Twain*, 4, 33. Henry Nash Smith and William M. Gibson tell the full story of Winifred's death: "Winifred Howells had died 3 March 1889 in a country rest-home, after a regimen of forced feeding and treatment for 'hysteria' under the care of Howells's old friend, Dr. S. Weir Mitchell. She had suffered intermittently for a long time from a malady never fully diagnosed, but most often described as 'nervous exhaustion.' At her death 'Mitchell apparently ran an autopsy and discovered that nothing could really have saved Winifred. That her disease was organic, not merely psychic, and that her pain had been all too physiologically real' (Edwin H. Cady, *The Realist at War*, Syracuse, 1958, p. 98). The effect of this disclosure upon William and Elinor Howells was deep and lasting, for their grief was doubled with self-reproach that was no easier to bear for its being groundless" (*MTHL*, 2:603–4n3).

31. Howells, *My Mark Twain*, 3.

32. Weller Embler, *Metaphor and Meaning*, 4.

4. Figuring the End

1. For foundational arguments about the failure of *Connecticut Yankee*, see Henry Nash Smith, *Mark Twain: The Development of a Writer*, 138–70; and Cox, *Mark Twain*, 198–221. For more recent discussions of the novel, see David E. E. Sloane, *Mark Twain as a Literary Comedian*, 146–67; Michelson, *Mark Twain on the Loose*, 150–71; and Howe, *Mark Twain and the Novel*, 118–73.

2. Smith, *Mark Twain*, 138; Cox, *Mark Twain*, 224.

3. Cox, *Mark Twain*, 215–16.

4. Ibid., 219.

5. Smith, *Mark Twain*, 143, 144, 145.

6. Mikhail Bakhtin, *The Dialogic Imagination*, 538, 539.

7. For influential arguments that largely set the terms for modern discussion of *Pudd'nhead Wilson*, see Smith, *Mark Twain*, 171–83; and Cox, *Mark Twain*, 222–46. See also Sloane, *Mark Twain as a Literary Comedian*, 177–88; Howe, *Mark Twain and the Novel*, 182–208; Gillman, *Dark Twins*, 53–95; Michelson, *Mark Twain on the Loose*, 188–202; Messent, *Mark Twain*, 134–56; Wonham, *Art of the Tall Tale*, 165–73; and Sewell, *Mark Twain's Languages*, 110–25. For an influential argument about the composition of the novel, see Hershel Parker, *Flawed Texts and Verbal Icons: Literary Authority in American Fiction*, 115–46. Of special interest are the essays in Susan Gillman and Forrest G. Robinson, eds., *Mark Twain's "Pudd'nhead Wilson": Race, Conflict, and Culture*.

8. Gerber, *Mark Twain*, 135.

9. Gillman and Robinson, *Mark Twain's "Pudd'nhead Wilson,"* vii.

10. Lodge, *Modes of Modern Writing*, 112.

11. Ibid., 107.

12. Tracing Roxy's one-sixteenth-black blood reveals the full extent of the miscegenation. Her great-great-grandmother would have been fully black, and her child from, one surmises, her white owner, must also have been a girl, one-half black, Roxy's great-grandmother. The pattern would have been repeated with each generation, her

one-quarter black grandmother and one-eighth mother each sexually joined with a white man, a girl child always the result. (A male offspring coupled with a white woman is possible, but not as likely or as common.) Roxy, then, would have been the product of four generations of miscegenation, a fact Mark Twain only hints at.

13. Murray Krieger, *A Reopening of Closure: Organicism against Itself*, 65.

14. Leslie Fiedler, "As Free as Any Cretur . . . ," 220, 221–22.

15. Some critics do call for reading both texts. Susan Gillman makes this argument: "[T]hese twin novels must . . . be read together, despite the fact that the farce makes a mockery of the Siamese twins' grotesque attachment, whereas the tragedy, obsessed with genealogy, race, and miscegenation, offers a critique of an American historical actuality." *Dark Twins*, 55. Peter Messent devotes a chapter to the twinned novels, arguing persuasively for their connections to one another: "A symbiotic bond, in other words, continues to exist between the two parts of the original body of the work. The stories may have been pulled apart, but they remain, none the less, connected." *Mark Twain*, 135. Rather than Gillman's political argument, Messent emphasizes reader-response: "The quest for meaning in *Pudd'nhead Wilson and Those Extraordinary Twins* becomes a form of collaborative project, as the reader puts the two together to find one broken whole." *Mark Twain*, 138. His chapter makes a forceful argument for reading both texts.

16. Cox, *Mark Twain*, 227. Wonham calls into question the metaphor of the literary caesarean, arguing that "the final revision amounted less to a sanitary operation than to a messy subversion of the original tall tale and of the identity riddle that the Cappello twins were intended to embody." *Art of the Tall Tale*, 167. Howe also comments on Twain's metaphor: "Corresponding to his reluctance to claim literary paternity, the obstetric-surgeon metaphor might seem to distance Twain from the creative act by aligning the process of literary production with maternity, to which he serves as technical assistant." *Mark Twain and the Novel*, 201.

17. Robert A. Wiggins, *Mark Twain: Jackleg Novelist*, 108, 109.

18. Parker, *Flawed Texts and Verbal Icons*, 136; Messent, *Mark Twain*, 155–56.

19. For a good overview and argument, see Marvin Fischer and Michael Elliott, "*Pudd'nhead Wilson*: Half a Dog Is Worse than None," 533–47. See also Cox, *Mark Twain*, 234–35; and Sloane, *Mark Twain as a Literary Comedian*, 178–79. Sloane traces the metaphorical implications of the joke for the novel: the repeated metaphorical comparisons between characters and dogs. As Sloane asserts, "In this context the joke conveys the misery implicit in disregarding the real, living object" (179). See also George E. Marcus, "'What did he reckon would become of the other half if he killed his half?': Doubled, Divided, and Crossed Selves in *Pudd'nhead Wilson*; or, Mark Twain as Cultural Critic in His Own Times and Ours," in Gillman and Robinson, *Mark Twain's "Pudd'nhead Wilson*," 190–210.

20. Studies of Mark Twain's humor are voluminous; an important book-length study is Covici, *Mark Twain's Humor: The Image of a World*. For excellent overviews, see Covici, "Humor"; and Gregg Camfield, "Humor," in his *Oxford Companion to Mark Twain*, 275–80. For an excellent recent argument about humor, see Bruce Michelson, *Literary Wit*. Camfield and Michelson make compelling arguments about the limitations of Freud's humor theory.

21. Ted Cohen, "Metaphor and the Cultivation of Intimacy," 8, 6.

22. Cox, *Mark Twain*, vi.

23. Sigmund Freud, *Jokes and Their Relation to the Unconscious*, 9.

24. Ibid., 11, 14, 13.

25. Ibid., 61.

26. Ibid., 50.

27. Ibid., 107.

28. Ibid., 124, 125.

29. Ibid., 182–83, 8.

30. Ibid., 107, 103.

31. Gibson, *Art of Mark Twain*, 162. Sloane notes the way these jokes build community: "Specific mottoes reflect the post–Civil War literary comedians and serve the function, as does Twain's humor elsewhere, of making the novel carry overtones that are contemporaneous with the experience of Twain's readers." *Mark Twain as a Literary Comedian*, 180.

32. Freud, *Jokes and Their Relation to the Unconscious*, 29, 165, 179.

33. Ibid., 179–80.

34. Sigmund Freud, *The Interpretation of Dreams*, 608; Jakobson, "Two Types of Language," 95; Jacques Lacan, *Écrits: A Selection*, 167, 234.

35. Freud, *Interpretation of Dreams*, 279; Meredith Anne Skura, *The Literary Use of the Psychoanalytic Process*, 137, 138.

36. An excellent recent discussion of Mark Twain's later writings is Tom Quirk, "Mark Twain in Large and Small: The Infinite and the Infinitesimal in Twain's Later Writing." Another excellent recent overview is Forrest G. Robinson, "Dreaming Better Dreams: The Late Writing of Mark Twain."

37. For an especially good discussion of the late dream fragments, ably setting them in historical context, see Gillman, *Dark Twins*, 136–80. See also Maria Ornella Marotti, *The Duplicating Imagination: Twain and the Twain Papers*.

38. Lacan, *Écrits*, 166.

39. Freud, *Interpretation of Dreams*, 322–23.

40. Jonathan Scott Lee, *Jacques Lacan*, 19, 22.

41. Ellie Ragland-Sullivan, *Jacques Lacan and the Philosophy of Psychoanalysis*, 60.

42. Ragland-Sullivan, *Jacques Lacan and the Philosophy of Psychoanalysis*, 78. I agree with Jason Gary Horn, who reaches this conclusion about *The Mysterious Stranger*: "The important point for Twain and James is that the other side of the self, rather than an essentially evil influence, as commonly portrayed in the literature of doubling, or the bearer of psychotic ills, as psychoanalysis generally defined it, is a potential conduit for spiritually enlightening experience." *Mark Twain and William James: Crafting a Free Self*, 139.

43. For the definitive study of the manuscripts, see Sholom Kahn, *Mark Twain's "Mysterious Stranger": A Study of the Manuscript Texts*.

44. Gibson points out "this metaphor of the doppelgänger created by a reflection in a mirror in a passage of the holograph manuscript, later canceled, of *A Connecticut Yankee in King Arthur's Court*" (*MTMSM*, 480–81).

45. Typesetting can be seen as a demonstration of the opposition between metaphor and metonymy: the typesetter creates a horizontal axis, a syntagmatic pole, by choosing from a vertical axis of type, a paradigmatic pole. Several critics have noted Twain's wish fulfillment in his description of the automatic typesetting in *No. 44, The Mysterious Stranger*: the actions of the Duplicates in magically setting type closely resemble the hoped-for success of the Paige typesetter. For a full discussion of the Paige typesetter and issues of print technology, as well as a discussion of the print-shop elements of *No. 44, The Mysterious Stranger*, see Bruce Michelson, *Printer's Devil: Mark Twain and the American Publishing Revolution*, esp. 208–23.

46. Ben Stoltzfus, *Lacan and Literature: Purloined Pretexts*, 72.

Coda. Mark Twain Studies and the Myth of Metaphor

1. Turbayne, *Myth of Metaphor*, 22.

2. Quirk makes a similar point in his annual review of Mark Twain criticism: "If Samuel Clemens had taken as his alias the name 'Mark Multiplicity' or 'Mark Monad,'

I wonder whether the character and emphasis of Twain criticism might have been different." Quirk, "Mark Twain," in *American Literary Scholarship: An Annual 1994*, 99.

3. Turbayne, *Myth of Metaphor*, 60.

4. Brooks, *The Ordeal of Mark Twain*, 38, 40–41.

5. DeVoto, *Mark Twain's America*, 320–21, 192, 193, 195.

6. Waugh and Monville-Burston, eds., in Jakobson, *On Language*, 17.

7. Peter Stoneley, *Mark Twain and the Feminine Aesthetic*, 8; Susan K. Harris, *The Courtship of Olivia Langdon and Mark Twain*, 9–10.

8. Robinson, *In Bad Faith*, 114; Turbayne, *Myth of Metaphor*, 66.

9. Gillman, *Dark Twins*, 1, 3.

10. Cardwell, *The Man Who Was Mark Twain*, 5, 7.

11. Turbayne, *Myth of Metaphor*, 64; Laura E. Skandera Trombley, *Mark Twain in the Company of Women*, xvi.

12. Turbayne, *Myth of Metaphor*, 64–65.

13. Fishkin, *Was Huck Black?*, 4.

14. Michelson, *Mark Twain on the Loose*, 3, 4, 8, 2.

15. Stahl, *Mark Twain, Culture, and Gender*, x; Camfield, *Sentimental Twain*, 17. Camfield does not, however, deny the presence of oppositions; he is trying "to relocate the site of that opposition from between conflicting world-views, to within the rather multiform and paradoxical ideology of American liberalism" (18–19).

16. Andrew Hoffman, *Twain's Heroes, Twain's Worlds: Mark Twain's "Adventures of Huckleberry Finn," "A Connecticut Yankee in King Arthur's Court," and "Pudd'nhead Wilson,"* xiv.

17. Lowry, "Littery Man," 51–64; Marotti, *The Duplicating Imagination*, 117–27, 3, 51; Harris, *Courtship of Olivia Langdon and Mark Twain*, 86. Harris has long been cognizant of the metaphorical implications of Mark Twain's work; see her *Mark Twain's Escape from Time: A Study of Patterns and Images*, one of the most metaphorically aware books in Mark Twain studies.

18. Turbayne, *Myth of Metaphor*, 65, 214; Tom Quirk, *Coming to Grips with "Huckleberry Finn": Essays on a Book, a Boy, and a Man*, 152.

19. Louis J. Budd, *Our Mark Twain: The Making of His Public Personality*, xiv–xv.

Bibliography

Arac, Jonathan. *"Huckleberry Finn" as Idol and Target: The Functions of Criticism in Our Time.* Madison: University of Wisconsin Press, 1997.

Aristotle. *On Rhetoric: A Theory of Civic Discourse.* Trans. George A. Kennedy. New York: Oxford University Press, 1991.

———. *The Rhetoric and the Poetics.* Trans. W. Rhys Roberts and Ingram Bywater. New York: Modern Library, 1954.

Baender, Paul. "'The Jumping Frog' as a Comedian's First Virtue." *Modern Philology* 60 (1962): 192–200.

Baetzhold, Howard. *Mark Twain and John Bull.* Bloomington: Indiana University Press, 1970.

Bakhtin, Mikhail. *The Dialogic Imagination: Four Essays.* Ed. Michael Holquist. Trans. Caryl Emerson and Michael Holquist. Austin: University of Texas Press, 1981.

———. *Rabelais and His World.* Trans. Helene Iswolsky. Cambridge: The MIT Press, 1968.

Beidler, Philip D. "Realistic Style and the Problem of Context in *The Innocents Abroad* and *Roughing It.*" *American Literature* 52 (1980–1981): 33–49.

Berkove, Lawrence I. "The Trickster God in *Roughing It.*" *Thalia: Studies in Literary Humor* 18, nos. 1–2 (1998): 21–30.

Berret, Anthony J. *Mark Twain and Shakespeare: A Cultural Legacy.* Lanham, MD: University Press of America, 1993.

Blair, Walter. *Mark Twain and Huck Finn.* Berkeley: University of California Press, 1960.

Blair, Walter, and Hamlin Hill. *America's Humor from Poor Richard to Doonesbury.* Oxford: Oxford University Press, 1978.

Booth, Wayne C. "Metaphor as Rhetoric: The Problem of Evaluation." In *On Metaphor*, ed. Sheldon Sacks, 47–70. Chicago: University of Chicago Press, 1978.

Branch, Edgar M. "'My voice is still for Setchell': A Background Study of 'Jim Smiley and His Jumping Frog.'" *PMLA* 82, no. 2 (1967): 591–601.

Bredin, Hugh. "Roman Jakobson on Metaphor and Metonymy." *Philosophy and Literature* 8 (1994): 89–103.

Bridgman, Richard. *Traveling in Mark Twain*. Berkeley: University of California Press, 1987.

Brooke-Rose, Christina. *A Structural Analysis of Pound's "Usura Canto": Jakobson's Method Extended and Applied to Free Verse*. The Hague: Mouton, 1976.

Brooks, Van Wyck. *The Ordeal of Mark Twain*. Rev. ed. New York: E. P. Dutton, 1933.

Budd, Louis J. *Our Mark Twain: The Making of His Public Personality*. Philadelphia: University of Philadelphia Press, 1983.

Burke, Kenneth. *A Grammar of Motives*. Berkeley: University of California Press, 1969.

Burns, Philip. "Fabrication and Faultline: Language as Experience in *Roughing It*." *Midwest Quarterly* 29, no. 2 (1988): 249–63.

Camfield, Gregg. *The Oxford Companion to Mark Twain*. Oxford: Oxford University Press, 2003.

———. *Sentimental Twain: Samuel Clemens in the Maze of Moral Philosophy*. Philadelphia: University of Pennsylvania Press, 1994.

Cardwell, Guy. *The Man Who Was Mark Twain: Images and Ideologies*. New Haven: Yale University Press, 1991.

———. "Mark Twain: The Metaphoric Hero as Battleground." *ESQ* 23 (1977): 52–66.

Chadwick-Joshua, Jocelyn. *The Jim Dilemma: Reading Race in "Huckleberry Finn."* Jackson: University of Mississippi Press, 1998.

Cohen, Ted. "Metaphor and the Cultivation of Intimacy." In *On Metaphor*, ed. Sheldon Sacks, 1–10. Chicago: University of Chicago Press, 1978.

Covici, Pascal, Jr. "Buck Fanshaw's Funeral." In *The Mark Twain Encyclopedia*, ed. J. R. LeMaster and James D. Wilson, 102–3. New York: Garland, 1993.

———. "Humor." In *The Mark Twain Encyclopedia*, ed. J. R. LeMaster and James D. Wilson, 377–80. New York: Garland, 1993.

———. *Mark Twain's Humor: The Image of a World*. Dallas: Southern Methodist University Press, 1962.

Cox, James M. *Mark Twain: The Fate of Humor.* Princeton: Princeton University Press, 1966.

Cummings, Sherwood. *Mark Twain and Science: Adventures of a Mind.* Baton Rouge: Louisiana State University Press, 1988.

DeVoto, Bernard. *Mark Twain's America.* Boston: Little, Brown, 1932.

Dolmetsch, Carl. *"Our Famous Guest": Mark Twain in Vienna.* Athens: University of Georgia Press, 1992.

Doyno, Victor A. "Presentations of Violence in *Adventures of Huckleberry Finn.*" *The Mark Twain Annual* 2 (2004): 82–83.

———. *Writing "Huck Finn": Mark Twain's Creative Process.* Philadelphia: University of Pennsylvania Press, 1991.

Doyno, Victor A., and Robert Berthoff, eds. *"Huck Finn" CD-ROM: The Complete Buffalo and Erie County Public Library Manuscript — Teaching and Research Digital Edition.* Buffalo and Erie County Foundation Board, 2003.

Eble, Kenneth E. *Old Clemens and W.D.H.: The Story of a Remarkable Friendship.* Baton Rouge: Louisiana State University Press, 1985.

Embler, Weller. *Metaphor and Meaning.* Deland: Everett/Edwards, 1966.

Emerson, Everett. *The Authentic Mark Twain: A Literary Biography of Samuel L. Clemens.* Philadelphia: University of Pennsylvania Press, 1984.

———. *Mark Twain: A Literary Life.* Philadelphia: University of Pennsylvania Press, 2000.

Fanning, Philip Ashley. *Mark Twain and Orion Clemens: Brothers, Partners, Strangers.* Tuscaloosa: University of Alabama Press, 2003.

Fiedler, Leslie. "As Free as Any Cretur . . ." *The New Republic,* August 15 and 22, 1955, 130–39.

Fischer, Marvin, and Michael Elliott. "*Pudd'nhead Wilson:* Half a Dog Is Worse than None." *The Southern Review,* n.s., 8 (Summer 1972): 533–47.

Fishkin, Shelley Fisher. *Was Huck Black?: Mark Twain and African-American Voices.* New York: Oxford University Press, 1993.

Florence, Don. *Persona and Humor in Mark Twain's Early Writings.* Columbia: University of Missouri Press, 1995.

Freud, Sigmund. *The Interpretation of Dreams.* Trans. and ed. James Strachey. New York: Science Editions, 1961.

———. *Jokes and Their Relation to the Unconscious.* Trans. and ed. James Strachey. New York: Norton, 1960.

Genette, Gérard. *Figures of Literary Discourse.* Trans. Alan Sheridan. New York: Columbia University Press, 1982.

Gerber, John C. "*Adventures of Tom Sawyer, The.*" In *The Mark Twain Encyclopedia*, ed. J. R. LeMaster and James D. Wilson, 12–15. New York: Garland Publishing, 1993.

——. "Mark Twain's Use of the Comic Pose." *PMLA* 77 (1962): 297–304.

——. *Mark Twain.* Boston: Twayne Publishers, 1988.

Gibson, William M. *The Art of Mark Twain.* New York: Oxford University Press, 1976.

Gillman, Susan. *Dark Twins: Imposture and Identity in Mark Twain's America.* Chicago: University of Chicago Press, 1989.

Gillman, Susan, and Forrest G. Robinson, eds. *Mark Twain's "Pudd'nhead Wilson": Race, Conflict, and Culture.* Durham: Duke University Press, 1990.

Graff, Gerald, and James Phelan, eds. *Adventures of Huckleberry Finn.* 2nd ed. Boston: Bedford/St. Martin's, 2004.

Gribben, Alan. "'I did wish Tom Sawyer was there': Boy-Book Elements in *Tom Sawyer* and *Huckleberry Finn.*" In *One Hundred Years of Huckleberry Finn: The Boy, His Book, and American Culture,* ed. Robert Sattelmeyer and J. Donald Crowley, 149–70. Columbia: University of Missouri Press, 1985.

Harris, Susan K. *The Courtship of Olivia Langdon and Mark Twain.* Cambridge: Cambridge University Press, 1996.

——. *Mark Twain's Escape from Time: A Study of Patterns and Images.* Columbia: University of Missouri Press, 1982.

Hoffman, Andrew. *Inventing Mark Twain: The Lives of Samuel Langhorne Clemens.* New York: William Morrow, 1997.

——. *Twain's Heroes, Twain's Worlds: Mark Twain's "Adventures of Huckleberry Finn," "A Connecticut Yankee in King Arthur's Court," and "Pudd'nhead Wilson."* Philadelphia: University of Pennsylvania Press, 1988.

Horn, Jason Gary. *Mark Twain and William James: Crafting a Free Self.* Columbia: University of Missouri Press, 1996.

Howe, Lawrence. *Mark Twain and the Novel: The Double-Cross of Authority.* Cambridge: Cambridge University Press, 1998.

Howells, William Dean. *My Mark Twain.* New York: Harper, 1910.

Jacobson, Marcia. *Being a Boy Again: Autobiography and the American Boy Book.* Tuscaloosa: University of Alabama Press, 1994.

Jakobson, Roman. *On Language.* Ed. Linda R. Waugh and Monique Monville-Burston. Cambridge: Harvard University Press, 1990.

————. "Two Aspects of Language and Two Types of Aphasic Disturbances." In *Fundamentals of Language,* ed. Roman Jakobson and Morris Halle, 69–96. 2nd ed. The Hague: Mouton, 1971.

Jong, Erica. Introduction to *"1601" and "Is Shakespeare Dead?,"* ed. Shelley Fisher Fishkin, xxxi–xlii. The Oxford Mark Twain. New York: Oxford University Press, 1996.

Kahn, Sholom. *Mark Twain's "Mysterious Stranger": A Study of the Manuscript Texts.* Columbia: University of Missouri Press, 1978.

Kiskis, Michael J. "Critical Humbug: Samuel Clemens' *Adventures of Huckleberry Finn." The Mark Twain Annual* 3 (2005): 13–22.

Knoper, Randall. *Acting Naturally: Mark Twain in the Culture of Performance.* Berkeley: University of California Press, 1995.

Krause, Sydney J. "The Art and Satire of Twain's 'Jumping Frog' Story." *American Quarterly* 16 (1965): 562–76.

Krieger, Murray. *A Reopening of Closure: Organicism against Itself.* New York: Columbia University Press, 1989.

Kruse, Horst H. "Mark Twain's *Nom de Plume:* Some Mysteries Resolved." *Mark Twain Journal* 30 (1992): 1–32.

Lacan, Jacques. *Écrits: A Selection.* Trans. Alan Sheridan. New York: Norton, 1977.

Lakoff, George, and Mark Johnson. *Metaphors We Live By.* Chicago: University of Chicago Press, 1980.

Leavis, F. R. "Mark Twain's Neglected Classic: The Moral Astringency of Pudd'nhead Wilson." *Commentary,* February 1956, 128–36.

Lee, Jonathan Scott. *Jacques Lacan.* Twayne's World Author Series. Boston: G. K. Hall, 1990.

Leonard, James S. "Huck, Jim, and the 'Black-and-White' Fallacy." In *Constructing Mark Twain,* ed. Laura E. Skandera Trombley and Michael J. Kiskis, 139–50. Columbia: University of Missouri Press, 2001.

Leonard, James S., Thomas A. Tenney, and Thadious M. Davis, eds. *Satire or Evasion?: Black Perspectives on "Huckleberry Finn."* Durham: Duke University Press, 1992.

Lodge, David. *The Modes of Modern Writing: Metaphor, Metonymy, and the Typology of Modern Literature.* London: Edward Arnold, 1977.

Lott, Eric. *Love and Theft: Blackface Minstrelsy and the American Working Class.* Race and American Culture, ed. Arnold Rampersad and Shelley Fisher Fishkin. New York: Oxford University Press, 1993.

Lowry, Richard S. *"Littery Man": Mark Twain and Modern Authorship.* New York: Oxford University Press, 1996.

Lynn, Kenneth S. *Mark Twain and Southwestern Humor.* Boston: Little, Brown, 1959.

Marcus, George E. "'What did he reckon would become of the other half if he killed his half?': Doubled, Divided, and Crossed Selves in *Pudd'nhead Wilson;* or, Mark Twain as Cultural Critic in His Own Times and Ours." In *Mark Twain's "Pudd'nhead Wilson,"* ed. Susan Gillman and Forrest G. Robinson, 190–210. Durham: Duke University Press, 1990.

Marotti, Maria Ornella. *The Duplicating Imagination: Twain and the Twain Papers.* University Park: Pennsylvania State University Press, 1990.

Marx, Leo. *The Machine in the Garden: Technology and the Pastoral Ideal in America.* Oxford: Oxford University Press, 1964.

———. "The Pilot and the Passenger." In *Mark Twain: A Collection of Critical Essays,* ed. Henry Nash Smith, 47–63. Englewood Cliffs, NJ: Prentice-Hall, 1963.

Mensh, Elaine, and Harry Mensh. *Black, White, and "Huckleberry Finn."* Tuscaloosa: University of Alabama Press, 2000.

Messent, Peter. "Caught on the Hop: Interpretive Dislocation in 'The Notorious Jumping Frog of Calaveras County.'" *Thalia: Studies in Literary Humor* 15, nos. 1–2 (1995): 33–49.

———. *Mark Twain.* New York: St. Martin's Press, 1997.

———. *The Short Works of Mark Twain.* Philadelphia: University of Pennsylvania Press, 2001.

"Metaphor." In *The Princeton Handbook of Poetic Terms,* ed. Alex Preminger, 136–41. Princeton: Princeton University Press, 1986.

Michelson, Bruce. *Literary Wit.* Amherst: University of Massachusetts Press, 2000.

———. *Mark Twain on the Loose: A Comic Writer and the American Self.* Amherst: University of Massachusetts Press, 1995.

———. *Printer's Devil: Mark Twain and the American Publishing Revolution.* Berkeley: University of California Press, 2006.

Morrison, Toni. *Playing in the Dark: Whiteness and the Literary Imagination.* Cambridge: Harvard University Press, 1992.

Ong, Walter J. "Metaphor and the Twinned Vision." In *The Barbarian Within and Other Fugitive Essays and Studies,* 41–48. New York: Macmillan, 1962.

Oxford English Dictionary, Compact Edition. Oxford: Oxford University Press, 1971.

Parker, Hershel. *Flawed Texts and Verbal Icons: Literary Authority in American Fiction.* Evanston: Northwestern University Press, 1984.

Partridge, Eric. *A Dictionary of Slang and Unconventional English.* Ed. Paul Beale. 8th ed. New York: Macmillan, 1984.

Pomorska, Krystyna, and Stephen Rudy, eds. *Verbal Art, Verbal Sign, Verbal Time.* Minneapolis: University of Minnesota Press, 1985.

Quirk, Tom. *Coming to Grips with "Huckleberry Finn": Essays on a Book, a Boy, and a Man.* Columbia: University of Missouri Press, 1993.

———. "Mark Twain." In *American Literary Scholarship: An Annual 1994,* ed. David J. Nordloh. Durham: Duke University Press, 1996.

———. *Mark Twain: A Study of the Short Fiction.* New York: Twayne Publishers, 1997.

———. "Mark Twain in Large and Small: The Infinite and the Infinitesimal in Twain's Later Writing." In *Constructing Mark Twain,* ed. Laura E. Skandera Trombley and Michael J. Kiskis, 191–202. Columbia: University of Missouri Press, 2001.

Ragland-Sullivan, Ellie. *Jacques Lacan and the Philosophy of Psychoanalysis.* Urbana and Chicago: University of Illinois Press, 1986.

Rasmussen, R. Kent. *Mark Twain A to Z.* New York: Facts on File, 1995.

Regan, Robert. *Unpromising Heroes: Mark Twain and His Characters.* Berkeley and Los Angeles: University of California Press, 1966.

Richards, I. A. *The Philosophy of Rhetoric.* New York: Oxford University Press, 1936.

Ricoeur, Paul. *The Rule of Metaphor: Multidisciplinary Studies of the Creation of Meaning in Language.* Trans. Robert Czerny. London: Routledge and Kegan Paul, 1978.

Robinson, Forrest G. "Dreaming Better Dreams: The Late Writing of Mark Twain." In *A Companion to Mark Twain,* ed. Peter Messent and Louis J. Budd, 450–65. Oxford: Blackwell Publishing, 2005.

———. *In Bad Faith: The Dynamics of Deception in Mark Twain's America.* Cambridge: Harvard University Press, 1986.

Rodgers, Paul C., Jr. "Artemus Ward and Mark Twain's 'Jumping Frog.'" *Nineteenth-Century Fiction* 28 (1974): 273–86.

Rogers, Franklin R. *Mark Twain's Burlesque Patterns.* Dallas: Southern Methodist University Press, 1960.

Rogers, Robert. *Metaphor: A Psychoanalytic View.* Berkeley: University of California Press, 1978.

Ruegg, Maria. "Metaphor and Metonymy: The Logic of Structuralist Rhetoric." In *Glyph 6: Johns Hopkins Textual Studies,* 141–57. Baltimore: Johns Hopkins University Press, 1979.

Searle, J. R. *Expression and Meaning.* Cambridge: Cambridge University Press, 1979.

Sewell, David R. *Mark Twain's Languages: Discourse, Dialogue, and Linguistic Variety.* Berkeley: University of California Press, 1987.

Shapiro, Michael, and Marianne Shapiro. *Figuration in Verbal Art.* Princeton: Princeton University Press, 1988.

Skandera Trombley, Laura E. *Mark Twain in the Company of Women.* Philadelphia: University of Pennsylvania Press, 1994.

Skura, Meredith Anne. *The Literary Use of the Psychoanalytic Process.* New Haven: Yale University Press, 1981.

Sloane, David E. E. *"Adventures of Huckleberry Finn": American Comic Vision.* Twayne's Masterwork Series. Boston: Twayne Publishers, 1988.

————. *Mark Twain as a Literary Comedian.* Baton Rouge: Louisiana State University Press, 1979.

Smith, David L. "Huck, Jim, and American Racial Discourse." In *Satire or Evasion?: Black Perspectives on Huckleberry Finn*, ed. Thomas A. Tenney, James S. Leonard, and Thadious M. Davis, 103–20. Durham: Duke University Press, 1992.

Smith, Henry Nash. *Mark Twain: The Development of a Writer.* Cambridge: Harvard University Press, Belknap Press, 1962.

Stahl, J. D. *Mark Twain, Culture and Gender: Envisioning America through Europe.* Athens: University of Georgia Press, 1994.

Stambovsky, Phillip. *The Depictive Image: Metaphor and Literary Experience.* Amherst: University of Massachusetts Press, 1988.

Steinbrink, Jeffrey. *Getting to Be Mark Twain.* Berkeley: University of California Press, 1991.

Stoltzfus, Ben. *Lacan and Literature: Purloined Pretexts.* Albany: State University of New York Press, 1996.

Stoneley, Peter. *Mark Twain and the Feminine Aesthetic.* Cambridge: Cambridge University Press, 1992.

Towers, Tom. "'Hateful Reality': The Failure of the Territory in *Roughing It.*" *Western American Literature* 9 (1974): 3–15.

Turbayne, Colin Murray. *The Myth of Metaphor.* New Haven: Yale University Press, 1962.

Turner, Martha Anne. "Mark Twain's *1601* through Fifty Editions." *Mark Twain Journal* 12, no. 3 (1965): 10–15.

Twain, Mark. *Adventures of Huckleberry Finn.* Ed. Victor Fischer and Lin Salamo with Walter Blair. Berkeley: University of California Press, 2003.

————. *The Adventures of Tom Sawyer.* Ed. John C. Gerber and Paul Baender. Berkeley: University of California Press, 1982.

————. *The Autobiography of Mark Twain.* Ed. Charles Neider. New York: Harper, 1959.

————. *A Connecticut Yankee in King Arthur's Court.* Ed. Bernard L. Stein. Berkeley: University of California Press, 1979.

————. *The Devil's Race-Track: Mark Twain's "Great Dark" Writings.* Ed. John S. Tuckey. Berkeley: University of California Press, 1980.

————. *Early Tales and Sketches.* Vol. 1, *1851–1864,* ed. Edgar Marquess Branch and Robert H. Hirst. Berkeley: University of California Press, 1979.

————. *Early Tales and Sketches.* Vol. 2, *1864–1865,* ed. Edgar Marquess Branch and Robert H. Hirst. Berkeley: University of California Press, 1981.

————. *Following the Equator.* Ed. Shelley Fisher Fishkin. The Oxford Mark Twain. New York: Oxford University Press, 1996.

————. *The Innocents Abroad.* Ed. Shelley Fisher Fishkin. The Oxford Mark Twain. New York: Oxford University Press, 1996.

————. *Letters from the Earth.* Ed. Bernard DeVoto. New York: Harper and Row, 1962.

————. *Life on the Mississippi.* Ed. John Seelye. New York: Oxford University Press, 1990.

————. *Mark Twain: Collected Tales, Sketches, Speeches, and Essays.* Vol. 1, *1852–1890.* Ed. Louis J. Budd. New York: Library of America, 1992.

————. *Mark Twain: Collected Tales, Sketches, Speeches, and Essays.* Vol. 2, *1891–1910.* Ed. Louis J. Budd. New York: Library of America, 1992.

————. *Mark Twain's "Mysterious Stranger" Manuscripts.* Ed. William M. Gibson. Berkeley: University of California Press, 1969.

————. *"Pudd'nhead Wilson" and "Those Extraordinary Twins."* Ed. Sidney E. Berger. Norton Critical Editions. New York: Norton, 1980.

————. *Roughing It.* Ed. Harriet Elinor Smith and Edgar Marquess Branch. Berkeley: University of California Press, 1993.

————. *Selected Shorter Writings of Mark Twain.* Ed. Walter Blair. Boston: Houghton Mifflin, 1962.

Twain, Mark, and William Dean Howells. *Mark Twain–Howells Letters: The Correspondence of Samuel L. Clemens and William D. Howells, 1872–1910.* 2 vols. Ed. Henry Nash Smith and William M. Gibson. Cambridge: Harvard University Press, Belknap Press, 1960.

Wellek, René, and Austin Warren. *Theory of Literature.* 3rd ed. New York: Harcourt Brace Jovanovich, 1977.

Wheelwright, Philip. *Metaphor and Reality.* Bloomington: Indiana University Press, 1962.

Wieck, Carl F. *Refiguring "Huckleberry Finn."* Athens: University of Georgia Press, 2000.

Wiggins, Robert A. *Mark Twain: Jackleg Novelist.* Seattle: University of Washington Press, 1964.

Wilbur, Richard. *New and Collected Poems.* San Diego: Harcourt Brace Jovanovich, 1988.

Wilson, James D. *A Reader's Guide to the Short Stories of Mark Twain.* Boston: G. K. Hall, 1987.

Wisbey, Herbert. "The True Story of Auntie Cord." *Mark Twain Society Bulletin,* 4 (June 1981): 1, 3–4.

Wonham, Henry B. *Mark Twain and the Art of the Tall Tale.* New York: Oxford University Press, 1993.

———. "Undoing Romance: The Contest for Narrative Authority in *The Adventures of Tom Sawyer.*" In *Critical Essays on "The Adventures of Tom Sawyer,"* ed. Gary Scharnhorst, 228–41. New York: G. K. Hall, 1993.

Index

Adams, Henry, 63–64

Adventures of Huckleberry Finn (Twain): Aunt Sally in, 78; Ben Harper in, 121; Buck's death in, 74; Buck's riddle in, 168–69; censorship of, 74, 121, 224*n*30; compared with *A Connecticut Yankee in King Arthur's Court*, 138, 140; on conscience, 20; T. S. Eliot on, 41; Emmeline Grangerford's artwork in, 81–82; ending of, 78, 224*n*33; Grangerford-Shepherdson feud in, 74; Huck's crisis of conscience in, 74–76; Huck's decision to scratch himself in, 120–21; Huck's literal vision in, 66, 68–71, 117–27, 168–69; Huck's poetic passages and use of metaphor in, 118–19, 124, 127–29; Huck's tricks on Jim in, 73, 84; Jackson's Island in, 118–19, 123–24; Jim's hair-ball prophecy in, 72, 79–80, 84, 119; Jim's metaphorical vision in, 72–74, 76–78, 224*n*30; jokes in, 121, 168–69; King and Duke in, 83; libidinalized speech in, 104; and minstrelsy tradition, 225*n*40; Miss Watson's metaphorical vision in, 69–76; "nigger" as word in, 83–85; Pap's drunkenness in, 118; Pap's metaphorical vision in, 72, 74, 75, 76; Pap's physical appearance in, 72, 80–81, 119, 123; Pap's speech on "govment" in, 81, 84, 119, 225*n*40; prayer, Providence, and heaven in, 69–70, 71, 74–76, 119–20, 121;

publication of, 132; racial metaphor in, 72, 78–86; recovery of first half of manuscript of, 117, 227*n*24; revisions of and (de)composing metaphor in, 117–29; river as metaphor for book in, 52; slave traders in, 82–83; sweat/bodily discharge in, 104; Tom Sawyer's Gang in, 70–71, 121–22; Tom Sawyer's metaphorical vision in, 70–72, 74, 75, 76; "trash" as word in, 84–85, 225*n*41; typesetting of, 132; and victims of metaphor, 66–78; white-and-black images in, 72, 78–86, 119, 225*n*40; Widow Douglas's metaphorical vision in, 68–70, 72, 74, 75, 76, 123

Adventures of Tom Sawyer, The (Twain): and bad faith, 63–65; Becky Thatcher's rejection of Tom in, 61; clichéd and dead metaphors in, 9, 50, 56–57, 59, 61, 65, 115; conventional narrator (Author) versus lively narrator in, 55–66, 140, 223*n*18, 223–24*n*21; Examination Evening scene in, 60, 63; extended metaphor in, 58; idyllic set pieces in chapter openings of, 57; Injun Joe's death in, 61–62; lampooning of overwrought literary language in, 60–62; publication of, 65; similes in, 58; Sunday school superintendent in, 58; Tom after bath in, 58; Tom's and Joe's pipe-smoking attempt in, 58; whitewashing scene in, 57, 59

Printed in the United States
142089LV00002B/1/P